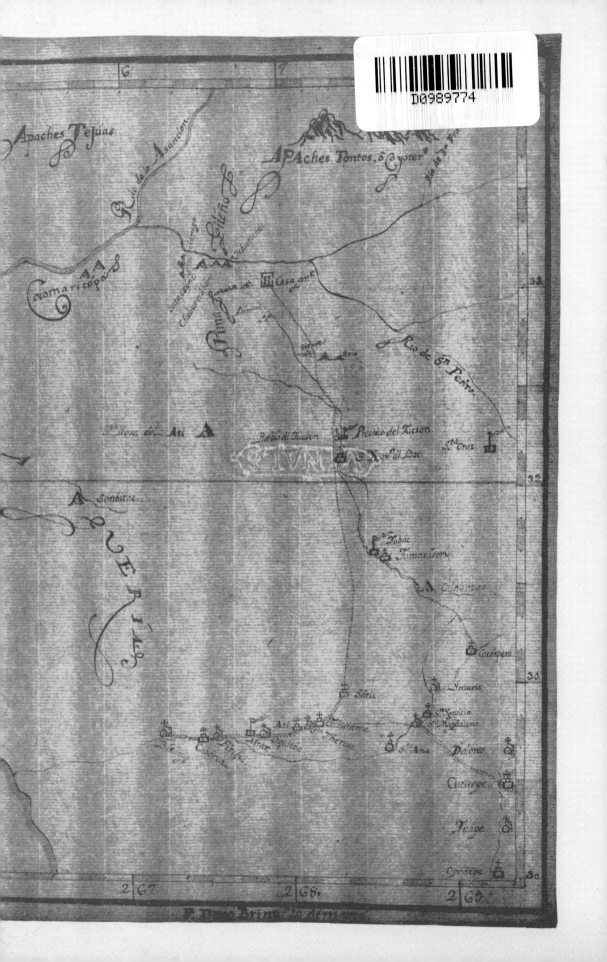

Apaches Tejuas.

APAches Tontos, ô Coyoteros

Rio de la Asuncion.

Cocomaricopas

Gileño

Casa grande

Pima

Rio de S.n Pedro

M.sa del Ati

Reduto de Tucson

Presidio del Tucson.

S. TVBAC

X S.n Xav.l del Bac.

S.ta Cruz

Sonoitac

P A P A V E R I A

S. Zubac

Tumacácori

Calabazas

Cocospera

Imuris

Sáric

S.n Ygnacio

Magdalena

Ati

Tubutama

Oquitoa

S.ta Theresa

S. Ana

Dolores

Busanic

Caborca

Pitiqui

Abar

Cucurpe

Tuape

Opodepe

F. Dieno Brino, la delin.

FRIAR BRINGAS
REPORTS
TO THE KING

El Colegio de la Santa Cruz de Querétaro, where Friar Bringas was a student and later procurator. As an official visitor for this institution, he made his 1796-97 report to the king of Spain.

Friar Bringas Reports to the King

Methods of Indoctrination on the Frontier of New Spain 1796-97

Father Diego Miguel Bringas de Manzaneda y Encinas, O.F.M.

Translated and Edited by
DANIEL S. MATSON
and **BERNARD L. FONTANA**

THE UNIVERSITY OF ARIZONA PRESS · Tucson, Arizona

About the Editors...

DANIEL S. MATSON's career as a linguist and translator began with a bilingual upbringing on the United States and Mexican border at Douglas, Arizona. In 1930 he added German to his list of languages with a B.A. from the University of Arizona. Between 1940 and 1944 he worked among the Papago Indians, becoming fluent in their tongue and immersing himself in their culture. He earned an M.A. degree in social studies at San Luis Rey College in California.

In 1950 Matson joined the faculty of the Department of Anthropology at the University of Arizona. The author of many articles and reviews, he and Albert Schroeder translated and edited the 1590-91 journal of Gaspar Castaño de Sosa, which was published in 1965 under the title *A Colony on the Move.*

BERNARD L. FONTANA, well-known specialist in the history of the Piman Indians and the missions of Pimería Alta, received his Ph.D. degree in cultural anthropology from the University of Arizona in 1960. An ethnologist at the Arizona State Museum and president of the Southwestern Mission Research Center, he has been editor of both *Ethnohistory* and *The Kiva* and has edited and coauthored numerous articles and books.

This volume is in the Franciscan Relations category of the series entitled *The Documentary Relations of the Southwest.*

THE UNIVERSITY OF ARIZONA PRESS

Copyright © 1977
The Arizona Board of Regents
All Rights Reserved
Manufactured in the U.S.A.

I. S. B. N. 0-8165-0599-3 cloth
I. S. B. N. 0-8165-0524-1 paper
L. C. No. 76-11987

CONTENTS

MAPS

PREFACE

When thirty-five-year-old Father Diego Bringas penned his 1796–97 report on conditions in northern New Spain, he was flushed with ambition and an enthusiastic drive for reform. How frustrated he must have felt when his carefully worded, lengthy document, instead of being delivered to the Spanish king, was relegated to territorial archives.

Events combined to dash the young Franciscan's plans for reforming the Pimería Alta. Spain and France had declared war against England in 1796; the demands of this conflict, along with revolutionary unrest in Mexico and empty coffers in Spain, made Father Bringas' fairly costly proposals seem futile. His handwritten report was copied by an episcopal scribe, then both manuscripts were put on file. The scribe's copy stayed in Hermosillo, while Bringas' original probably ended up in Querétaro.

Only in the early nineteenth century, almost one hundred years after Father Bringas' death, was his report to the Spanish king finally shipped across the Atlantic. Its destination, however, was Rome, not Madrid. Father Marcellino da Civezza consulted the manuscript, along with thousands of others, in support of his multivolume history of the Franciscan Order. Eventually it was filed in some boxes containing similar unclassified documents in the library of the Antonianum College in Rome.

More than 150 years passed before the Bringas report came to light again. This time a Franciscan brother rummaging through the Civezza boxes discovered the document and thoughtfully sent a microfilm of it and other manuscripts to Franciscan historian Father Kieran McCarty. McCarty, who was then at the Academy of American Franciscan History in Washington, D.C., arranged for microfilmed copies of the documents to be deposited in the University of Arizona Library and in the Oblasser Memorial Library of Mission San Xavier del Bac.

Coincidentally, editor Bernard Fontana, with the aid of ethnohistorian Henry Dobyns, had recently discovered that he had microfilmed the scribe's copy of the Bringas report along with a large number of other nineteenth-century documents in the Archivo del Gobierno de la Mitra de Sonora in Hermosillo. Events were conspiring to permit Father Bringas' magnum opus to be read widely.

In 1964, Father Kieran, who subsequently became pastor of Mission San Xavier del Bac, arranged for María Antonia Rodrígues of Nogales, Sonora, Mexico, to undertake the tremendous labor of converting Father Bringas' handwritten Spanish into typewritten copy. Carrying the process further, in 1964 University of Arizona student T. Scott Higgins partially translated the Bringas report as a term paper for a course on the history of the Indians of North America.

It was Higgins' rough translation that first brought the significance of Father Bringas' manuscript to the attention of the editors, Daniel Matson and Bernard Fontana. It was obvious that this Franciscan father's efficient plans for reform were an important contribution to the history of the Pimería Alta.

But both of us also felt strongly that the Bringas report offered more than history. We believed that if it were at all possible for man to learn from the experiences of the past, this document might be of burning interest to those in the modern world who are busily engaged in what are essentially the same pursuits as those depicted by Father Bringas — trying to manage the affairs of other countries instead of settling their own problems at home.

Both of us became convinced that such a pointedly relevant document should appear in published form. In the end we decided to collaborate on a complete translation of the Bringas report, including introduction, notes, lexicon, and references.

Matson, who is fluent in Spanish, provided the raw English translation. Fontana's job was to convert the manuscript into more flowing English, always struggling to preserve the meanings intended by Father Bringas in 1796. In the process of translation we mainly worked from the excellent typescript of María Antonia Rodrígues, although we also made repeated references to the microfilm of Bringas' original. We further checked unclear or questionable portions against the scribe's copy from Hermosillo.

The decision was made not to translate status titles, such as *comandante general,* from Spanish into English, because the translated titles often convey different obligations and prerogatives than those intended in the original Spanish. We have provided a lexicon to explain terms left untranslated.

We should also point out that the titles *father* and *friar* do not mean the same thing. All priests are *fathers,* but only priests or brothers who are members of one of the mendicant orders within the Catholic church, i.e., Franciscans, Augustinians, Benedictines, or Carmelites, qualify as *friars.* The fifth order within the Catholic church, the Society of Jesus (Jesuits), is not, strictly speaking, a mendicant order. Its members, therefore, do not qualify as friars. Diego Bringas, a Franciscan, was both a father and a friar, and appears with both titles used interchangeably throughout the manuscript.

The original Bringas report was divided into unparagraphed numbered sections, as was traditional for this sort of document. We have retained the original section numbers, but in most instances have broken the sections into paragraphs as part of the translating process to improve readability in English.

Even though we are the products of twentieth-century American culture, we tried throughout the translation to see things through the eighteenth-century eyes of a friar in whose view something had gone wrong with the Spanish involvement with the Piman Indians and who felt compelled to make the whole matter clear to the king of Spain. At all events, we have pooled our joint intellectual resources in an effort to present an important essay in what can happen when a great power embarks on the tortuous and treacherous path of changing the world about it into its own likeness and image.

Acknowledgments

Over the four-year period required to bring Father Bringas' report into published form, we have become indebted to many historians, linguists, and anthropologists for the time they spent with us in constructive discussions. These include Father Kieran McCarty, O.F.M.; ethnohistorian Father Charles Polzer, S.J.; historian John Kessell, and anthropologists Edward H. Spicer, Emory Sekaquaptewa, Thomas B. Hinton, Paul Turner, and Gordon Krutz.

We would have been doomed without the labors of our typists — Della Antone, Marilyn Hill, Annette Schiffer, Teresa Chico, and Susan Brew. Theirs has been yeoman effort.

For the Bringas maps we extend our gratitude to librarian Chad Flake and the Brigham Young University Library. Mr. Flake responded quickly and efficiently when we solicited the loan of the original maps now in the permanent care of the B.Y.U. library in Provo, Utah.

We also thank the University of Arizona Press for the skill and cooperation of its professional staff in projecting this book into published form.

DANIEL S. MATSON
BERNARD L. FONTANA

INTRODUCTION
TO THE
BRINGAS REPORT:
A MICROCOSM OF
INDOCTRINATION

INTRODUCTION

"Put it that Spain had swarmed," wrote Mary Austin (1924:26). "Whatever the urge that compels great populations to sow themselves to all four quarters of the earth, the desire to spread the blessings of Christianity was, in the sixteenth century, a popular way of rationalizing it."

And Spain had indeed swarmed. She hived on the mainland of Mexico in 1519, and for nearly the next three hundred years members of her colony moved out in every direction until New Spain encompassed all of modern Mexico, islands in the West Indies, half of Central America, the Philippine Islands, and the southwestern portion of what today we know as the United States of America.

Always at the vanguard of the movement — whether alone, with explorers, with troops, or with settlers — were missionaries of the Roman Catholic church. Their principal concern was with native Americans, the Indians, peoples deemed by Spain to be in need of conversion and civilization. It was up to the missionaries to fashion American Indians into Christianized, civilized, law-abiding, tax-paying citizens of the Spanish crown. "These missionaries became a veritable corps of Indian agents, serving both Church and State . . . [T]he rulers of Spain . . . made use of the religious and humanitarian zeal of the missionaries, choosing them to be to the Indians not only preachers, but also teachers and disciplinarians" (Bolton 1960a: 4, 13).

Viewed in another way, missionaries are agents of directed culture change. In the process of converting the religious disposition of a person to one's own disposition, cultural traditions in addition to those we label as "religious" inevitably come under attack. In working toward the "civilization" of the Indians, Spain's missionaries made no bones about it. They were purveyors of Spanish or other European customs, beliefs and habits in nearly all realms of human activity; they were the promoters of assimilation.

Rarely in the annals of human history has one nation devised so intricate and detailed a system to bring about the assimilation of native populations within the boundaries of her empire as did Spain during the three hundred years of her heyday on the world scene. Herbert Bolton (1960a: 2, 12) has argued that it was because Spain had little population of her own to export that she elected to extend her religion, language, law, and traditions through the conversion of populations of native inhabitants to function as colonists. In doing so, Spain evolved a complex set of laws, royal orders, and heavily bureaucratized religious, military, and civil institutions to cope with a single problem: how to make loyal Spanish subjects out of native peoples. The 1796–97 report of Friar Diego Bringas de Manzaneda addressed to the king of Spain provides us with a valuable microcosm of these indoctrination policies in action.

Father Bringas: Scholar, Soldier, Spy

Diego Miguel Bringas de Manzaneda y Encinas was a *criollo,* a creole born in New Spain in 1762 of European parents. His birthplace was the Real de Minas of Alamos in the western foothills of the Sierra Madre Occidental in Sonora about twenty-four miles north of the present northern boundary of the Mexican state of Sinaloa.

The young Bringas became a student at the Royal College of San Francisco Xavier in the city of Querétaro, from which he passed to attend the Royal and Pontifical University of Mexico in Mexico City. Upon graduation he returned to Querétaro, where he entered the College of Santa Cruz de Querétaro and took the Franciscan habit. In a confidential report on the secular and regular clergy in 1793 prepared for the viceroy by the sub-delegate of Querétaro, Bringas was described as:

. . . outstandingly religious and of outstanding talent, instructed in the fine arts, especially in geography, sacred history, ecclesiastical and profane. He deals easily with any subject. He is dedicated. His discussions are profound and clear, organized to achieve his ends. He is an excellent orator and he has produced a quarto volume of sermons, both panegyric and moral, as well as two small volumes in dozavo [twelfths] of meditations on the Most Holy Sacrament (Bringas 1960: vii).

By 1795, at age thirty-three, Bringas had become the procurator of his Quere-taran college. That same year he was sent by that institution as an official visitor to the missions of the Pimería Alta, delivering nine additional missionaries to these posts at the same time. One of the results of this journey was his subsequent report to the king, a document which was never delivered due to embroilments resulting from the war between Spain and England.

When the Mexican war of independence from Spain erupted in 1810, Father Bringas, although a *criollo,* enlisted in the royalist army. He served as chief chaplain of the 6,000 troops in the army of General Félix María Calleja, and he saw service in major battles at Aculco, Guanajuato, Puente de Calderón, and Zitácuaro. He later served in the Spanish Regiment of San Carlos, thus earning for himself the title of *Predicador del Rey* (King's Preacher).

Bringas' loyalty to the royalist cause against an independent Mexico remained constant throughout the eleven years of revolution. He remained at the Queretaran college even after Mexico had won her independence, but in February 1827 he armed Indians in the mountains surrounding Querétaro and instigated a revolt. He planned to form battalions of natives at whose front would march friars carrying the cross. But the plan aborted when the Indians were arrested. Bringas and sixteen other religious were expelled from Mexico, and in October 1827 they embarked on the British merchant frigate *La Hibernia* bound for New Orleans.

On board the ship a new plot was hatched in Bringas' fertile brain, this one to invade Mexico by forming a colony in Texas of Indians and Negroes who would eliminate the Texas criollos. Once in control of Texas, he would make agreements with Mexican *mestizo* (part Spanish and part Indian) generals. But the Mexican government got wind of the plot and sent troops to make sure that Bringas' colonists would not gain control of Texas.

Hearing of these developments, the scholarly friar decided instead to lay before King Ferdinand VII of Spain a proposal that would have Indians and Negroes throughout Mexico rise in revolt against the new republic. In 1828 Bringas sailed to Havana with his plan in hand. He was told it was unnecessary for him to see the king, that his royal majesty wanted Mexico re-taken by any means possible.

Bringas was on board the ship *Soberano* when Spaniards launched a Mexican invasion from Cuba through Tampico. This 1829 Spanish enterprise turned into embarrassment for the invaders. Mexico remained independent, and Father Bringas spent the rest of his life involved in intrigue and espionage in futile attempts to regain for Spain the land of his birth.

Before his death, probably in Cuba and sometime after late 1829, Father Diego Miguel Bringas de Manzaneda y Encinas published thirty-two pamphlets and articles. He also left behind at least two maps of Sonora and the Pimería Alta; an unknown quantity of unpublished letters and other manuscripts; and his important 1796-97 report to the king of Spain (Bringas 1960: vii-xi; Ezell 1958; Franco 1961: xciv-xcvi).

Father Bringas reveals himself as an intelligent, alert, even pushy planner and manager. He arranged for future operations and critiqued the errors and failures of the past. He probably would have made a good corporation executive. Had he not been a priest he would probably have been a lawyer.

The Bringas Report: A Cry for Reform

By early 1795, the threat of secularization of the missions of Pimería Alta hung cloud-like over the College of Santa Cruz de Querétaro. Many of the other missions in the Provincias Internas had become *doctrinas* or *curatos*, and the temporalities of the missions had thereby been turned over to the natives and to local justices. Added to the problems of the college was the fact that some of her friars, according to rumor and report, had not been behaving themselves very admirably in their mission posts. Indeed, it had been alleged "that all was evil, dissolute, and fraught with licentiousness" (Kessell 1976: 183).

One solution would be to send a father visitor vested with authority to correct the abuses and to give a full account. A second solution would be to send more friars so that two could serve in each mission, the better to monitor one another's behavior — as well as to assure that one would receive last rites should he die in his post. A third solution would be to do both.

Father Diego Bringas was the man chosen to carry out the third plan. He was young, just thirty-three years old; he was scholarly and persuasive; and, having had no mission experience among the Indians, he was aligned with no particular mission faction. By his own account (section 5), Father Bringas and his nine missionary companions set out from Querétaro on April 16, 1795. Toward the end of May the father visitor and the *comandante general,* Pedro de Nava, had a long discussion in which they explored the matters of the need for more missions and more military protection; the need to have two friars in each mission; and moving Papago Indians into the San Pedro Valley from which Pimans had been driven by Apaches in the 1760s (Kessell 1976: 184).

From his visit with Nava, Father Bringas traveled to Aconchi in Sonora to talk with Father Barbastro, president of the missions. Bringas informed Barbastro, who because of old age had written a letter of resignation in January 1795, that he was being replaced as president by Father Francisco Yturralde (see notes 46 and 112). The latter's post was at Tubutama, and it was part of the Pimería Alta — not a hundred miles to the south of it as was Aconchi (Gómez Canedo 1971: 17-18; Kessell 1976: 184).

From Aconchi Bringas rode on to Tumacácori. It was here he met with Father Yturralde, who had come from Tubutama for the occasion. From Tumacácori the visitor continued northward — this time to see for himself the situation of the Piman Indians living on the Gila River with the Cocomaricopas and thereby to discern the feasibility of New Spain's continued expansion northward and northwestward toward Alta California (Kessell 1976: 185-186). Captain José de Zúñiga, commander of the troops at the presidio of Tucson, supplied Bringas with a military escort and an interpreter, Pedro Ríos, for his trip to the Gila River villages (Kessell 1976: 186). The maps resulting from this trip appear on pp. 53 and 98 of this book. Bringas' account of the Gileños and of his other impressions of the frontier are given in his report to the king, one which he started to write late in 1796 and which he finished early in 1797.

Were the Bringas report being written today, we would think of it as a grant proposal. And knowing that the potential grantor was totally ignorant of the background against which the proposal was being made, Father Bringas elected to tell the king of the history, the laws, the geography, the ethnography, and the general political and military circumstances on this northern outpost of New Spain. As well he may have. Maps of Mexico and of the New World continued to be published early in the nineteenth century which showed the region of the Pimería Alta as "unknown" (Tejas Galleries 1974: 25-26). Northern Sonora was certainly not the center of the Spanish universe.

Bringas' requests to the king are summed up in section 101 of his report. For Sinaloa and Sonora he wanted two religious hospices to be founded as commodious way stations between Querétaro and the frontier. He wanted the mission at Pitic to be returned to the Queretaran friars for the Sonoran hospice, with assistance being provided by the presidio at Pitic. He wanted two ministers in each of the eight missions of the Pimería Alta, and he wanted the missions governed strictly as *reducciones,* with no Spaniards other than the missionaries to live in them.

Bringas also asked for six new missions to be founded, one at Sonoita (see notes 78 and 91) and the other at the Papago village of Santa Rosa, west of Tucson about sixty miles. The third and fourth missions were requested for the Gila River

Pimas and the fifth and sixth for the Cocomaricopas, farther west down the Gila. In support of these he wanted two new presidios, one at Sonoita and one at the junction of the Gila and Colorado rivers, where the friars had been killed in 1781. The presidios were to be manned chiefly by the inexpensive Opata and Pima troops.

Finally, having had nothing but bad luck with the penny-wise and pound-foolish Galindo Navarro and the impenetrable bureaucracy of Nava's *comandancia general*, Bringas asked that Sonora, like the two Californias, be returned to the administrative jurisdiction of the viceroy.

From his limited perspective of the world scene, Father Bringas couldn't know that the days of Spain's expansion were over. His focus was upon matters of church and state in northwest Mexico and the Pimería Alta — of the many errors and few successes of Spain's Indian policy there. To understand Father Bringas' fervent recommendations to the king, it is necessary to understand the setting that was his world, as well as the culture of the Piman Indians he sought to dominate.

Church and State in New Spain: A Firm Partnership

Citizens of the United States tend to take for granted the doctrine of separation of church and state. The assumption is that this policy has been an American principle from the very beginning, one of the self-evident truths discussed in the Declaration of Independence. But in truth church and state were married in the arena of Indian affairs in the United States in the nineteenth century, with the state paying direct subsidies to churches to instruct Indians in schools and fostering a policy whereby Christian church organizations nominated the men to be selected as Indian agents (Beaver 1966).

An eighteenth-century Spaniard would have seen nothing incompatible in such a policy. Indeed, to have had it otherwise would have struck him as altogether peculiar.

The welding together of church and state in Spain and her possessions took the form of *patronato*, the essential provisions of the patronage having been set forth in a bull of Pope Julian II in 1508. The idea, and it is one which became elaborated as the history of New Spain unfolded, was that the crown would over-see the spread of Christianity and maintenance of the Catholic church, while the church would support the crown and permit royal intervention in ecclesiastical affairs (Farriss 1968: 7, 15).

Patronage, or *patronato*, is a legally regulated grant of the church, a grant which entails certain rights and obligations and which is given by the church in gratitude to a benefactor — in this case, to the crown of Spain. Patronage may be either personal or real, that is, bestowed on a person as such or affixing to one in possession for the time being of a status position or office to which a patronage is connected (Sägmüller 1939: 560).

It was the *patronato real* which enabled the crown to maintain control over the colonial clergy in New Spain. The king was considered to be the pope's representative in the Indies, with the result that members of the clergy accepted almost without question the right of royal supervision over church affairs. The king was de facto head of the church in America, and through the *patronato real* the clergy became a branch of civil service, a loyal auxiliary of the crown (Farriss 1968: 10, 15). It is not surprising, then, to discover that viceroys of New Spain were sometimes archbishops of New Spain as well.

Civil Government in Northwest New Spain

The supreme legislative and administrative agency of Spain with respect to the New World, one with authority over New Spain as well as over Spain's other American possessions, was the Council of the Indies, created in 1524 and based in Madrid. The laws under which all of Spain's New World empire was governed initially took the form of a variety of edicts, the first codification of some of them appearing in 1512 as the "Laws of Burgos" and the second codification, that of 1542 and 1543, being known as the "New Laws."

In 1680 some 400,000 orders and regulations were reduced to 6,400 laws in the *Recopilación de Leyes de los Reynos de las Indias* (*Recapitulation of the Laws of the Indies*). This remarkable document and its two predecessors stood as the first codifications of colonial laws by a world power, and they provided the models after which other European nations fashioned their own laws for the governing of colonies. The body of the *Recopilación* was never revised, although it was published three times in the eighteenth century and twice in the nineteenth. A *Nuevo Código de las Leyes de Indias* (*New Code of the Laws of the Indies*) was formulated in 1790, and its provisions superseded the *Recopilación* on nearly all ecclesiastical matters. It was never published in whole, however, appearing only as individual laws on specific topics as these arose and were submitted to the king by the Council of the Indies (Bancroft 1883a: 516-534; Bernstein 1963: 744A; Ewing 1966: 16; Farriss 1968: 11, 105-106; and Parry 1963).

The king, moreover, as absolute monarch of the Spanish empire, could issue orders (*cédulas*) at will, and all of these had the effect of law. The viceregal government under which New Spain was governed was instituted in Mexico in 1535 (Bancroft 1883b: 375-385). The viceroy, as the highest-ranking official in New Spain, was in charge of civil, political, and economic administration; he was in charge of the royal treasury; as captain-general he was commander of the armed forces; and he exercised the right of royal patronage (patronato real) (Fisher 1926: 3). Under patronato real, the crown appointed all ecclesiastical beneficiaries, although it usually delegated to vice-patrons (viceroys or governors) the right to appoint individuals to church offices beneath those of archbishop and bishop. As early as 1522 the crown gained the right to license missionaries destined for the Indies, none of whom could travel to the New World or return without royal permission. Once in New Spain, however, missionaries — unlike secular clergy — could be appointed to posts by their own superiors, and the superiors were themselves elected by members of their own orders without royal interference (Farriss 1968: 16, 18-19).

As a vice-patron, it was the viceroy's job to promote the extension of missions on the frontier. This included having to pay the salaries of missionaries and various other mission expenses as well as having to provide protection for the religious who manned these frontier posts (Fisher 1926: 197).

Throughout most of New Spain's history, the viceroy was also president of the *audiencia* in Mexico City. The audiencias wielded power in New Spain second only to that of the viceroy. They were administrative bodies and courts of law; they could communicate directly with the crown without the viceroy's intervention. There were two audiencias in New Spain, that in Mexico City having been founded in 1527 and that in Guadalajara in 1548. Most of their members, as judges, were Spanish lawyers appointed by the crown (Ewing 1966: 17).

With the death of the last of Spain's Hapsburg kings in 1700, the Bourbon line ascended to the throne. The Bourbon kings, beginning with Philip V, began a program of reconstruction of the Spanish empire, an empire whose navy had shrunk to twenty ships, whose army was comprised of 20,000 men, and whose mother country was virtually bankrupt, "without roads, without commerce, without agriculture, and without industries" (Priestly 1916: 13). The program of reconstruction came to full fruit with the accession to the throne in 1759 of Charles III, one of the "enlightened despots" in whose court the French exercised a considerable influence. Two of Charles III's overriding goals were to extend royal absolutism and to develop the material wealth of Spain. The French, especially, urged him to effect increased revenues from Spain's New World possessions (Bancroft 1883b: 367 n. 14; Farriss 1968: 91; Lynch 1958: 1-17).

In support of these goals, Charles dispatched to New Spain as "Most Illustrious Visitor General of the Indies" one of his most able ministers, José de Gálvez. He arrived in Mexico in 1765 with a commission from the crown to inspect and arrange administration of the royal revenues. Although his achievements were many (see, for example, Navarro García 1964 and Priestly 1916), his two principal administrative reforms involved the creation of the comandancia general as the governmental organization for northwestern New Spain and the institution of the Spanish intendancy form of government for all of New Spain (Priestly 1916: 289).

While the plan for the intendancies was signed by Gálvez and Viceroy Carlos Francisco de Croix in January 1768, it was August 1769, before it was approved by the king. The first intendant to be appointed, Pedro Corbalán, assumed his duties in 1770 with ad interim powers of intendancy for Sonora and Sinaloa, where revenues were expected to increase because of new mines (Fisher 1929: 15; Priestly 1916: 287).

But it was 1786 before the Ordinance of Intendants for New Spain became officially promulgated and before the intendancy system covered all of New Spain. A dozen intendancies and three provinces were created, including the Intendencia de Sonora, with its capital at Arizpe. Although the intendants were in charge of justice, general administration, war and finance, they were still under the viceroy with respect to the former three departments. Intendants took complete charge of finances, however, thus relieving the viceroyalty of some of its tasks connected with the supervision of the royal treasury and its various branches. Regarding finances, the intendants were immediately responsible to the intendant-general in Mexico City, who in turn answered to the Council of the Indies (Fisher 1926: 3; also see Fisher 1929 and Navarro García 1959).

The institution by Gálvez of the comandancia general was far more important in the history of northwestern New Spain than the creation of intendancies. In

1763 Spain acquired the Louisiana Territory from France, and it was proposed to occupy California with Spanish colonists — the latter at least partly in response to the threat of Russian encroachment headed southward down the Pacific coast. Simultaneously, the situation of the northern provinces was a precarious one because of Indian attack. These were the considerations which entered into Gálvez's thinking when he proposed the amputation of the northern provinces from the viceroyalty by means of a comandancia general under control of a comandante general, whose government would be essentially a military one (Thomas 1941: 16-17).

On August 22, 1776, the king of Spain set aside the Provincias Internas as a single governmental unit. It was comprised of the northern provinces of Nueva Viscaya, Coahuila, Texas, New Mexico, Sinaloa, and Sonora, including, to a lesser extent, the Californias. The comandante general was given authority entirely independent of that of the viceroy, although the audiencia of Guadalajara retained its powers as before. The comandante general had authority over governors of individual provinces as well as over their judicial officers and treasury officials. He was a vice-patron in that he had the prerogatives of the patronato real and thereby controlled appointments of secular curates to their church posts. And like the viceroy, he was responsible for payment of salaries to missionaries and for their protection against hostile Indians.

The first comandante general of the Provincias Internas was Teodoro de Croix, a nephew of Carlos Francisco de Croix, the immediate past-viceroy of New Spain. Appointed on May 16, 1776, he arrived in Mexico City in December of that year and set off immediately to familiarize himself with the region he was to command. His legal advisor (asesor), Pedro Galindo Navarro, assumed his post in the administration of the Provincias Internas in 1777 (Bancroft 1884b: 637-638; Thomas 1941).

With respect to the clergy — including the exercise of patronato and concern with missionaries — Pedro Galindo Navarro appears to have played a more active role within the government of the Provincias Internas than did Croix or any of the subsequent comandantes generales. This asesor, who seems always to have had a watchful eye on the royal treasury and its expenditures, was blamed by Father Bringas for the disaster which befell two abortive Spanish settlements on the lower Colorado River in 1781. It was Galindo Navarro, moreover, with whom Bringas had his lengthiest written debate in his relations with the Provincias Internas. During his long, if occasionally interrupted tenure as asesor, which lasted at least until August 1797, Galindo Navarro repeatedly and consistently took a stand in favor of thrift and economy of the royal treasury against requests of bishops, missionaries, and of anyone else connected with the religious establishment (see, for example, Bancroft 1884b: 652-653; Castañeda 1942: 26-27, 60-61, 65, 194-195). In an argument in 1791 between the comandancia general and the bishop of Durango, Esteban Lorenzo de Tristan, concerning the prerogatives of patronato, Tristan characterized Navarro as one who was "fidgety, debauched, confused, and a paper-shuffler" (Porras Muñoz 1966: 639-640). It is likely that Father Bringas would have agreed.

The comandancia general of the Provincias Internas underwent several changes through the last quarter of the eighteenth century. On June 9, 1783, Felipe de Neve became comandante general replacing Croix, but he died in August of the following year, to be succeeded by José Rengel, whose appointment was ad interim and whose authority was circumscribed by the audencia of Guadalajara (Bancroft 1884b: 639; Loomis 1969: 265). Jacobo Ugarte y Loyola was named ad interim to command the Provincias Internas on October 6, 1785, but on June 17 of that year Bernardo de Gálvez, who had been a soldier on the frontier, was made viceroy of New Spain. Because of his frontier experience, Gálvez was given authority over all military, political, and economic matters involving the Provincias Internas (Bancroft 1884b: 639; Moorhead 1968: 64-66).

In August 1786, Gálvez divided the Provincias Internas into three military commands, one of which included Sinaloa, Sonora, and the Californias and which was commanded by Ugarte. The viceroy died on November 30, 1786, and for a brief time Ugarte enjoyed some of the viceregal authority held by his predecessors in the comandancia general. But in March 1787, the vacancy created by Gálvez's death was filled by Viceroy Manuel Antonio Flores, and he resumed viceregal control over the Provincias Internas. Moreover, the new viceroy consolidated the three military commands into two, making Ugarte commander of the Provincias Internas del Occidente (or Poniente), comprised of Nueva Vizcaya, Sonora, Sinaloa, and the Californias (Bancroft 1884b: 639-640; French 1962: 2; Loomis 1969: 265; Gálvez 1951: 31-32; Moorhead 1968: 66-79).

In March 1790, Pedro Romualdo de Nava Grimón y Porlier became comandante general of the Provincias Internas del Occidente, and the following year he became comandante general of the eastern provinces as well (Bancroft 1884b: 641). The eastern and western military commands of the Provincias Internas were reunited by a royal order of November 1792, with the Californias being removed from the comandancia general and with the capital being established permanently at the Villa de Chihuahua. Pedro de Nava continued as comandante general, but again independent of the viceroy and again the vice-patron. This independent status of the Provincias Internas continued throughout Nava's tenure. He was replaced in August 1800, by Nemesio Salcedo y Salcedo (Bancroft 1884b: 641; Loomis 1969: 266; Simmons 1968: 42).

Civil and military affairs in the northwest were inextricably intertwined during the last half of the eighteenth century, particularly after the formation of the comandancia general of the Provincias Internas in 1776. Indians, especially Apaches but including Seris and apostate Pimans, kept Spanish troops in Sonora and Sinaloa on the run and on the gallop. The so-called Pima Revolt of 1751 led to the erection of two additional Spanish presidios in Sonora — one at Tubac (1752) and a second at Altar (1754). The Tubac presidio was moved to Tucson in 1776.

Soon after the Quechan (Yuma) Indians destroyed the two Spanish settlements which had been founded among them on the lower Colorado River, the Spaniards organized military companies of friendly Indians for service on the frontier. In 1782 a company of Piman troops began their service at San Ignacio, and in the years that followed they saw service at the presidios of Altar, Buenavista, Santa Cruz, and Tubac (Dobyns 1972: 328-331). In 1784 an Opata Indian company was organized with headquarters at Bacoachi, also in Sonora (Bancroft 1884b: 681).

Civil and military government in Sonora and elsewhere throughout the Provincias Internas were further coalesced in 1786 when Viceroy Bernardo de Gálvez issued his "Instructions for Governing the Interior Provinces of New Spain." It was here that Gálvez's "peace policy" was set forth, in which it was his stated intention "to establish with the Indians [principally Apaches] a commerce which will attract them to us, which will interest them, and which in time will put them under our dependency." To do this he urged his field commanders to bend every effort toward making Apaches dependent on Spanish clothing, food, drinks, and weapons. He proposed that Apaches be helped in becoming addicted to brandy or mescal; that they be given long guns "with barrels, stocks, and weak bolts without the best temper," thus forcing their reliance on Spanish gunsmiths for their repair; and that if they did make armistices, they be given regular rations of food (Gálvez 1951: 36-51). It was this policy which led eventually to the establishment of small settlements of "tame" Apaches immediately adjacent to the presidios of Bacoachi and Tucson.

If it fell to the military to tend to Apaches, however, it was the lot of the missionaries to bring peaceful Indians to full citizenship status, to "bring them to vassalage" of his royal highness, the king of Spain. And the church bureaucracy was hardly less complex than that of secular government.

Ecclesiastical Organization in the New World

Catholic clergymen in New Spain, as elsewhere, were either seculars or regulars. Secular clergy "live in the world" rather than in monasteries or religious cloisters. They owe obedience to the bishop because of canonical law rather than through a religious vow of obedience in which one renounces his own will. Seculars practice celibacy; like laymen, they own private property. The religious hierarchy of the church resides in the secular clergy.

Regular clergy are members of religious orders. They take vows of poverty, chastity, and obedience in addition to special vows sometimes required by a particular order. Regulars cannot own private property; they are members of religious communities and, as such, do not "live in the world" (Boudinhon 1912).

Although several religious orders were represented in New Spain, two of them — the Jesuits, regulars of the Society of Jesus (S.J.), and the Franciscans, regulars of the Order of Friars Minor (O.F.M.) — were destined to play the largest role in the missionary history of northwestern New Spain. Indeed, in Sonora, theirs were the exclusive roles except for occasional filling-in by seculars.

Every order which had as one of its apostolates the conversion of non-Catholics to the Catholic faith evolved its own missionary methodology. These "mission systems" varied from religious order to religious order, and within the orders from time to time and, sometimes, from location to location.

As originally conceived in the history of the church, the "mission" was not a building or place; it was an activity. "The 'missions' of Europe," which predated those of the New World, "were bands of itinerant preachers bent on haranguing virtue back into the lives of the graceless mob." As for mission beginnings in the New World, "Throughout the liturgical year priests and friars left their residences and colleges in the major cities to evangelize the neighboring Indian towns and to preach the jubileos. Their express purpose, like that of their European counterparts, was to bring about a change in the 'vicious' living habits of the populace — Indian and Spaniard alike" (Polzer 1972: 22-23).

As the frontiers of New Spain came to be pushed ever farther outward during the sixteenth century, itinerant missionaries found themselves farther afield from their administrative headquarters. In 1577 the Jesuits in New Spain formally suggested that residences or "houses of habitation" be constructed in Indian communities for the missionaries (Polzer 1972: 28). As the decades passed and the frontier continued to expand, the residences became a whole complex of buildings, including a church edifice, and the mission became an institutionalized activity, a place as well as something à missionary did.

Each religious order had its own internal sets of rules and regulations, its own bureaucratic structure, its own organization of administrative hierarchy. Those of the Jesuits, who laid the groundwork of missionary activity in Sonora, have been described in detail by Charles Polzer (1972). The structure of the Order of Friars Minor (Franciscans), whose members followed the Jesuits in many of their mission posts in Sonora when the former were expelled from all of New Spain in 1767, was equally complex.

The highest-ranking Franciscan authority in New Spain was the *comisario general*, who answered only to the comisario general of the Indies at the royal court in Madrid (McCarty 1973: 11). At the very end of the eighteenth century, the crown succeeded in persuading the pope to eliminate the office of comisario general in the colonial branches of the religious orders (Farriss 1968: 64), but this occurred after Father Bringas had written his report to the crown.

Franciscans in New Spain were assigned either to Franciscan provinces, geographical and administrative units under direction of a father provincial, or to apostolic colleges of the propagation of the faith, which were under direction of a father guardian. A group of missionaries in a certain region under jurisdiction of a province was headed by a priest whose title was *comisario*. The functionally equivalent position for a group of missionaries under jurisdiction of a college bore the title *presidente* (Carlisle and Fontana 1969: 41 n. 4).

In 1768, when the Franciscans took over the Sonoran missions from the deported Jesuits, the region fell under the jurisdiction of the Province of Saint James of Jalisco (Provincia de Santiago de Xalisco) and of the Missionary College of the Holy Cross at Querétaro (El Colegio de Santa Cruz de Querétaro), which appears as the frontispiece of this book. The guardian of the college and the provincial of the Jaliscan province were entirely independent of one another, both answering directly to the Franciscan comisario general of New Spain (Carlisle and Fontana 1969: 41 n. 4), although the colleges had a liaison with the viceroy who bore the title of *procurator*. The college of Santa Cruz, like the other apostolic colleges in New Spain, was founded to train friars specifically in "the propagation of the faith and the conversion of heretics and other unbelievers." From its founding date in 1682 as the first such Franciscan college in the New World until the suppression of apostolic colleges by the Franciscan Minister General in 1908, there were at least thirty-six such institutions altogether in Spain's western hemisphere possessions (McCarty 1962: 54, 57).

The initial institution implanted by the crown in New Spain to bring about the integration of the natives into the religious, legal, economic, and social network of the Spanish empire was the *encomienda-doctrina* system. In its simplest terms, the Spanish conquistador was given a grant by Spain to collect tribute from the natives so long as he agreed to protect them and to Christianize them. As summarized by Antonine Tibesar (1957: 115-116):

In accordance with this method as embodied in the royal laws, a team composed of soldiers, merchants, priests, and royal political officials would enter a pagan country to destroy insofar as possible all aspects of pagan culture, political, social, and religious, which were opposed to the Spanish Christian culture. The destruction of the old and the construction of the new culture often went ahead at the same time.

Under this plan, the soldier or conquistador was the opening wedge. By force, or at least a show of force, he gained the submission of the native rulers and thus opened the door for the merchant, the royal official, and the priest [i.e., the doctrinero]. With native opposition overcome or silenced, these could then undertake their own special tasks. The royal officials supported by the soldier settled the natives in larger towns and villages, called reductions, imposed upon them the political system of Spain, and maintained them in peace and harmony, conditions prerequisite for the success of the merchant and the priest.

Success in their respective endeavors brought to each class its own reward. The conquistador became an encomendero, *the royal official could look forward to increased salary and prestige and royal preferment, while the priest would profit by the successes of all because through their endeavors he had been presented with a large field of prospective converts, who had been conditioned to receive his message. The Indians were peaceful, gathered in large groups, and mentally prepared to abandon their old beliefs and to accept those of their present rulers and conquerors.*

Abuses in the encomienda-doctrina system, such as the "unbridled cruelties and debasing depravities" committed by soldiers during conquest and unfair advantages taken of Indians by encomenderos — to say nothing of the drastic decline in sedentary native population — led to its demise. The "New Laws" of 1542-43 declared that Indians could no longer be given in encomienda, and that upon the death of incumbent encomenderos, their holdings, including the labor of Indians, would revert to the crown. Needless to say, the encomenderos and others profiting from the system resisted the laws, but to no permanent avail. In 1573 King Philip II banned the conquest system in those parts of the Americas not already conquered, and by the early part of the seventeenth century, encomienda was lapsing into history. In northwestern New Spain, it saw its last gasps with the 1598 colonization by Don Juan de Oñate of New Mexico and with early seventeenth century government in that new province (Hammond and Rey 1953: 36, 508-509; Simpson 1950: 130; Tibesar 1957: 116-117; also see Scholes 1937).

By the onset of the eighteenth century, the methodology of bringing Indians to the Holy Faith and to royal vassalage had become the "mission system," one rather narrowly prescribed through royal orders (cédulas), in the Laws of the Indies and other laws, through the rules of particular religious orders, and by tradition. The Spanish view seems to have become that the New World Indians were as clean slates, blank sheets of paper upon whom the Word — of the king as well as of God — had only to be written.

But the writing would take time and the natives were to be advanced by stages. It was a program of planned assimilation which began with founding a mission (misión) for pagans, that is, those presumed to be without religion, which advanced either to reductions (reducciones) or conversions (conversiones) for beginners in the Christian faith; which further progressed to doctrines (doctrinas) for those who were at least partially instructed in the Catholic faith; culminating in curacies (curatos), fully secularized churches administering to the religious needs of full-fledged Catholics who by now had also become tax-paying vassals of the crown. It was with these first three stages of development that missionaries of religious orders were concerned: from simple presence (misión) to conversión (or reducción) to doctrinal formation (doctrina). With the curacies, there was no missionary involvement. They were in the hands of secular clergy (Polzer 1972: 4-9).

In a narrowly defined sense — and it is in this sense that Father Bringas makes most of his definitions — there is a distinction between misión and conversión that relates to the process of promoting the assimilation of Indians.

. . . Although the two terms, misión and conversión, are nearly synonymous, the stress of conversión is on the actual activity of a change in belief and subsequent cultural practices. A misión might be for several years hardly more than an outpost of example for people who refuse to accept the basic teachings of the missionaries. The use of the term misión need not imply effectiveness or success. Conversión, however, usually connotes a process of acceptance and change. When the terms are used interchangeably in a document, the connotative quality of conversión is usually controlling the intended meaning of misión. But the exclusion of the term conversión in a document can lead to the suspicion that progress in conversión was minimal. As a matter of fact, the acceptance of Christian beliefs by the Indians of northwestern New Spain would seldom allow anything but a nearly synonymous use of the term (Polzer 1972: 5).

Father Bringas, in his report to the king, characterized reducciones and conversiones as being "essentially the same institution" (section 16). The notion of reducción, however, implies something more than conversión alone. A reducción involved the bringing together of Indians into settlements around churches and placing the Indians under sole jurisdiction of the missionary. "The intention behind forming reducciones was to 'lead the Indian back' from the mountains and woods into a community where he could better learn the rudiments of Christian belief and the elementary forms of Spanish social and political organization" (Polzer 1972: 10).

In the New World, where the concept of reducción developed, the freedom of the missionary to deal with his Indian neophytes in isolation was backed by the Laws of the Indies. Ideally, the missionary wanted his Indian charges in a wholly segregated community, one free of the taint of worldly civilians or Spanish troops. Moreover, so long as Indians were under a missionary — whether in conversión or reducción — they were free of paying tribute to the crown and tithes to the bishop. In short, they were exempt from taxes.

The missionary and his order alone were responsible for the administration of religious as well as temporal affairs in the community. The *conversor,* who was subject to the rules of his order, was in charge of the physical property of the church, its buildings and their contents, grounds, fields, and produce of its fields, even as he was in charge of religious instruction and the daily and weekly routine of the community. The rules, precepts, and methodology of Jesuit missionaries in Sonora — including their relation to the reducción — are detailed in the study by Charles Polzer (1972: 40-128). The actual routine of life in a conversión as perceived by a Jesuit missionary who served in Sonoran missions is described in "The Relation of Philipp Segesser" (Segesser 1945).

The next institution on the path to Indian assimilation was the evolved doctrina, a descendant of the encomendero-doctrina system. The doctrina may be viewed as half-mission and half-secular parish or curacy. A regular who served as a *doctrinero* was appointed to his post by his own provincial or guardian, although technically a doctrina came under patronato real. The vice-patron was supposed to be notified by the regular clergy of appointments to a doctrina (Farriss 1968: 190). The bishops, moreover, supposedly had the right to pass on appointments of doctrineros within the areas of their episcopal jurisdictions. Bishops could also "visit the *doctrinas,* inspect the records, examine the doctrinero or incumbent, correct abuses should any be found to exist, and finally, what is more pertinent to the present question, receive tithes from the members of the particular doctrina for support, the crown having granted a part of the tithes which is enjoyed under the Patronato Real to the bishops for their support" (Geary 1934: 20).

In effect, the doctrina was turned over to the jurisdiction of the local bishop and was thereby secularized. Whether the priest was a regular or secular, his charge was limited to spiritual ministration. Modern Indian parishes in the American Southwest administered by Franciscans operate in a somewhat similar fashion, especially regarding the relationship between the local bishops and the Franciscan provincial hierarchy.

Although either regular or secular clergy could serve in doctrinas, for the most part only the former did so. Moreover, they were Franciscans from provinces with whom the role of doctrinero rested most easily, missionaries from the colleges seeing themselves instead as conversores — specialists in converting Indians to the faith. Doctrineros were dependent on the royal treasury for their income, and the income was such that few seculars would be attracted by it. The stipend was more in keeping with the vows of poverty taken by regulars (Polzer 1972: 7-9).

Since the Indians in a doctrina were not exempt from payment of tithes, and since they were at least in part under episcopal jurisdiction, it is no wonder missionaries such as Father Bringas argued in favor of a lesser status for churches cared for by friars from apostolic colleges. The doctrina was the last step before the religious would have to relinquish all responsibility for Indians. It was in the doctrina that the real job of instilling doctrinal integrity was carried out. It was at this stage that Indians were taught Spanish and how to read, write, do arithmetic, and recite the catechism (Polzer 1972: 111-113).

No other phase in mission development is more difficult to recognize and describe than the pre-parochial [i.e., doctrina phase]. It is precisely in the evaluation of this stage that the thorny problem of secularization arose. Missionaries insisted the Indians were still learning the rudiments of the Faith; the Bishops insisted that they had attained sufficient levels of knowledge and self-support to become parishes. And the disputes raged for decades, proving that adequate norms for determining the extent of change were non-existent (Polzer 1972: 116).

As a final argument against secularization — a status toward which bishops and vice-patrons in New Spain continually pushed, especially after Charles III inaugurated the Enlightenment in Spain's possessions — the regulars would assert "that the Indians were not adequately prepared to compete with Spanish society" (Polzer 1972: 117).

Father Bringas cites a *cédula real* dated January 30, 1607, as well as another of December 5, 1608, which he says support the claim that missions were to be exempted for ten years from the time of their founding from tribute to the crown, tithes to the bishops, and any interference from viceroys, governors, presidents, bishops, or other religious superiors. They were to be left solely to the care of the conversores. What the cédulas actually stated, as published in the *Recopilación* (Book 6, Title 5, Law 3 of the 1681 edition) was:

We order that those pagan Indians who of their own free will embrace our Holy Catholic Faith and receive Baptism solely as a result of the preaching of the Holy Gospel, shall not be subject to the encomienda, nor pay tribute for ten years, nor be compelled to any service (Geary 1934: 18).

The rationale behind these orders seems clear enough. They were aimed at preventing the oppression of Indians by force which would thereby provoke their aversion toward the religion of the oppressors (Huonder 1911: 689), to say nothing of their open revolt.

The laws of 1607 and 1608 said nothing about the exemption of missions from jurisdiction of the bishops. But for whatever reasons, the interpretation of these laws became expanded through time until it was understood that automatically after ten years misiones or reducciones should be made subject to episcopal jurisdiction — at least as doctrinas if not as curatos. In point of fact, this "ten-year plan" was rarely, if ever, carried out in New Spain, but the understanding (or misunderstanding) of it remained as a bone of contention between regulars and seculars, missionaries and the civil government (Geary 1934: 22–23).

Perhaps with more of an eye on the royal treasury than on the principle of Indians' being made loyal Catholic vassals, in October 1749 King Ferdinand VI issued the order that all regulars serving in doctrinas and curas in the Spanish New World be replaced by secular clergy. The vice-patron in New Spain, the Viceroy Conde de Revillagigedo, apparently saw a chance to relieve the crown and himself of the burden of having to pay upkeep for missions and salaries of missionaries while simultaneously bringing in new revenues in the form of tithes and tribute from previously tax-exempt subjects.

Revillagigedo meant more by secularization than the mere replacement of regulars by diocesan priests, as the king had ordered. He further intended that the missions should be turned over to the bishops; that mission lands and properties be distributed to the Indians; that Indians should be placed under a form of pueblo government and laws and made exempt from missionary control; and that tithes be paid by Indians for support of their diocesan priests (Geary 1934: 28–29). The views of this viceroy of New Spain are worth noting, especially since they stand in almost total opposition to the opinions expressed by Father Bringas some forty-seven years later in his report to the king:

The missions should in conformity with the law have been reduced to doctrinas long ago, and the Treasury would have been freed of the increased expenses which have been and are being maintained; because it is more than a hundred and thirty and a hundred and twenty years since some of these missions were established and subjected completely to the direction of their respective missionaries. During so long a time none of them have been restored [to the bishops], as should have been done after ten years, in virtue of the law. As a result of this, the Royal Treasury has been injured not only by the expenses which the missions occasion it as long as they continue to exist, but also by the fact that it is deprived of the tributes which the Indians would have contributed if the missions had been given their diocesan bishops in the stated time; and the damage goes further still because the Indians have no property in common in their missions nor liberty since they live with great servitude and subjection, depending on and subject to the will of the missionary fathers. So great is this that it might be said without fear of mistake that the missionaries, under the pretext of their [the Indians,] being neophytes and other pretexts advanced, want to perpetuate their despotic rule over them. As a result, if the governors of the provinces and their subalterns attempt to enforce the municipal laws of the kindom for the sake of good government and in order that the pueblos of the Indians might be ruled in conformity to them and in opposition to that which the missionaries have established and ordered in their own form of government, then the wrath of these missionaries conspires against these just provisions, so that the governors in order to escape this anger and avoid an inexorable persecution find themselves obliged to yield to the policy of the missionaries. The Viceroy, perplexed by the fights and quarrels and in danger of being accused of disloyalty, impiety and stubbornness toward the religious order in charge of the particular missions, cannot make a decision, since his position demands that he avoid the inconveniences and ill consequences that would follow, with injury to the reputation of his employees and his own person. . . .

The source of all this evil comes from the fact that under the pretext of a misinterpreted and misconceived law, Spaniards have been excluded from the Indian community villages at the missions. But the damage of this was recognized too late for the evils which I already specified were permitted to arise and we suffered revolts of the Indians. If, on the contrary, the congregation and population of Spaniards had not been hindered, those evils would not have occurred. The Indians would now be better disciplined and advanced in the spiritual as well as the temporal, and imbued with a greater spirit of subordination and obedience; in a few years the missions would have been abolished and the Indians would be enjoying freedom and the fruits of their labors, while the King would be enjoying the payment of tribute; the dominion would have been more populated and its most distant provinces developed, provinces that are very rich in fruits and mines; and finally, with the Indians instructed and accustomed to everything pertaining to their Christian, political, civil and social life, there would be no fear of the danger of their insurrection (Geary 1934: 27-28).

In spite of the king's order and of the viceroy's opinions, secularization of the missions failed to occur all at once. The principal reason, no doubt, was simply that there weren't enough secular priests in New Spain to take over the missions — especially since most of them were in fact poverty-stricken and did, indeed, have to rely on the royal treasury for their continued existence. Such assignments were not within the tradition of the secular clergy.

A large step in the general direction of secularization of the Sonoran missions was taken in 1767. On February 27, King Charles III issued a mandate for the expulsion of the Jesuits from all of Spain's dominions in Europe, America, and Asia. The order was opened and read by the viceroy of New Spain, the Marqués de Croix, on June 24, and it reached the governor of Sonora, Juan Claudio de Pineda, at San Miguel de Horcasitas, the provincial capital, on July 11 (Bancroft 1883b: 432, 438; McCarty 1973: 5; also see Pradeau 1959).

Whatever the immediate reasons for the decision of Charles III to expel the Jesuits, and these were surely many and complex, the move was one which fit into the general mood of the Enlightenment; the influence of France (and of Jansenism and Voltaireism) in the Spanish court; the need of Spain to unburden herself of the cost of missions and missionaries as well as to extract more money from her possessions; and the trend toward a secularist bureaucracy and the pulling away of Spain from Rome. Ignatius of Loyola, the founder of the Jesuit order, had stressed obedience to the pope as one of the principal underpinnings of the Society of Jesus. Obedience to Rome in a nation jealous of its prerogatives under patronato real could only have been viewed by that nation's ministers with some mistrust.

Governor Pineda ordered that the expulsion of the Jesuits in Sonora be carried out by the military, and that Indians in the conversiones be assured of continued royal protection. His instructions further were to tell the Indians that the Jesuit fathers would be replaced by doctrineros and curas, and that they now had "the civil liberty of treating and living with Spaniards as brothers" (McCarty 1973: 6). In short, what the royal order of 1749 had decreed was about to be carried out — at least partially so — on the Sonoran frontier.

In terms of ordinary ecclesiastical jurisdiction, Sinaloa and Sonora, as a part of Nueva Viscaya, fell under the bishopric of Guadalajara at the time of its founding in 1544. But in 1620 the bishopric of Durango (Guadiana) was created, and Sonora became part of its episcopal jurisdiction. Other than its military chaplains, however, Sonora was almost wholly without secular clergy until there were a few mining towns large enough to support them. But in 1767, with the expulsion of the Jesuits, the bishop of Durango, Pedro Tamarón y Romeral, thought he saw an opportunity to extend the authority of his office throughout the settlements vacated by the black-robed regulars. As it turned out, however, Tamarón had an insufficient number of diocesan priests to man the former mission posts.

There were fifty-two vacancies to be filled in Sonora alone, to say nothing of missions in other parts of the diocese. The end result was that very few Sonoran missions fell into the hands of secular clergy, and those that did were largely in the south along the lower Yaqui River, where Yaqui Indian parishes or curatos were begun (Bancroft 1883b: 692; 1884b: 97, 595; McCarty 1973: 9-10, 55-58).

Most of the mission stations in Sonora went to the Franciscans, both those from the College of Santa Cruz de Querétaro and from the Province of Santiago de Jalisco. The friars were granted diocesan faculties of preaching and hearing confession by Bishop Tamarón, who let it be known to others than the friars themselves that he expected them to minister only to the religious needs of Indians (McCarty 1973: 33-34).

After a series of adventures and misadventures at sea, overland, and in the confused administrative situation which followed in the wake of the Jesuit expulsion — some of which is reminiscent of a Gilbert and Sullivan scenario (see McCarty 1973: 22-58) — the friars began arriving at their Sonoran missions the spring and summer of 1768. It would appear that the Jaliscans took over the former Jesuit posts at Aconchi, Bacadehuachi, Banámichi, Cuquiárachi, Sahuaripa, Onapa, Gusavas, Baserac, Arivechi, Mátape, and Arizpe, including the *visitas,* or mission visiting stations of these headquarters. The Queretarans took over at Guevavi (Father Juan Crisóstomo Gil de Bernabé), Caborca (Father Juan Díaz), San Ignacio de Cabúrica (Father Diego Martín García), Opodepe (Father Antonio Canals), Ures (Father Esteban Salazar), Cumuripa (Father Enrique Echaso), Tecoripa (Father Juan Sarobe), Onavas (Father José Antonio Caxa), Cucurpe (Father Antonio Reyes), Saric (Father Juan José Agorreta), San Xavier del Bac (Father Francisco Garcés), Ati (Father José Soler), Suamca (Father Francisco Roch), and Tubutama (Father Mariano Antonio de Buena y Alcalde, President of the Missions, and Father José del Río) (Carlisle and Fontana 1969; McCarty 1973: 60-71). Of the latter, Guevavi, Caborca, San Ignacio, Saric, Ati, Suamca, San Xavier, and Tubutama were in the land of the Upper Piman Indians, the Pimería Alta, while Opodepe, Ures, Tecoripa, Onavas, Cumuripa, and Cucurpe were in the so-called Pimería Baja.

In keeping with the intention of the crown, the visitor general, the vice-patron, the governor, and the bishop of Durango to strive for secularization of the missions, the College of Santa Cruz de Querétaro instructed its missionaries bound for Sonora to allow Indians in the villages to have free communication with Spaniards, even to the extent of allowing Spaniards to settle in the villages; to encourage Indians to trade with Spaniards; to open formal schools with non-Indian teachers in the mission settlements; and to explore and become familiar with the country beyond the mission frontier. The immediate policy was to administer the churches as doctrinas rather than as conversiones (McCarty 1973: 14-15).

What characterized Franciscan missions in Sonora during their first years from about mid-1768 to June 13, 1769, has been labeled the "civil commissioner" system of government. Civil commissioners (*comisarios*) were initially placed in charge of all mission properties when the Jesuits departed, the position of government authorities being that the properties had belonged to the Jesuits rather than to the Indians. The newly arrived Franciscans were placed in the role of doctrinero, spiritual chaplain rather than conversor in the control of their Indian charges, and they were expected to live solely from their income in the form of the royal stipend (*sínodo*).

Moreover, the only property turned over to the friars by the civil commissioners were the priests' residences and their furnishings and the churches and their necessary contents. Mission lands, stock, agricultural produce, and the fruits of Indian labor in theory were given to the Indians thus "set at liberty," but in fact the Indians, except village headmen or governors, were now expected to pay royal tribute. From the point of view of the native, it must have seemed a small matter whether his efforts were being expended in behalf of missionary or civil commissioner. His labors certainly weren't intended by the crown to be expended solely in his own behalf (McCarty 1973: 73-106).

The civil commissioner system proved to be a disaster from the point of view of Spanish administrators. The friars, although used to poverty, were for all practical purposes unable to subsist on their small salaries. Indians "went over the hill" and failed to become a source of tax revenue as had been anticipated. Mission property disappeared. Church structures began to fall apart, and there were no funds for their repair. All of this was taken into account when José de Gálvez, visitor general of the Indies, made his tour of Sonora in the first half of 1769. The result was that on June 3 of that year, Gálvez issued an order that the temporal goods of the missions in the Pimería be turned back to the care of the Queretaran friars. On September 29, he further

. . . issued a list of five special orders for observance in the Pimería missions. The first commanded attendance at Christian instruction under pain of punishment. The second laid down the same conditions for agriculture and communal work for the good of the village. The third decreed that the missionaries could administer all of the Sacraments to Spaniards and other non-Indians living in their mission districts without the permission of nearby' diocesan pastors; diocesan pastors, moreover, could no longer collect tithes within the mission districts. The fourth order clarified the third; residents of mission districts, Indians and non-Indians, were obliged to Christian instruction and worship on Sundays and holydays.

*. . . The fifth and last order imposed the obligation of giving Spanish surnames
to Indian families and of discontinuing the use of pagan surnames. The order
forbade the Indians from calling people their relatives because they belonged
to the same Piman nation [some of whom were at war with the Spaniards]. Gálvez
wanted to break all ties with the rebels and Pimas outside the mission system. In
the same order, he reiterated the obligation incumbent on everybody to learn and
speak the Spanish language (McCarty 1973: 153-154).*

As a result of Gálvez's orders, the Franciscan missions of the Pimería continued to be operated as conversiones or reducciones, much in the manner as they
had been administered by the Jesuits. In 1771 the Queretarans added San José
de los Pimas to their list of permanently manned missions in the Pimería Baja,
even as in 1772 they assigned a resident priest to La Santísima Trinidad de Pitic
(Roca 1967: 172-173, 244-245). But in 1774, all eight Queretaran missions south
of the Pimería Alta were turned over to the Jaliscan friars, although the actual
change didn't take place until 1776 (Bancroft 1884b: 685, 688; Roca 1967: 387
n. 58). It was the view of Father Bringas, as expressed in his report (section 12),
that the Pimería Baja churches by then were more than ready for doctrina status
if not to become curacies, and he felt that being freed of their care would enable
the Queretarans to concentrate on the expansion of the mission frontier to the
Gila and Colorado rivers and beyond.

In 1776 the Franciscans in the Pimería Alta found themselves looking to the
comandante general of the newly formed comandancia general of the Provincias
Internas for financial support and military protection, and in 1780 they realized
their hopes of expansion through the founding of two new settlements among the
Quechan (Yuma) Indians on the lower Colorado River near the mouth of the
Gila. As Father Bringas describes in considerable detail in his report (sections
68-69), however, these two settlements were not quite missions and neither were
they quite Spanish colonial pueblos. In any case, they were short-lived. In July
1781, the Yumas destroyed both towns and made martyrs of four sons of the College
of Santa Cruz de Querétaro: Francisco Garcés, Juan Díaz, Juan Barreneche, and
José Moreno (Bancroft 1884b: 684; Forbes 1965: 175-205; Roca 1967: 354 n. 24).

Earlier, on May 7, 1779, on recommendation from Madrid, the Holy Father,
Pope Pius VI, had created the Diocese of Sonora. Carved in part from the Diocese
of Durango, it consisted of Sinaloa, Sonora, Lower California, and Upper California. Its first bishop, appointed December 12, 1780, and consecrated September
15, 1782, was none other than one of the Queretarans' own, Father Antonio de los
Reyes, O.F.M., the priest who had been assigned to Cucurpe in 1768 (Geiger
1959: II: 343).

Reyes was in his mission post only until early 1771, when he was appointed
procurator of the Querétaro college. As such, he was the official liaison between
the college and the viceregal government, and his headquarters were in Mexico
City. While Reyes was in Mexico he worked out a plan of his own for the administration of the missions. It was a plan which called for the establishment of four
Franciscan custodies (*custodias*) for the Provincias Internas, a custody being a

kind of minor or incipient Franciscan province. Reyes' plan, which was approved by the king and submitted to the Council of the Indies in 1777 and without any consultation on Reyes' part with his own College of Querétaro or with any of the other apostolic colleges in New Spain, said that the staffing of the four custodies should be by Franciscans (Geiger 1959: II: 345; Stagg 1974: 66-71).

. . . [T]he mode of life [was to be] similar to that led in the colleges. Each custody was to be ruled by a custos or custodian and he and his friars were to be independent of the colleges though the missionaries were to be supplied by the colleges. The custodies were to have their own statutes in general conformity to those of the colleges. The missionaries belonging to the custodies would enjoy the same canonical privileges and favors as those belonging to the apostolic colleges.

Since the missionaries in the field would nevertheless often be far away from the headquarters of the custodian, Reyes suggested that substitute superiors, called vicars or presidents and subject to the custodian, be placed in the mission field to watch over the personal lives of the friars as well as their external employment. The terms of the custodian and vicars were to be three years, at the end of which they were to assemble for chapter and as voters elect a new custodian and new vicars, according to the constitution and statutes of the Order.

Such organization, Reyes pointed out, called for a commodious residence at the principal place where the custodian was to live, with at least six religious in residence and as many more as could maintain themselves from the alms of the faithful. This central house was to be empowered to receive novices and should provide shelter for the sick and aged missionaries of the custody. Where the vicars resided, other small convents were to be built where three or more religious were to dwell (Geiger 1959: II: 345-346).

In 1779 the idea was approved in Rome, and in 1781 Pope Pius VI published a forty-two-page apostolic brief on the custodies and their statutes. On May 20, 1782, after Reyes had been made bishop of Sonora, the king decreed the founding of the four custodies Reyes had recommended. They were intended for Sonora as well as the two Californias, New Mexico, and Nueva Vizcaya (Geiger 1959: II: 347-349).

It is not surprising that the three apostolic colleges (San Fernando, Zacatecas, and Querétaro), who felt that the administration of their missions in the Provincias Internas was being threatened, reacted negatively to the idea of custodies. The protests of the friars were largely effectual, and only the Custodia de San Carlos de Sonora ever took actual shape on the ground. On October 23, 1783, in a meeting which took place at Ures in Sonora, Reyes appointed Father Sebastián Flores the first custodian. The next day, nine of the missions were raised to the status of hospices or convents and Banamichi became the custodial seat. At last, the Custodia de San Carlos, in addition to the nine hospices, ended up with sixteen missions with resident friars and twenty-five visitas, outlying mission stations without resident clergy. There were thirty-four missionaries in all, eight of them from the

Queretaran college, twelve from the Jaliscan province, and fourteen other Spanish Franciscans who had recently come from Spain (Geiger 1959: II: 358).

The San Carlos custody was beset with difficulties from the very beginning. Father Sebastián Flores, the custodian, died in January 1784, when he had been in office barely two months. His replacement was the former Queretaran, Antonio Barbastro, whose sympathies most probably had never been with the idea in the first place. Moreover, the missions were not able to support themselves through alms, and Santa Cruz de Querétaro had to continue to supply the missionaries with their salaries as before and to supply replacements for men who died, became ill, or retired.

Bishop Reyes died March 6, 1787 (Stagg 1974: 71). The next year, 1788, Father Barbastro himself informed the king that the custody form of administration had retarded, rather than advanced, the mission cause, and he asked the king to abolish it. Finally, on August 17, 1791, the king complied with Barbastro's request, and the Custodia de San Carlos de Sonora passed out of existence. The missions were returned to their pre-custody status, the Queretarans again in charge of the missions of Pimería Alta (Geiger 1959: II: 359, 362-364). In 1793 Father Barbastro compiled a lengthy report on the entire situation on the Sonoran frontier, a study which complements the report of Father Bringas translated in this book (see Gómez Canedo 1971).

In spite of the experience of the San Carlos custody, the move in the direction of secularization continued to grind relentlessly forward in the Provincias Internas. On April 10, 1794, Pedro de Nava, comandante general of the Provincias Internas and royal vice-patron, ordered that in all missions which had been in existence longer than ten years "every mission Indian was . . . to enjoy all the liberty, freedom, and privileges granted by Spanish laws to Spaniards and *gente de razon* (beings endowed with reason)." Moreover:

They were individually to take care of their own cattle, cultivate and plant their own lands, enjoy the returns of their crops, engage freely in trade, pursue the work they preferred, and seek gainful employment as laborers to provide for the needs and care of their families. But the justices and other public officials were to exercise particular zeal to prevent them from falling into idle habits or evil ways and to keep them from indulging in drunkenness and other excesses to which they were prone.

The new administrative officers, the *justicias* (justices), were given all the powers formerly exercised by the missionaries in supervising the natives and in protecting their interests (Castañeda 1942: 46-47).

Where had the friars of Pimería Alta heard this before? The doctrinas were being proposed all over again; it looked like a replay of their first active year in the Sonoran missions. Again it was Father Barbastro, now president of the missions, to the rescue. He appealed to Nava that such a move would destroy the Pimería Alta missions altogether. Nava responded by suspending the order for that region (see section 96). It was in such an atmosphere that Friar Diego Bringas de Manzaneda y Encinas set out from his College of Santa Cruz de Querétaro on April 16, 1795, in the role of father visitor (Kessell 1976: 183). Among other things, he would take it on himself to straighten out the relationship between church and state in northern Sonora and thereby strengthen the mission cause.

Indian Culture in the Pimería Alta: A Model of Adaptation

When the Jesuit priest Eusebio Francisco Kino crossed over the imaginary line in northern Sonora poetically labeled the "rim of Christendom" (Bolton 1960b), he became the first European known to establish a prolonged relationship with northern Piman Indians. The year was 1687, and the Indians consisted of diverse groups whose common bond was that of language. They all spoke mutually intelligible dialects of Piman, a language which belongs in the larger Uto-Aztecan stock, a group of related languages spoken all the way from southern Idaho to Nicaragua.

The Spaniards applied various names to these Pimans, calling some of them simply "Pimas," while others were variously "Papagos," "Sobas," "Sobaipuris," "Gileños," "Imuris," and "Piatos." The ethnographic reality appears to have been that there were at least two or three dozen Piman groups in northern Sonora, each independent of the other and each with its own local dialect. Some of these people survived as hunting-gathering nomads in the deserts of what are today northwesternmost Sonora and southwesternmost Arizona. Others, those called "Papagos" during most of the eighteenth century, lived where Papagos continue to reside, in the vast riverless desert watered largely by summer monsoons that bring enough moisture to make agriculture possible. During the winter they lived in villages near permanent springs at the bases of mountain ranges. In the summer their villages were in the intermontane valleys in which they planted their fields of corn, tepary beans, and other native crops where rain-filled arroyos debouched onto the flats (Fontana 1974).

Piman life took its most luxuriant and anchored form in the riverine perimeters of the northern portion of the Sonoran Desert. The Gila, Santa Cruz, San Pedro, Magdalena, Concepción, Altar, and Sonoita rivers provided a year-round source of water, that most precious of all desert commodities — water that enabled the human species to live permanently in larger villages with fixed locations next to streams. Fields of crops could either be planted in the floodplain of rivers or they could be encouraged in their growth with the help of irrigation ditches.

It was here the Spaniards found the "Pimas," the "Sobaipuris," and the "Gileños." It was here, among the larger villages, that the missions were founded, the churches constructed, and — as history would have it — the Spanish towns and later Mexican and Anglo-American cities grew. Tucson, the largest city in Arizona south of the Gila River, owes more than its name, *stuk-son*, to the Pimas. They were Indians who began the settlement in time immemorial, no doubt because they found the Santa Cruz River to their liking. And it was because of the Piman settlement that Spanish missionaries and soldiers were attracted to the place. The Spanish presidio became a ruined Mexican outpost; the Mexican town of mud-brick houses became an Anglo-American desert metropolis.

In pre-European times and, indeed, throughout the Spanish colonial period there was no such entity as a Piman "tribe," if by "tribe" one understands some kind of political linkage of units. What there were instead were "no-village" people in the west, perhaps two or three bands of extended family members; from nine to a dozen dialect groups of "two-village" people, each group comprised of a series of related settlements; and perhaps another six or eight dialect groups of "one-village" people living in the river valleys.

The villages were laid out in similar fashion with widely scattered structures, both public and private. The private structures were arranged in family compounds, and they consisted of brush houses and storage units, cooking enclosure, and a sunshade, or ramada. The public structure was a brush building in which the men held their nightly council meetings. It was usually near the compound of the headman of the local group because he was in charge of its upkeep. It also had to be located within shouting distance of all the other houses, because announcements were made from it in that manner (Bahr 1973: 4).

Local groups were encompassed by larger units called regional bands. The dialect spoken by members of a band was the same; village groups within the bands attended each other's ceremonies; and the villages within a band often recognized the "headship" status of an individual in what was regarded as a parent village (Bahr 1973: 21-22; Underhill 1939: 70-89). The headman held his office because of his personal abilities, not through inheritance. He could be a ritual orator ("wise speaker"), the organizer and principal speaker at council meetings ("fire maker" or "keeper of the smoke"), the person in charge of the group's sacred bundle ("keeper of the plaited basket"), and the person who had "great man" social status ("the one above") (Bahr 1973: 18-19). Government was by consensus of adult males and thereby strictly through consent of the governed. The headman could not be an autocrat.

The headman could have younger assistants to help him in his duties, assistants in roles such as "legs," "eyes," and "voice," and there were other men who led on specific occasions, as the war leader, hunt leader, game leader, and song leader (Bahr 1973: 19). This was about the extent of the political organization of Piman Indians during the eighteenth century.

Piman economics was based on sharing and on devising means — whether through ceremonial exchanges, betting, or gifts — to spread wealth fairly evenly throughout the group and regional band (Bahr 1973: 24-37). Cooperation lay at the root of village subsistence, and the whole was cemented together by a world view spoken of as '*ó'odahm himdag*, the "Piman Way." The term '*ó'odahm* is used universally by Pimans in referring to themselves. It means "The People."

In its narrowest sense, we would translate '*ó'odahm himdag* as "Piman religion," but the concept of "way," meaning virtually a whole way of life, comes closer to expressing its genuine character. Pimans had no religion as something separate and apart from the rest of their lives. What they had was a way of life which saw the essence of religion in all things, all people, and all actions. Just as people had a "way," so did other living beings and some things that people did, such as ceremonies. Just as people had rights and dignity and propriety, so did other living beings and ceremonies.

The Piman Way was reinforced among its followers by the threat of the diseases which could befall one who transgressed against it — the principal role of the shaman being to diagnose and direct the cures for such illnesses. It was further supported by a rich ceremonial life, with ceremonies involving growth of crops, hunting, warfare, community health, and, above all, the bringing down of life-sustaining rain (see Bahr and others 1974; Underhill n.d., 1946, 1968).

The language the Pimans spoke was as complex as any in the world. It was and continues to be capable of expressing ideas as intricate and as abstract as any concepts peculiar to Indo-European cultural traditions, whether Spanish, Latin or English. The vocabulary is enormous — running into many thousands of words (Mathiot 1973) — and is capable of expressing whatever it is Pimans might have occasion to say within the context of their real universe.

In short, the Piman Indians whom the missionaries encountered in the late seventeenth century in northern Sonora had political organizations, social organizations, economic organizations, a complex language, and a religion which was the embodiment of their various ways of life. They had developed a technology admirably adapted to desert subsistence, one which appears to have been well suited to extracting a maximal living from the natural surroundings while imposing the least amount of long-range environmental damage.

Even so, existence must have been harsh. Life expectancy was very short. In dry years there were probably starvations; in good years people weren't likely to get fat. The only major sources of meat were game animals like antelope, deer, and mountain sheep, all hard to kill with the bow-and-arrow and an uncertain source of food at best. Spanish cattle, sheep, and horses — to say nothing of new crops such as wheat — must have looked very good to the Pimans. It is small wonder that Piman villages sometimes sent out emissaries to urge a visit by the missionary. It was he who distributed the largesse of European foodstuffs.

The Pimans of northern Sonora were not a cultural island. There were other Pimans to the south, even as there were Opatas and Seris. There were Yuman-speaking Indians on the west and northwest; there were Apaches to the north, northeast, and east (see Spicer 1962). But on the overland route to California from Mexico, the Pimería Alta was an essential steppingstone. Its natives had to be "brought to vassalage" if Spain's manifest destiny were to be fulfilled.

The Friars and the Pimans: Directed Culture Change

We who view historically Spain's involvement with the Indians of the Pimería Alta must ask ourselves specifically what it was that Father Bringas and his fellow friars meant when they spoke of bringing the Pimans to the vassalage of the crown of Spain. This phrase of theirs assumed that Indians occupied a pre-ordained, subordinate position in the social structure of contact culture, and that Indians owed allegiance to the king. In time, they would owe him taxes as well. In return, the king was to provide Indians protection.

Bringas further talks of wanting Indians to learn of and to appreciate "social, political and intellectual life," implying they had none of their own. He wanted them to cease to be "at complete liberty," to stop their "idleness and continual wandering." He further wished them to become interested in Spanish trade and commerce.

The report notes the need to promote good among the Indians as a device to "keep the vast dominions of Your Royal Majesty in the most flourishing state." Indians should not be "lazy" in working and cultivating their fields; they should be good farmers (in the Spanish model). They should adjust to the laws and policies of "civil society." They should be peaceful; become expert in mining; useful in trades; weaned away from insubordination, lack of foresight, distrust, and "instability"; and encouraged to live in settlements with uniform and straight streets "in order to avoid disorderly appearance," "disorderly" being a Spanish definition. Indians should also be made to work for private as well as community good.

If these were the civil aims of the Indians' conversion, they were also to be brought to the Holy Faith, "Holy Faith" being the kind of Roman Catholicism practiced in eighteenth century New Spain under the patronato real and as implemented locally by Franciscan friars. Conversion to the faith and subsequent perseverance in the holy religion are often-expressed ideals.

To accomplish these ends, the religious and civil authorities would lead Indians through institutionalized stages progressing from mission to conversion or reduction to doctrina to curacy. Indians would be the recipients of preaching. They would be baptized, and sacraments would be administered to them. The regular clergy would control the temporal goods in Indian communities that were to be isolated and segregated, and Indians themselves would be under the sole and exclusive charge of the missionaries.

Indians would receive instruction; their "excesses" would be controlled. Their "true happiness" would be promoted, suggesting they were not already happy. They would be put to work in agriculture and made to work communal farm plots as well as privately owned plots which would be distributed among them, two private plots going to the more industrious workers. People were to be fully clothed, especially the women and children, and they were to forsake those vices enjoyed by Spaniards, such as gambling, drinking, and dancing. They were to be instructed, made to learn, won over, transformed. Spanish was intended to become their language.

What we are looking at in the Bringas report were not the spontaneous efforts of zealous men, both secular and religious. What we see were the attempts of obedient civil servants to put into effect the measures decided upon in ever-increasing detail at a multitude of council tables by managers and lawyers and soldiers and churchmen. We are looking at the outlines of a non-random, totally planned effort.

To understand fully the nature of this effort, we should know something of the agents of change — the Franciscan missionaries of the College of Santa Cruz de Querétaro. The kind of training these friars received beginning in the late seventeenth century has been described by Father Isidro Félix de Espinosa, one of three official chroniclers of the history of the college, the other two being Arrici-vita (1792) and Bringas (1960) himself. Writes Father Espinosa (1964: 173-176):

Since the venerable founder of this college was an ecstatic man, he arranged the regular life of the missionaries in such a way that they had no idle time and so that the common Enemy would always find them occupied. The time was and still is to this day divided thus: at midnight, as is the custom in our seraphic order, the religious rise for Matins which they recite slowly and devoutly. Then they recite the litany of Our Lady. Then there is an hour of meditation from which none are dispensed. This holy work is kept up so tenaciously that it is interrupted only for the three days of Holy Week and the happy morning of the Resurrection, when Matins are at four o'clock.

In the mornings at five-thirty in summer and six o'clock in winter, Prime is recited. Then Masses are said, one after the other. A long time is used for this. At eight o'clock the three other little Hours [Terce, Sext and None] are said, followed by the conventual Mass [i.e., the Mass officially celebrated for the whole convent].

The Apostolic Bulls order that there is to be a conference on languages or on mystical theology after None if there are no confessions to be heard. They give faculties to the Guardian to dispense if the latter is the case. The confessions inside and outside are so many and so continuous that they fill the whole morning, and noon comes without finishing the hard labor. From the start it has been a praise-worthy custom not to dismiss the penitent until he has been comforted and admonished, even though time was lacking.

After the noon meal, on the days when they did not march to church reciting a psalm, the community washed the dishes. On no day, no matter how great the feast, is there any lack of a great number of religious who go to church to adore the Most Holy or to perform other devout exercises to which each may be inspired by his own piety. They then retire in religious silence until Vespers, which they recite with the same gravity and devotion as the rest of the Office. On leaving the choir, they go directly to a conference on moral subjects so as to be able better to administer the sacrament of penance. . . . Ordinarily there are two-and-a-half hours left for study, but those who go to hear the confessions of the sick do not get there. They do not let a bit of time be lost, in accordance with the admonition of the Holy Spirit to the Just.

At five-thirty there follows the complete litany and then a whole hour of meditation which is ended by reciting the prayer to the Most Holy Sacrament with arms extended like a cross. Then they go to the refectory for the evening meal. At its conclusion they all go to sing the "Tota Pulchra" to the Immaculate Conception with other devout prayers for the good of Holy Church, for those at sea, for the extirpation of error, for the sick, for rain and for other needs of Christian people. Then they take the discipline [i.e., flail themselves with a scourge] on the days customary in the whole Order. During the time that remains until silence, which begins at eight, those who so desire are reconciled and others visit the altars or are busy about some virtuous activity. When the bell rings for silence, all retire to their cells. With this, the cycle of virtuous activity is complete.

. . . In addition to all this, which God's goodness has maintained, the first missionaries did many additional works. They spent more time in meditation, using for it the time not assigned to other things by the rules. So little time was spent in sleep they had barely enough rest. When choir was over at two-thirty, they all engaged in the holy exercise of making the Stations of the Cross in the cloister bearing crosses, and wearing nooses and crowns of thorns. Some took the discipline in the meantime. Some remained in prayer. Each one performed whatever penitential exercise to which he was inspired by the Holy Spirit.

The fervent Chief [i.e., Father Guardian], aware of the ardor of his soldiers, spurred them on by exhortation and example, not permitting self love to cause any cessation of these battles of the spirit. He well knew by experience that in this spiritual warfare there is more danger in idleness than in combat.

Lovers of the cross and of their crucified lord represented thereon, devised new ways of imitating the sorrowful image by causing suffering for themselves. With pious insults they obliged the lay religious and the oblates to perform the office of tormentors by striking them, jerking on their nooses and even kicking them in disgust. This painful mortification cost some not a little effort, but all profited from it though some gained merit for their suffering and others gained considerably by their resignation in obediently causing it.

On the Vespers of great feasts, they added other penances to the mortification of fasting while in the refectory. Some ate seated on the floor. Others walked around the tables bearing heavy crosses. Others kissed the feet of their brothers, confessing their defects and faults, and since permission to do this was not given all at the same time, in order to preserve the decorum of the community, some mortified themselves by suffering pain and others by not suffering it. Oh! How little appreciated is the joy of those who live in such monasteries! Those who perform such penances succeed in humbling themselves. Those who watch them humble themselves still more, for they see themselves as men of little zeal. These are fruitful gains which are of manifest profit to those who perform the acts as well as those who do not.

The prudent prelate [father guardian] saw that by the continual exercise of the virtues, the strength of his beloved sons became greater each day. And so he did not limit their fervor. He realized that his missionaries, like plants, grew into trees owing to the water of grace, and that to do the works expected of them, one could not be bound by lazy laws of the world. He saw them as the gleaming torches of enlightenment and instruction. His heart would not let their rays be extinguished by idleness when they might serve to inflame souls in the fire of their Maker.

For this purpose he ordered them to hold a mission in this city of Querétaro, which they began on the first Sunday of September. The first day there was a fervent sermon in every church; then one every day for fifteen days in the parish church and for a week in the churches of Guadalupe and Saint Anthony. The seed of the divine word was scattered throughout the plazas and public streets in all quarters of the city where the missionaries were distributed. They preached with words full of the Spirit, admonishing the world to practice virtue and detest vice. They reprehended with holy freedom, striking the sins but without injuring those guilty of them. Thus they bore fruit without causing any scandal and with credit to the teaching. Nor were they satisfied with having achieved the universal reformation of customs with this one mission.

For many years two or three missionaries would go out in the quietest part of the night singing moral couplets and preaching on the street corners. On Christmas the whole community [of friars] went out before Matins carrying two holy images of Most Holy Mary and her most chaste Spouse, begging for a lodging at the portals of human hearts. This was done with such tender feeling that the noisy gatherings that usually accompany the licentious doings of the worldly did not take place.

With the continuous fire of the divine word which the missionaries spread about, the tares of the abuses which had deformed the Christianity of the citizens were consumed. Some of the festivities were abandoned which had been celebrated with bull fights, parades and the ostentatious show of Moors and Christians [see Warman 1972]. Many of the poor, in order to make a show, had either sold or pawned what they needed for the support of their children. Others had spent thousands of pesos impersonating the Grand Turk and his captains. They had bought dangerous contrivances made of gun powder with their money. At the end of the feasts they began to regret their activities. But now they are thankful that they were freed from illusion by what they had regretted.

Another abuse as full as the arroyo that fertilizes the lands of Querétaro was that of scandalous public bathing in which men and women came together on the banks of the streams with music, food, and festivity. Imagine the evil that this could produce, that is if one can imagine it without becoming stained. Public games were done away with; dancing and fun making ceased; laxity of conduct was interdicted, and now the celebrated amenity of the gardens of Querétaro was unknown.

I do not say that vice was completely wiped out. Like the venemous hydra, when one head is cut off another is born. What was achieved was that the scandalous conduct which took place in the plazas without shame is today politely hidden. Even though the malice of sins is not eliminated, it is no longer a cause of scandal.

Finally, this city was so reformed by the arrival of the missionaries that [this incident occurred when] a common man who was well born and God fearing returned from a trip which had kept him away for some time. He met a well born local resident who was also God fearing, and asked him if there was anything new in the city. He replied, "Sir, Querétaro is no longer Querétaro. Some meddling fathers have come to "la Cruz" and now there are no more fandangos. Everything is now very sad. No harp or guitar is heard. Everything is praying and sermons, and the city has lost its joy."

No doubt this man was one of those of whom the Holy Spirit says that they rejoice in doing evil and that they glory in their worst deed. He knew by experience that Querétaro was no longer the same. Formerly it was the cause of many sins due to the delights it offered. Today, owing to the moderation of life and the frequent reception of the sacraments, it can be numbered among the most exemplary cities of the world.

Friars from this college and of these persuasions were the ones who went forth in the eighteenth century to bring Piman Indians to the Holy Faith. If the message they had to convey was good news, the messengers were of dispositions quite unlike those among whom they were to spread the word.

That Spain's conversion effort among the northern Piman Indians generally failed is a matter of historical record. Many Pimans were outwardly Christianized in that they accepted a number of the formal aspects of the new religion, but few, if any, of the intended meanings of those forms survived. And most certainly Pimans never became loyal vassals of the Spanish crown. They reacted to Spanish aggression in a variety of ways, all of them aimed at preserving their identity as viable peoples. Sometimes they withdrew; at others they were themselves the physical aggressors; they adapted; they were accommodating. Above all, they seem to have gone only so far as they had to go to give the appearance of change. They discovered soon that what the Spaniard wanted was Indians to have the *appearance* of being like themselves rather than to undergo genuine assimilation.

A Second Look at the Bringas Report: An Editorial Appraisal

In terms of purely regional interest, study of a Spanish colonial document such as Father Bringas' manuscript supplies descriptive and statistical information which, even if known by a few archivist scholars, has not previously been published. Included in this category are the statistical summaries showing more than 750 baptisms which took place in the Pimería Alta from the period between the Franciscan takeover in 1768 and the time of Bringas' writing in 1796. Considered with other kinds of records, they provide the raw data for possibly worthwhile analyses involving the age distributions in various populations and their changes through time; the movement of Indians of particular tribes; the relative successes or failures of particular missionaries; and other kinds of demographic concerns. Father Bringas had before him copies of mission registers, some of which have subsequently disappeared — most notably those for the Franciscan period of San Xavier del Bac.

Although the Yuma massacre of the priests and Spanish colonists has been described in print in several places, Bringas provides us with the first verbatim reporting of the orders issued by Comandante General Teodoro de Croix for the establishment of these ill-fated settlements. We also are given a glimpse of the involvement of Pedro Galindo Navarro.

From most extant documents it is difficult to get a view of what life for the average person was like in a Sonoran town during the final thirty years of the eighteenth century. Population figures and accounts of values of extracted minerals don't offer much help. However, through the reports of Father Arriquibar on Bacoachi's Apache community, as well as discussions by Father Llorens and by Bringas alluding to Tucson, we can get at least a hint of what was going on behind the scenes of most official reports.

Thanks to his October 1795 journey to the Gila River, we also have from Father Bringas an important ethnographic description of the Gila River Pimas — important because it fills a large gap in the history of descriptions of these people.

In some ways, moreover, it is the most complete such description for the whole of the eighteenth century.

Finally, historians of northern Sonora and what has become southern Arizona will appreciate Bringas' information relating to the missions of Pimería Alta, information on their numbers and their physical conditions and changes through the years.

But these items of regional interest are not what make the Bringas report outstanding. It seems to us the real significance of this document lies in the fact that it provides a blueprint of Spanish attempts at directed culture change. It contains a full-blown, detailed, step-by-step discussion of many of the means conceived by Spain to effect a sweeping reformation of native cultures in the New World. As such, it is a study in the efforts everywhere and at any time — ancient and modern — of peoples of one set of cultural persuasions to convert to their point of view peoples of a quite different set of persuasions.

We see in this document many points of similarity between Spanish indigenist programs and later United States programs for Indians. The Spaniards had reducciones in which the natives were tax exempt; the United States has reservations whose governments and lands are tax exempt. The Spaniards had doctrinas whose Indian-owned lands were held in trust by the crown; lands within Indian reservations in the United States are held in federal trust. Funds for the administration of missions came out of the Spanish Ramo de Guerra, or "War Fund" (Bolton 1960: 11). Until 1849, the administration of Indian affairs in the United States was vested in the War Department. The Spanish reducción was an all-Indian community presided over by a missionary whose task it was to bring about the re-enculturation of Indians into the dominant society. United States Indian reservations until the turn of the century — and to a large extent after — were segregated communities of Indians who were subjects of directed culture change being presided over by missionaries and various selected agents of the federal government. In both cases, Indians were being asked to adopt the ways of the dominant society while being expected to remain in near-total isolation from it.

Thus, in the final analysis, the Spanish conquest was more than the coming together of Spanish culture and the cultures of native peoples. It was the establishment of an integrated system of domination, that of a minority who were dependent on a system of power exercised over a native majority. In this sense, the role of the missionary has been the role of the aggressor. Simply to "spread news of great joy" is one matter; to invade the most sacred inner precincts of another man's being, and thereby to defile him, is something else again. It seems to us there can be no greater form of violence than this.

The implications in this matter in terms of the modern world should be clear. As highly industrialized, technology-dependent state societies continue to broaden their spheres of influence and compete with one another for the resources and allegiances of so-called third world or underdeveloped nations, we are witnessing a modern counterpart of the European age of discovery and expansion which was touched off in the fifteenth century. Cultures continue to come into contact and conflict; nations whose members believe they share similar values, ideals, and traditions continue to attempt to impose these — whether by peaceful persuasion or less subtle forms — on peoples whose whole cultural stances are radically different. Leaders of superordinate powers no longer speak of "civilizing" those whom they would subordinate. Instead they are "assisting the developing nations of the world" in their own development; they are "liberating the people from imperialistic exploitation" by capitalists and others; or they are "preserving the freedom" of other countries and protecting their citizens against communist aggression.

It occurs to us that only the slogans and rhetoric are different. State societies continue to broadcast portions of their various value systems to all four quarters of the earth, and underlying principles of cultural proselytism, directed culture change, and the kinds of resistance or lack of resistance to such change are the same as they were in New Spain during the sixteenth, seventeenth, and eighteenth centuries.

Which brings us to the largest question of all: Why? We can suggest two answers, both of them related. There are doubtless more possible responses, but it is better they should be proposed by others with the same concerns.

First of all, life is a series of encounters. One's culture orders these encounters to make it possible for human beings to cope with them. Western, rational, "scientific" culture abhors mysteries. We therefore make mysterious aspects of life intelligible either by applying our own labels to them or by attempting to make them over into forms with which we are familiar and can manipulate. Thus we often attempt to make people over in our own image.

Indians, on the other hand, tend to tolerate and accommodate the unintelligible. Strangers are kept conceptually segregated into "stranger" categories in their mythologies.

It may also be that rather than speak of "Indian" in contrast to "Western" man, we should be speaking instead of "state societies" versus societies which are not — whether tribal or band or local group or extended family organization. There is evidence that the Aztecs and Incas, for example, used techniques not unlike those of the Spaniards in extending their pre-Conquest empires. And any modern state — be it Chinese, European, or American — which can speak of its policies toward "native" peoples can be thought of as a colonial power bent on the manipulation of those peoples — which brings us to our second suggestion concerning why anyone wants others to look, act, talk and think like himself.

It has been argued that "the missions were preparing the indigenous populations for non-existent places in a [New World Spanish] society dominated by aristocracy and elitism" (Polzer 1972: 128). Although the missionary may have believed he was preparing the natives for a new place in a new society, he was in fact assuring that the "native" remained just that.

The category "native" applies to the subordinated sector in the colonial situation; it has nothing to do with the specific content of the native cultures. In the early days of the colonial era, the "native" was a pagan and an idolator; that provided the rationalization and justification for the regime to which he was subjected. Today, the Indian may be Catholic or Protestant, he will certainly no longer be an idolator, but he will be regarded as backward or lazy or depraved, in short, ethnically inferior, which is the appropriate assumption required to rationalize the colonial situation. This kind of Indian, in short, is the product of a colonial relationship, not a culture (Bonfíl Batalla 1972: 25-26).

Viewed in this framework, the need of members of state societies to work toward the appearance of assimilation in their "native" population becomes clear. Our pretense at making them be like us, while settling for appearances alone, is a salve to individual conscience. But their continuance as "natives" is an important economic asset in support of the state. As Bonfíl Batalla (1972: 22, 28) has pointed out, non-Indians control the economy of Indian groups. This applies to sales to Indians as well as to purchases from them. Indian producers have no choice of markets. Indian economies are subverted by the changing demands of non-Indian economy such that Indians' lands and manpower are given over in response. And finally, Indians are manipulated as a consumer market. This status among modern Pima and Papago Indians living in southern Arizona has changed almost not at all from its eighteenth century beginnings.

As final questions, we must ask, Is it really worth it, worth it for any of us as human beings? Is the drive toward the appearance of assimilation in others really desirable? Are the individual cries of pain and the little agonies of little people engendered by their encounter with an unsuspected and undreamed of world system to the long-range advantage of humanity? Or is it possible to have harmony with the greatest possible diversity? Is it possible to impregnate the ways of others without destroying the richness inherent in their own identities? Can we abolish the "Indian" as a colonial category, allowing for the emergence of ethnic identities in all their vigour?

These are the issues raised by Father Bringas' report to the king.

DANIEL S. MATSON
BERNARD L. FONTANA

N° 15

K
Bundle 18, N° 25

1796
202/42

Report to the King concerning the missions of
Pimería Alta; new establishments; inadequate
measures of the Comandancia; the fragile
peace with the Apaches; and many other
important matters. Its transmission to Spain
was suspended due to the war, 1796.

Bringas

1799

THE REPORT OF
FATHER DIEGO MIGUEL BRINGAS
DE MANZANEDA Y ENCINAS, O.F.M.
TO THE KING OF SPAIN
1796~97

FRIAR BRINGAS
REPORTS TO THE KING

Señor: The Guardian and Discreets of the Apostolic Seminary of Santa Cruz of the City of Querétaro in New Spain, present themselves with the submission and respect owed to the sovereign and royal person of your Majesty, and say:

 I

The eight missions situated on the border of the Provincia Interna de San Juan Bautista de Sonora in the nation of the Pimas Altos[1] have been placed in our charge and under our management through the patronage and trust of Your Royal Majesty. Likewise, we are also in charge of bringing to our Holy Faith and to the vassalage of Your Royal Majesty the many and diverse nations which are in the vicinity of our missions and the Pimas Altos. Two thousand eight hundred pesos a year are needed for the support of 16 *ministros,* sons of this college, for the pious and holy purpose of helping the reduced Indians to persevere in our holy religion; to enable them to learn and appreciate social, political and intellectual life; and to motivate the gentiles to embrace these important aims. For our part, we have undertaken all the ordinary and extraordinary labors which were incumbent upon us in the discharge of our obligation, ministry and duty to fulfill the royal trust of Your Catholic Majesty. Those *conversiones* have suffered many vicissitudes up to the present time, although these have not succeeded in completely obstructing our efforts. We have made use of the most efficacious means possible in order to achieve this. Now, however, the most serious peril threatens the very existence of those eight missions. We foresee obstacles which may be insurmountable or which may give us a very difficult time during the reduction of the frontier nations. We have believed it to be part of our duty to inform Your Royal Majesty clearly and in detail of whatever we thought necessary to achieve these ends as well as to assist in promoting Your Majesty's efforts to cover the increased expenses incurred in the recruitment and travel costs of ministers for this seminary. All this is in order that Your Royal Majesty might condescend to take steps in accordance with his royal pleasure. Thus our conscience will remain clear because we have taken that most powerful and efficacious recourse to the clemency and catholic zeal of Your Royal Majesty.

---

1. Bringas here refers to the Piman Indians of northern Sonora and Arizona as distinguished from those living in southern Sonora and farther south.

2

We must go back, Señor, to the eighth day of July, 1767, in order to inform Your Majesty with the proper exactitude. On that day by order of the Marquis de Croix, Viceroy of Mexico, this College took charge of the administration of the 14 missions of the Pimería Alta and Pimería Baja of the Provincia de Sonora. It never ceased to promote the ends to which the royal confidence has destined it until through the sovereign decisions of May 20, 1782, Señor Don Carlos III, august father of Your Majesty, commanded that the aforesaid missions be turned over for the creation of the Custodia de San Carlos de Sonora.[2] This was done in obedience to such a superior order. However, with the passage of years difficulties arose with respect to the Custodia. In view of them, Your Majesty commanded in the *cédula real* of July 16, 1790,[3] that the Guardian and Discreets of this Seminary should collect opinions and information, such as they might deem opportune, from persons who were honest and zealous in the service of God and Your Majesty and report the results to him. This sovereign order of Your Majesty was obeyed. Finally, in the cédula real of August 17, 1791, you commanded that the missions should continue temporarily in the old manner until the best method should be finally determined.[4]

---

2. Carlos Francisco de Croix, Marquis de Croix, was the forty-fifth viceroy of New Spain. He served in that capacity from August 24, 1766, to September 21, 1771. He was the uncle of Teodoro de Croix, who in 1776 became the first comandante general of the newly organized comandancia general of the Provincias Internas of New Spain.

Don Carlos III, king of Spain from 1758 until his death in 1788, was born in 1716, the fifth son of Felipe V. His cédula real of May 20, 1782, actually decreed the erection of four custodias: de la Concepción in New Mexico; San Carlos of Sonora; San Gabriel in Upper and Lower California; and San Antonio in Nueva Vizcaya. It also "ordered the viceroy of New Spain, the *audiencias* of Mexico and Guadalajara, the commandant general of the Provincias Internas, the archbishop of Mexico City, the bishops of Puebla, Valladolid (Morelia today), Oaxaca, Guadalajara, Yucatan, Durango, and Sonora, as well as the provincials and guardians of the provinces concerned, to see that the custodies were erected and the statutes observed. No one was to impede the work directly or indirectly but rather to provide all necessary to bring this 'so useful and charitable work' which 'redounded to God's service and mine' to a happy fruition" (Geiger 1959: II: 348-349). Of the four proposed custodias, that of San Carlos de Sonora was the only one which became a reality.

3. Maynard Geiger (1959: II: 364) writes: "Then the king addressed a letter [Bringas says cédula] to the college of Querétaro on July 16, 1790, asking it to investigate the matter and to see what steps could be taken in keeping with the royal intentions. Querétaro advised that the custody [of San Carlos of Sonora] be abolished to save the missions. It stated that [Bishop Antonio del los] Reyes 'in bringing the project before the king and before Rome had not represented or expressed the wishes of the colleges or missionaries but merely his own ideas which had been found impracticable.'"

4. "On August 17, 1791, the king abolished the custody of San Carlos and declared the old order of things restored. After fifteen years [Bishop Antonio de los] Reyes' plan had come to an end. The bishop did not live to see the dissolution of the custody he erected" (Geiger 1959: II: 364). Reyes died March 6, 1787 (Stagg 1974: 71).

3

By virtue of this mandate of Your Majesty this College resumed charge of the eight missions in the Pimería Alta. Zealous activity was begun at once to repair the damage the missions had suffered during the time of the Custodia. The College tried to make use of the means most conducive to this purpose without losing sight of the most important objective: the extension of our Holy Faith and the dominion of Your Majesty over the frontier nations. No measures considered opportune for the purpose were omitted.

4

For five years now, Señor, all of our efforts and hopes for an increase in conversions have been frustrated. We have been disappointed in thinking that only the catholic zeal of Your Majesty could accomplish this. It therefore becomes our obligation to explain to Your Majesty the steps which we have taken up to the present time in pursuit of these goals.

Three things especially have been the target of our efforts, and our feeble attempts have been extended to all three. These are characteristic of our Institute[5] and are in the service of God and Your Majesty.

The first is the care of the spiritual needs of the *pueblos, villas, minerales* and *lugares* which are scattered over more than 500 leagues.[6] The very distance makes it impossible for them to receive the regular encouragement of preaching without enormous expenditures and extraordinary measures.

The second is the restoration, stabilization and growth of the 14 pueblos which make up the eight missions of the Pimería Alta which are in our charge.[7]

The last is the conversion of more than 25,000 souls of poor gentile Indians who are on the frontier and beyond our missions. They are for the most part in a most advantageous state to receive the Gospel and to acknowledge vassalage to Your Majesty.

All these need Your Majesty's beneficent attention for their success.

---

5. That is to say, the Order of Friars Minor, or Franciscans.

6. See the terms *pueblo, villa, mineral, lugar* and *legua* in the Lexicon of Spanish Words in the back of this book.

7. Bringas lists these fourteen pueblos in section 22. His map, pictured on p. 98 of this book, was based on his 1795 trip (Ezell 1956: 156), and shows fifteen pueblos, with Ymuris [Imuris] being clearly indicated as a visita. Possibly between October 1795 and the date of Bringas' writing, Imuris was dropped from the rolls. The eight missions, or *cabeceras*, were Caborca, Ati, Tubutama, Saric, San Ignacio, Cocóspera, Tumacácori, and San Xavier del Bac. The other six pueblos were visitas. This was precisely the situation in September 1797, when Father Francisco Yturralde (1798) made his visit to these places. He, too, says nothing of Imuris.

As for the first matter, this College took the step of designating five religious who should travel along the hot coasts of Jalisco and Sinaloa preaching the divine word and administering the Holy Sacraments with faculties provided by the ordinaries of those places.[8] After having left this Seminary on September 25, 1793, they returned on April 20, 1795. They spent all this time in missionary work in more than twenty different locations where they remained for long periods to establish in each one a place of congregation for those in the surrounding country, thus satisfying so far as possible the needs of all. After they had exerted themselves to the point of becoming gravely ill, we discovered that the harvest was not plentiful and that for its cultivation even a large number of transient workers would not suffice. To bring it to fruition permanent workers would be necessary. The terminus of this *misión* was the Villa de Sinaloa, 350 leagues from this city. This College decided that some missionaries whom it designated to accompany the ministros of our missions should continue to cultivate the vineyard as opportunity offered until they reached the farthest away of the previously established misiones. From there on they should continue their preaching until they reach the end of this North America in a northwest direction and the locale of our missions in the Pimería. Ten missionaries actually went on April 16, 1795. They continued to look after all those peoples from the Villa de Montesclaros del Fuerte as far as the *real de minas* of San Ildefonso de la Cieneguilla and the Presidio of San Agustín del Tucson. The latter is the farthest outpost on the Sonora frontier, at 32.5° north latitude. They made lengthy stays in twelve places during a six months' period and traveled altogether a distance of more than 600 leagues to the farthest point from this city.[9]

This short exposition contains the important points which we will later explain to Your Majesty.

As for the second subject, as soon as this College again took charge of these missions, it gave orders to their President to take all measures necessary to maintain and extend them. He should put into effect all the orders issued for this purpose prior to the establishment of the Custodia. He should also request from this College the ministros needed to relieve missionaries and to fill vacancies. This was done. Twelve ministros were designated for this purpose. Measures were later taken by the Comandante General for the government of the missions, although they were

---

8. We have been unable to learn the names of the five religious or further details of this trip. An "ordinary" is usually either a bishop or head of a religious order. He possesses "ordinary" powers and authority under canon law, whereas other clergy possess only delegated authority.

9. We are unable to identify the specific settlements in which the nine Queretaran friars accompanying Father Bringas were placed. See note ten for the friars' names.

suspended at the request of the President, who explained to him the difficulties he would encounter in practice. He had solid grounds for fearing that very far from leading to the happiness which the Comandante intended to achieve for all concerned, these measures would doubtless contribute instead to the more rapid decadence and total ruin of the missions. We shall explain this to Your Majesty when we deal with this point.

As for the third item, from this time on our College began to work for the reduction of the Indians of the frontier who were in better shape before the erection of the Custodia. It made various representations to the office of the Comandante General of Chihuahua. Seeing that they had no effect it sent a religious who should be given sufficient authority as well as a pass by the Comandante General to visit all the missions. He was also to make arrangements to get them into the best shape possible and bring nine religious to serve internships with the missionaries so that in accordance with the many cédulas reales as well as with canon and civil law, they should be trained in the best possible way to discharge their ministry. He was also ordered to enter the country of the gentiles who populate the Gila River, discerning their condition, number, industries, relationships; the nature of the country; and the inclination of the gentiles toward the Gospel and vassalage. He was to note everything in detail and make the necessary plans. Finally, he was to present himself as the representative of the College to the Comandante General of the Provincias Internas and give him a detailed account of everything. He was to ask in our name whatsoever he should judge proper, both for the improvement of the eight missions as well as for the reduction of the gentiles. When all these matters had been taken care of, he was to return to inform us about them. This was actually done by the end of fourteen months for each of the points which have been mentioned.[10]

Since, Señor, these three points embody the obligations of our Seminary, and since no provisions were made up to the present to discharge them fittingly, our fidelity will not let us rest until we have informed Your Majesty of what is needed

---

10. Father Bringas is referring to himself. He set out with the nine missionaries on April 16, 1795, as described in the Introduction of this book. These were fathers Pascual Rodríguez, Mariano Bordoy, Francisco Covas, Ángel Alonso de Prado, Andrés Sánchez, Pablo Mata, Andrés Caraygorta, Ramón López, and Pedro Amorós (Rivera 1795). Bringas made his journey among the Indian villages along the Gila River in October 1795 (Ezell 1956:156;1958:18), and reported to the comandante general on March 15, 1796 (Section 36). The fourteen months to which he refers were probably those between the time he was ordered to make his inspection and the presentation of a final report to the college. This would seem to have been from about April 1795 to June 1796.

in each case, and until you have given us orders in accordance with your royal pleasure. The remedy, Señor, for all the ills, present and to come, relative to the three points under discussion seems to us, after the matter has been thoroughly considered, to be the following:

That aid is required to relieve the spiritual needs of the Provincias Internas of Sinaloa and Ostimuri together with the pueblos and other places on the southern coast, especially from the Río de las Cañas, which is where the new Diocese of Sonora begins, as well as the western boundary of the Diocese of Guadalajara, is a result of the vast distance of almost 300 leagues across the two aforementioned dioceses and the eastern section of the coast. A multitude of minerales, haciendas de campo, lugares, and pueblos are scattered throughout the region.[11] These are indeed few in comparison to the size of the area, but they include many thousands of souls who have only a few priests for pastors. Their zeal is insufficient to provide instruction for all. These people, consequently, often live without the use of the Sacraments and with no proper instruction in the Mysteries and Truths of the Faith. This lack, however, is not the fault of the ministros. It is quite impossible for them to look after sheep who are so widely scattered in such small groups over so many leagues, and who have to be thus scattered in order to live from the products of their lands and their crops. The considerable distance of those lands from any of the Missionary Colleges in North America deprives them of the ability to give aid which they could otherwise provide for the spiritual needs of the inhabitants through the activity of the missionaries. They only receive this help if the ministros destined by this College for the missions of Sonora happen to pass through, or when we take the extraordinary and painful measure of sending a special mission to help them at great expense and at the cost of the health of the missionaries — and all this merely for a transitory benefit which cannot be repeated without the same grave inconvenience. On a mission which was made to these regions, and which has been mentioned before, the five religious suffered the same very grave spiritual necessities as do many of those poor souls.

 9

The most effective remedy would seem to us to be the organization of a hospice made up of missionaries from our College in the suburbs of the Villa de Sinaloa which is 350 leagues to the northwest of Querétaro. In this hospice there would be stationed ten priests and two lay brothers, and the ministros could live in a religious community and observe the rules of the Order. They would take turns in the regular exercise of their ministry in different directions — just as we see them in these dioceses — so that as they extended their apostolic journeys to the southeast as far as the Río de las Cañas and to the northwest as far as the Real de los Alamos,

---

11. See *hacienda de campo* in the Lexicon of Spanish Words in the back of this book.

they would make up for the lack of secular ministers in those places, who are very scarce, and they could live on the alms collected over so many leagues without detriment to other religious bodies since there are no others in the whole region. This idea, which our zeal and the exercise of our ministry have inspired in us in order to fulfill one of the purposes of the Apostolic Seminaries, coincides with the wishes of the inhabitants of those provinces. And it seems to us useful, beneficial and favorable as represented in the reports which we herewith present to Your Majesty. Now, taking everything into consideration, Your Majesty may adopt whatever measures he desires. We can assure you that there will be no other expenses for the erection of this hospice to be met from the Royal Treasury except those required to cover cost of recruitment and travel expenses of some more workers. These will be added to those already authorized by Your Majesty, and who have been brought by the Comisario of this College to these realms. As far as added expenses are concerned, the advantages which the inhabitants of those regions will obtain from their presence motivates them to cooperate generously. Among them there is one person of considerable wealth and status. Nor do we doubt, Señor, that this seed of an Apostolic College sown in the heart of these fertile provinces will mature in a short time and will be in a position to bring about the spiritual happiness of so many souls whose health is one of the prime objects of the royal piety, catholic zeal and clemency of Your Majesty. In order to illustrate more completely all that we have said, we present to Your Majesty the following map. It has been drafted with the greatest possible exactness and includes the lands between the Río de las Cañas and the Real de los Alamos. Together with it is an explanation of everything included which contributes to this objective.[12]

10

The repair, stability and growth of the 14 pueblos which comprise the eight missions of Pimería Alta in our charge, depend, Señor, on explaining many points to which we can do no less than implore the attention of Your Majesty. From the time when the now-expelled Regulars of the Company of Jesus founded these missions until the year 1768, when the missionaries of this College took them over, they were always governed most rigorously as *misiones, conversiones,* or *reducciones.* These names really all mean the same thing in contrast to *doctrinas* and *curatos,* in spite of the fact that all have gone beyond the legal limits as defined in law from the time of their founding, for which reason they should have called

12. The Río de las Cañas forms a portion of the boundary separating the modern states of Nayarit and Sinaloa in Mexico. It formerly defined a part of the northern boundary of the Intendencia de Guadalaxara and the southern boundary of the Intendencia de Sonora (Priestly 1916: illustration 8). Unfortunately, we have been unable to locate the map of this region to which Father Bringas refers. It is not listed in the Torres Lanzas (1900) guide to the maps in the Archivo General de Indias.

themselves *doctrinas*. Actually, the royal will alone could have effected this change as in accordance with instructions contained in the real cédula of June 1, 1754.[13] However, the Catholic Kings, glorious predecessors of Your Majesty, did not approve of making this declaration by which these missions would pass from the state of *conversiones* to that of *doctrinas*. Although they had actually gone beyond the legal requirements, they were still not mature enough for such changes. As a consequence, the Jesuits were permitted to continue governing them as *reducciones*, which they actually were.

II

When the government of these missions was transferred to the missionaries of this College, it was recognized at once that innovations had been made in their government prior to our being put in charge — innovations which would lead to their total extinction.[14] The few possessions which had remained in the missions at the withdrawal of the Jesuits and which were intended for some of the *comisarios* were suffering from considerable diminution. The Indians were made aware that the royal order left them at complete liberty. They therefore lived in perpetual idleness and continual wanderings in the brush and in the various pueblos. Thus the aim of Your Majesty was not being achieved, namely, that the Indians should become acquainted with the Spaniards and become interested in the commerce of seeds and household goods — things they neither possess nor are able to acquire — due to the continual idleness and lack of government which is characteristic of them. Our experience has disclosed the harmful effects of all this. We recognize

---

13. We cannot locate the text of this particular cédula real, one issued by Fernando VI.

14. Bringas has in mind two principal innovations. The first of these was the immediate confiscation of mission property upon the departure of the Jesuits by the government. Royal soldier-commissaries were placed in charge of the temporal goods of the missions for two years. "Under the name of temporalities of the Jesuits, they were destined for various and strange uses without being applied in the least as useful and productive for the churches and common necessities of the villages. As a result of this, heavy damages began to appear in the structure of the churches and the houses of the ministers, and much sickness and hunger appeared among the Indians" (McCarty n.d.: 10).

The second "innovation" was the sudden and unexpected freedom of the Indians from control of the religious. Nineteenth-century historian Hubert H. Bancroft described what had happened by the time the Franciscans arrived on the scene in 1768: ". . . the neophytes had been for a year free from all control, and had not been improved by their freedom. Not only had they relapsed to a great extent into their roving and improvident habits, but they had imbibed new ideas of independence, fostered largely by settlers and soldiers. They regarded themselves as entirely free from all control by the missionaries, whose whole duty in these later times was to attend to religious matters. The padres might not, so these independent aborigines thought, give orders, but must refer requests to native officials; if they required work done for them they must pay for it" (Bancroft 1884b: 672-673). These first two years (1768–69) of the Franciscan takeover of the Pimería are the subject of a Ph.D. dissertation by Kieran McCarty (1973).

the fact that those pueblos do not merit the name of "misiones," since they lack the characteristics demanded by the Royal decrees. Neither are they doctrinas, because they cannot be provided with ministros under the Royal patronage. All these considerations moved the missionaries to lay the whole matter before the Señor Royal Visitor, Don José de Gálvez. When he had been informed about it in detail he decided to issue his own order dated June 3, 1769, at the Real de los Alamos. In it he directed the comisarios to turn over officially to the care of the missionaries all the temporal goods of the missions.[15] And after a period of seven years, during which time he continued in this assignment and during which he witnessed the use and distribution of the mission property, this same official had also observed the instruction and direction of the Indians, and he was convinced that those peoples were not sufficiently mature to be exempted from the inspections of their ministros. He was further convinced that it was necessary that they continue to be governed according to the Royal decrees for conversiones or reducciones for as long as prescribed by the Laws of the Indies, even though all these missions had already existed for many years.

12

After this decision had been made, the missionaries continued in the missions progressing as they could under their restored government. They did so as far as was possible in provinces which were under attack by the barbarous Apaches. This went on until 1774. In the meantime the college had added two missions to the Pimería Baja. These were San José de Pimas and Pitic. The latter was inhabited by the Seris who later rebelled and killed their ministro. In 1774 the college recognized it would have to give up the eight missions of the Pimería Baja because they now bore a classification which does not fall within the jurisdiction of our

---

15. On June 23, Gálvez also took care of church, Indian, and royal lands other than those in Pimería Alta. "By this decree the commissioners of Gálvez were to go to places of settlements, and in the presence of the parish priest, the 'captain-general' and the governor of each group of Indians, divide the lands. The first land to be set apart in each settlement was for the town site; next, four leagues of communal land. Pasture lands were then to be provided, and the priest was to have five *suertes* [one *suerte* equalled 20,000 square *varas*, or approximately four acres] adjoining the communal lands. The Indians were to have one *suerte* for each head of family, two for the governor, and three for the 'captain-general'. Titles to land were to be given and preserved in the new subtreasury at Alamos. No land might be alienated subsequently, but if any were left untilled two years it should revert to the crown. Royal lands outside the needs of the Indians might be leased in perpetuity to Spaniards or unobjectionable half-castes, at two pesos per annum for each *suerte*. When the lands should have been assigned the commissaries were to make lists of the tributaries; this tax was to be fifteen reals for Indians who were married, half that amount for single men, twenty reals for negroes and mulattoes married, ten reals for single men. Indian caciques, governors, etc., were to be free from tribute" (Priestly 1916: 257, 286-287).

In point of fact, as late as 1803 no taxes had been collected from Indians anywhere in Sonora (Priestly 1916: 285).

Order.[16] They did not now even deserve the name of "misiones." None of them were active in the propagation of the faith. The only one qualified to do this work was Pitic, and it could as well be done from one of the missions of the Pimería Alta which still remained in our charge. In this way the college was freed to concern itself with foundations being undertaken on the Gila and Colorado rivers.

The college continued to manage these missions this way from the time of the Custodia until 1794. At that time the present Comandante General of the Provincias Internas circulated an order to all the missions. There were to be no exceptions other than for new foundations which did not then exist, nor do they now. This order requires all of them to submit to the rules laid down for doctrinas. The serious problems which the President of our missions knew would certainly arise when the order was put into effect (even though the aforementioned *jefe* had intended only to improve the management of Indian affairs) forced him to inform the Comandante concerning them. In view of this information the Comandante condescended to suspend the order for a limited time. The opinions of the chaplains of the presidios near our missions were in agreement with those of our President. This was made effective in the major part of the territory of the other missions of the provinces of Ostimuri, Sonora and Nueva Vizcaya.

Señor, this is the status of the missions insofar as their government is concerned up to the present time.

But we consider that we must in conscience discharge our ministry. Our fidelity as subjects, as well as our Catholic Majesty's royal trust in us, oblige us to do our

16. San José de los Pimas was established as a visita of Tecoripa in 1653. It remained a visita throughout the Jesuit period, but in 1771, under orders issued by José de Gálvez two years earlier, Friar Juan Bautista Garcés was assigned there as resident missionary. Father Juan was replaced at San José by Father Pedro Font in 1773 (Rosa 1967: 245). Font turned the mission over to a fellow Queretaran, Father Joachín Belarde (Joaquín Velarde), on June 30, 1775, but he was back at San José in August of 1776 (Font 1930: 2, 527).

Pitic, which dates from at least 1704, was put in charge of Father Matías Gallo in 1772, who was replaced in 1775 by Friar Bartolomé Ximeno. In the interim, the Seri Indians rebelled at the mission of Carrizal in March 1773, making a martyr of Father Juan Crisóstomo Gil de Bernabé (Eckhart 1960: 42-43; Font 1776; Roca 1967: 172-175).

The eight missions of the Pimería Baja relinquished by the Quereterans to the Jaliscan friars were San José, Pitic, Onavas, Cumuripa, Tecoripa, Ures, Opodepe, and Cucurpe — including their various visitas. Although recognition of the need to turn these missions over seems to have taken place in 1774 (also see Bancroft 1884b: 688), the actual change did not occur until 1776 (Roca 1967: 387 n. 58).

part to avoid the ruin of the missions. We are required, therefore, to explain satisfactorily the great obstacles to the conversion of the Indians inherent in this measure and the reasons for our fears.

The wise and lofty dispositions of the Laws of the Indies were dictated by the zeal, wisdom, piety and experience dating from the beginnings of the conquest of America. With the greatest prudence and foresighted restraint they embrace all the purposes worthy of the attention of a pious Catholic Monarch. As long as they are respected and practiced they will be the source of spiritual and temporal good and will keep these vast dominions of Your Royal Majesty in the most flourishing state. In them there is always a remedy available for even the smallest problems. If to the Laws of the Indies we may add the cédulas reales which were issued to clarify and further perfect this legal system in accordance with what has been learned through the years of experience and the cases that have arisen, then there is nothing left to desire but obedience to and the practice of such lofty and just regulations — understanding them always in their legitimate and genuine sense and not taking the literal meaning only, especially when this is obviously contrary to the pious purposes and holy intentions which our kings and lords have always manifested up to the time of Your Majesty.

In the discharge of the Royal Patronage, their ardent zeal, morality, and desire for the prosperity of church and state have caused our Monarchs to issue many wise dispositions on the subjects of the better government of the churches, divine worship, reformation of procedures, administration of the Sacraments, and the better distribution of pastors. They have divided their respective duties and privileges among the various classes of clerics with the greatest success and in accordance with the nature and conditions of that portion of the flock of the faithful which is entrusted to their care. Insofar as the royal authority extends, they have given them all the faculties necessary for the satisfactory performance of their ministry. With regards to those which are proper to the ecclesiastical authority, they have obtained for them favors and suitable faculties. These are to be found in a great number of rescripts and pontifical bulls which have been issued at the instance of our Monarchs.

Thus we see the care of souls distributed among misiones, reducciones, and conversiones, which are essentially the same institution, and among doctrinas and curatos, which are completely different from each other as well as from the former. Each, however, corresponds to a specific spiritual condition: pagan, new Christian, and Catholic instructed in the qualities of a good vassal who is useful to church and state. The royal dispositions mentioned above, in agreement with church law, subject the curatos to the form of government which the councils have dictated, and which is fitting only for a church which has been established in the fullest sense of the word. The dispositions of the royal patronage provide different types of ministros for the doctrinas and the conversiones. It was necessary to recognize that this had to be done if the faith was to be propagated. This is the duty solely of the conversores or ministros. This contrasts with the doctrineros and curas, whose duties are to preserve the faith after it has already been propagated in the pueblos they minister.

17

The Catholic Kings, who are our lords, have wished the reducciones or misiones to be completely subject to the rule of the conversores alone. They were to be exempt from the jurisdiction of the bishops. They were also exempted from contributing that small tribute which every subject is required to pay in recognition of his status as a vassal. For this reason, the tribute was not to be asked of them until the time had come for them to pass under the government of the regular laws. The misioneros should have been preparing them for this. For the same reason, they are exempted from paying tithes although the government considers them during this period of time as subjects.

Our Sovereigns have ordered all this for the period of ten years, the time to be reckoned from the day that the education of the pueblo has begun. During this period of ten years the Sovereigns wanted to hear nothing about them. The Viceroys, Presidents, Governors, Bishops and other superiors are also prohibited during this time from interfering in the government of the Indians and are required to leave them completely to the rule of their conversores. All these matters are determined by Law 3a, Title 5, Book 4, of the *Recopiladas* as well as by the real cédula of Don Felipe III of January 30, 1607.[17] This law was restated to the Marqués de Montesclaros, Viceroy of Peru, December 5, 1608.[18] We may add to this the laws issued by the Catholic Kings, our lords, august progenitors of Your Majesty, *viz.* Don Felipe V on November 13, 1744, to the Count of Fuenclara, Viceroy of México, and by Don Fernando VI on December 4, 1747 — from Buen Retiro — addressed to

---

17. The third law of Title 5 of Book 4 of the *Recopiladas* is entitled, "That Indians who are willing may be taken for laborers and workmen," provided they are not already settled, living in a house on land which they would thus desert if they were to leave. The *cédula real* of January 30, 1607, issued by Philip III, "provided that the Indians who were converted and became Christians could not be made serfs, and should be exempt from taxation for a period of ten years" (Huonder 1911: 689).

18. The Marqués de Montesclaros was viceroy of Peru from 1607 to 1615. This cédula, like that of January 30, 1607, provided Indians with exemption from taxation during the first ten years after their conversion. It also exempted Christianized Indians from *encomienda* (Geary 1934: 18).

Don Juan Francisco de Huemes y Horcasitas, Viceroy of México.[19] Both of these laws were specially designed for the individual advancement of these same missions we now have in our charge. They provided for broader authority for the conversores and for greater exemptions from the regular laws. However, we never had the good fortune to see them put into practice in spite of the urging of the ministros. We will prove all this to Your Majesty.

18

But the purpose of our Sovereigns, the exalted progenitors of Your Majesty, in exempting the conversiones from all inspection except that of their misioneros, was solely to achieve the Indians' true reduction to the faith and to vassalage. They wished to remove every obstacle which could in any way retard the conversion of other gentiles who live near the reducciones. It should be understood that the designated period of ten years is neither so absolute nor so rigid as to keep it from being changed (always keeping the Sovereign informed) if the impediments which the law presumes to have been removed during this time continue to exist. The same is true if at the end of the period the attainment of the desired end is still remote or if serious obstacles to the reduction of the neighboring gentiles have arisen, thus adding to the difficulty.

This correct understanding of the law has been practiced and the royal will in the matter has been shown in the conversiones of the provinces of Paraguay, whose governors had been commanded that for the first twenty years the Indians should remain under this rule alone, knowing no other. We would never dare to

19. Felipe V, the first Bourbon king of Spain, was born in 1683. He succeeded to the throne in 1700 and reigned until his death in 1746. He founded the Royal Academy of History in 1738. His successor, Fernando VI, was born in 1712. He reigned as king of Spain until his death in 1758. Buen Retiro is the Madrid park where the royal Crystal Palace is located.

Pedro Cebrián y Agustín, count of Fuenclara, was the fortieth viceroy of New Spain, serving in that capacity from November 3, 1742, to July 9, 1746. His successor was Francisco de Güemes y Horcasitas, count of Revillagigedo, who remained in office until November 3, 1755.

These two cédulas reales, parts of which Bringas quotes later in his report (section 36) and which Father Antonio Barbastro found occasion to cite (quoted in section 98, Bringas report) were among the more important laws concerning missionary activities in Pimería Alta and Alta California. The cédula of November 13, 1744, provided that two missionaries should be in each mission, one to remain at the mission and the other to make explorations and journeys to convert Indians while traveling with an armed escort of which the priest was in command. It also called for information suggesting how the Pimería Alta might be made a safe route for overland parties of colonists headed for California and how it could become a springboard for conquest in the north. It also recommended that either the presidio at Pitic or at Terrenate be moved to the Gila or Colorado River (Bancroft 1884b: 537-538).

The cédula of December 4, 1747, ordered the viceroy in general terms to investigate the matter further and to enforce whatever provisions he might deem necessary to bring northern Pimería Alta under control (Bancroft 1884b: 539).

The College of San Fernando, which supplied missionaries for Upper California, similarly cited these cédulas in opposition to the idea of having a single missionary in each mission (Geiger 1959: II: 258).

imagine that Your Royal Majesty or that the Supreme Council of the Indies could have done better than to prolong the management of the conversiones in this way — when in the space of ten years it has not been possible to prepare all the Indians for baptism. Similarly, we believe that Your Majesty will prolong the time for as many decades as are needed to advance Indian nations to the state to which the law of ten years was originally intended to bring them. For example, whenever a nation is stupid and backward in learning the ineffable mysteries of the faith and is lazy in working and cultivating the fields. Another example is a nation which even after a long elapsed time has remained unable to adjust to the laws and policies of the civil society which is so close to them and knows them so well, and which has spent the greater part of the year in contact with them in their very own pueblos.

The high regard which we have for the sacred person of Your Royal Majesty convinces us you will give us whatever time is needed. This is expressly referred to in Law 8, Title 2, Book 2 of the *Recopiladas*.[20] In this law Don Felipe II and Don Felipe V use these words:

According to our obligation and duty as Lord of the Indies we desire nothing more than the publication and the spread of the law of the Gospel and the conversion of the Indians to the one catholic faith. To them we direct our thoughts and care as the chief object of our intentions. We order and command, so far as we are able, all members of our Council of the Indies that postponing all other important matters and our own interests they should have as their principal concern the conversiones and the doctrinas. Above all, they should apply all their efforts and skills as well as all other necessary means to station enough ministros among them so that the Indians and natives will be converted and preserved in the knowledge of God our Lord and in the honor and praise of His holy name. Thus, as we fulfill our obligations, which we so much desire to do, the members of our Council may also satisfy the demands of their consciences, which in turn will enable us to satisfy the demands of our own.

Finally, the catholic zeal and the inherited piety with which Your Royal Majesty keeps liberally opening the royal treasury for the purpose of supporting the conversiones during the most calamitous periods of the war, makes us believe you will comply with our request.

---

20. The title of Law 8, Title 2, Book 2, dating from 1636, is "That the principal care of the Council [of the Indies] should be the conversion of the Indians and assigning sufficient Ministers for the task." Bringas quotes it in full in section 19 of his report.

Now that we have concluded our brief summary of the means and management established by law for the government of the curatos, doctrinas, and misiones, we must undertake the task of proving two things: first, that our missions of Pimería Alta are in the strictest sense active conversiones; and second, that it is absolutely necessary they be governed as such in order to avoid their ruin, which would make the reduction of the frontier nations to the faith impossible. However, for both there is no difficulty. It is only a question of explaining simply the actual circumstances of the eight missions.

If the aforesaid missions, Señor, are without a single exception located on an active frontier; if all are near numerous groups of gentiles; if they are all engaged in propagating the faith, adding many souls to it, even though in small groups which are not from only one, but from ten or twelve different nations; if almost all of them see their towns filled with gentiles for the greater part of the year who are attracted there by their needs or by the friendliness of the ministros or by the bonds or relationships which many of them have with Christian Indians, and who for this reason are continually entering and leaving the pueblos; if this communication makes them feel free to bring the prisoners of war captured by some nations from others and to sell them there at very low prices, thus furnishing the opportunity for their baptism; if as a result of all this some of these nations are clamoring for the faith and to have missions established in their countries; if they continually watch to see what sort of treatment is given to the Indians who have been reduced and have found that the ministros regard them as sons and share with them even the stipends which the royal piety of Your Majesty gives them; if the ministros in addition to this give them special attention, teaching them to cultivate the land — if all this, it would seem that such missions have all the characteristics of genuine reducciones or conversiones, because, Señor, each and every one of the situations thus described are true at the present time in the eight missions of Pimería Alta.

As far as the first two points are concerned, Señor, they are evident from the map which we respectfully present to Your Royal Majesty. [See p. 53 of this book.] It was drawn with all possible accuracy based on frequent journeys which the missionaries of this College have made through the countries shown on it from the year 1768 to last year, 1795. They took the latitudes of the places where they found pueblos or congregations of gentiles.[21] It can be seen from the map, Señor, that the numerous nations of gentiles called "Papagos" — which includes more than 4,000 souls — is found spread among nineteen rancherías covering a distance of more than 80 leagues measured from southeast to northeast and just beyond the 14 pueblos which comprise our missions. The latter are designated on the map with the following names, starting from west to east, and going to the north: Bísanig; Caborca; Pitiquito; Oquitoa; Atil; Santa Teresa; Tubutama; Saric; Santa Magdalena; San Ignacio; Cocóspera; Tumacácori; San Xavier del Bac; and San Agustín del Tucson, this latter located at 32.5° of latitude and at the very terminal point of Christian pueblos.

If we look southward from these Christian pueblos, they have before them the island of Tauron [Tiburón] populated by the Seri Indians, who are gentiles.[22] If to the east, there are the Plains where the barbarous Apaches live; if northward, there are the numerous Coyotero Apaches and others. If to the northwest, there are the nations of the Pimas Gileños, and farther to the west, the Cocomaricopas, Apaches, Tejuas Yumas, Xalchedunes, Cajuenches, Jaliquamais or Quiquimas, Cucapas, and others.[23] With all this it is evident that these missions are not only on the frontier but are in the strictest sense in the midst of gentiles who number more than 25,000 souls according to the repeated observations of our missionaries.

21. This map appears on the opposite page. The original is in the Brigham Young University Library, Provo, Utah. It was first published by Ezell (1956: 154) as "Bringa's [sic] Map of the Gila River region and the Coast of California."

22. Close examination of Bringas' map suggests that the friar misread "I Tiburon" as "I Tauron." In any event, the island, in possession of the Seri Indians since time immemorial (see McGee 1898; 9 *et seq*), is certainly that of Tiburón.

23. The Apaches to the east, in terms of modern classification, included the Chiricahua and Mescalero, and beyond them, the Jicarilla and Lipan (see Berlandier 1969: 128-135; Forbes 1960; Opler 1946, 1965; Sonnichsen 1958; and Wilson 1964 for descriptions of these groups). The Coyotero Apaches are Apaches of the White Mountain group of the Western Apache tribe living on the San Carlos Reservation, but the term was used by Bringas to refer to the entire Western Apache tribe (Goodwin 1969: 2-3, 6). The Pimas Gileños are the modern Pima Indians of the Gila River and Salt River reservations (Ezell 1961; Russell 1908). The Cocomaricopas were a Yuman-speaking tribe that became extinct in the 1830s (Dobyns and others 1963). Other Yuman tribes are the Cajuenches (Kohuanas), amalgamated into the modern Maricopa tribe (Ezell 1963: 16; Spier 1933: 17); the Cucapas (Cocopas) (Gifford 1933); the "Jaliquamais or Quiquimas" (Halyikwamais), incorporated by the Kohuanas during the early nineteenth century, and who formerly lived north of the Cocopas and south of the Kohuanas (Spier 1933: 10); and the Yuma proper, known in modern times as the Quechan (Forde 1931). The Apaches Tejuas — the comma should be after "Tejuas" rather than "Apaches" in the Bringas manuscript — were Yavapais (Garcés 1900: I: 208-209). They are described by Gifford (1932, 1936). Among the "others" on the map are the Jamajabas (Mohaves), Chemeguabas (Chemehuevis), Payuitas (Paiutes), Yutas (Utes), Moqui (Hopi), Jeniqueches (Serraños), Jecuiches (Cahuillas), Quemeyas (Kamias), and Cuñeils (Kwinitls, a Diegueño group) (Ezell 1956: 154).

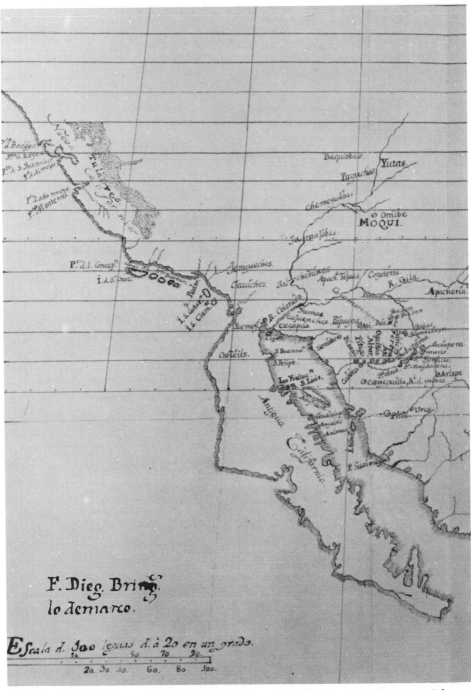

Map 1. Bringas' Map of the Gila River Region and the Coast of California

That the aforesaid missions are engaged in propagating the faith is true at the present time. In the last months alone more than 160 souls have been received and baptized. This has also been true from the time when we received the missions in the year 1768 until the present, as the appended lists show in detail. [See Friar Bringas' Appendix to this Report.] They were made up in legal form of entries extracted from the books of administration. It is clear from them that almost 1,000 souls from 12 different gentile nations have been baptized in those pueblos. In this same manner, each and all of the conditions mentioned above have been verified. However, referring to the sixth condition, which concerns the pressure of the gentiles to have missions in their land, the Pimas Gileños have been clamoring for them for half a century. We now have evidence of their perseverance from a new journey which was made to their country of which we have informed the Comandante General of Chihuahua and which we shall explain to Your Majesty.

From this array of facts it is clear, Señor, that our missions are conversiones or reducciones in the strictest sense. Of all the characteristics they should have for this, only that of the ten years provided by law is out of conformity. But this fact itself proves that the ten-year period has as its only purpose advancing the conversiones to the stage at which they could be properly changed into doctrinas. And this also proves the truth of the second assertion; that is, they ought to be ruled as reducciones to avoid their ruin which would make it impossible to bring the frontier nations to the faith.

To convince you of this need, it seems that we could be satisfied with the proof offered in section 23, above. However, we should add something of the great amount which we could not explain in detail without boring you. We shall therefore adduce a single example which, it seems, should leave no doubt at all. When the order had been circulated that all the missions should be governed and provided with ministros in accordance with the royal patronage; that the missionaries should turn over the temporalities to the secular comisarios; and that the Indians should cooperate in supporting their doctrineros with a half *fanega* [bushel] of maize every year or a dozen *reales* [$1.50], it seems that one would expect the most salutary results of this order in those missions which because of their age have a greater number of inhabitants and which are in locations totally separated and free from the hostilities of the barbarians. Such a place would be a rich and fertile land, where the Indians are really inclined to work, and are very civilized due to their Spanish contacts. They would be skillful in trade and commerce and expert in mining. Such conditions would offer the best hope for putting the new regulation into effect. However, Señor, the above is an exact picture of the Indian missions situated on the banks of the two large rivers, the Yaqui and the Mayo. We can see what effect it has produced there.

The regulation had barely been put into effect when the ministros recognized the impossibility of continuing to live with it. They saw they were losing Indians, and they recognized other grave consequences. They then abandoned that populous nation. At that time there were more than 20,000 souls with only three learned men in charge of 14 scattered pueblos with large populations in need of at least as many more ministros. If Law 46, Title 6, of Book I of the *Recopiladas de Indias* says that no doctrina should ever have more than 400 Indians, how could those pueblos adjust to the law?[24] Pueblos where there are at least 7,000 Indians for every ministro? And these Indians are scattered about in different pueblos, in swamps, in open country? However, Señor, those pueblos have been without ministros not only for the maximum time permitted by Law 48, Title 6, Book I, which is four months, but for more than two years. It is possible that these doctrinas will continue to have a regrettable loss of souls if this new rule for their provision and government is not suspended until a more auspicious time.

If this has been the regrettable situation in missions which have been in existence for 200 years, what ought we to expect if a new form of government is established in them? The *curas* of these pueblos have resided in them for a very long time. The first is Don Francisco Joaquín Valdés, who has been in charge of his pueblos for 27 years. The second is Don Miguel de Encinas, who has been there

---

24. This law promulgated in 1593, 1618, and 1643, reads: "We have been informed that the *Ministros de Doctrina* have not taken proper care in the education of the Indians and in teaching them the Articles of our Holy Roman Catholic Faith. This is our primary duty. For its fulfillment we have founded and endowed all the churches that seemed needed and have assigned adequate incomes for the curas and doctrineros from our own income, and we have made up for any lack from our Royal Treasury. In spite of this it happens that the curas and doctrineros are trying to take charge of more Indians than it is possible for them to teach and give the Holy Sacraments. We charge the archbishops and bishops to examine with particular care the numbers of Indians who can be conveniently taught by each doctrinero and cura, taking into account the local situation and the distance between populated places. In accord with these findings they should assign a district to each doctrina, and the number which seems proper must never exceed 400 Indians, unless particular circumstances should force the number to be greater or less. This we command the viceroys, presidents, and governors who shall account to us for the fulfillment of this law. . . ."

for 25 years.[25] Both of these, and another who died a short time ago, were in charge of the temporalities of their missions. They supported divine worship in a fitting manner. They taught the Indians Christian doctrine, since they were perfect masters of the language. Finally, the populous Yaqui nation, which has been so frequently commended by the august progenitors of Your Majesty, and who were so peaceful, so useful in the trades and in mining in the Provincias Internas, now remains with no other Christian teaching than what a much smaller number of ministros can give them. These ministros are widely dispersed in the attempt to satisfy the Indians' needs and they have no assistants for such a great harvest. According to the Laws of the Realm there should be at least 40 ministros, where actually there are barely three.

28

These curas who abandoned that favored country for the very natural joy of being able to live more easily in another location were much loved by their Indians. They were well acquainted with the products of the area, and consequently, if they had judged that these new regulations of the decree would be practical, even if it were only one-quarter part of what the Indians were supposed to contribute to them during the year, they could expect some millions of pesos annually with which they could live decently and bring in other workers to help them. But knowing that this contribution was contrary to laws which were purely the product of imagination, and knowing that when they were put into effect the curas would be in extremely grave difficulties resulting from the new system of management, they considered they had to give up the harvest of souls in order to be able to live and not to compromise the salvation of their own souls due to the

---

25. Spicer (1962: 54-55) writes: "The Yaquis were fortunate in one of the secular curates who was assigned to the church at Torim — Don Francisco Joaquín Valdez. He spent twenty-three years at his base in Torim [Sonora], becoming widely influential among Yaquis. He was a man of unusually high education, holding a university degree. His major interest lay in developing crafts and manufacturing as a balance to the agricultural subsistence economy which the Yaquis had developed. He instituted a program of technical assistance and set up a school in Potam. He encouraged sheep raising and cotton and indigo production. In 1774 he secured looms and a technician who knew textile manufacture and was successful in getting Yaquis to weave for commercial production. A stocking factory was set up in Potam and hatmaking was introduced. He also is reported to have trained Indians in carpentry, masonry, and metal-founding. How much further he carried this than the Jesuits had done earlier is not recorded, but it does appear that craft industry received a considerable impetus among Yaquis as a result of his efforts."

Data concerning Don Miguel de Encinas are more elusive. In the 1740s he was in the province of Ostimuri where he, Francisco Mijares, Joaquín Valdés, and Manuel de Huidobro were made "honorary servants of the militia" to help guard against potential Yaqui and Mayo Indian uprisings (Ocaranza 1933: 66). Bancroft (1884b: 687 n. 56) reports that seculars involved in the Yaqui villages after the Jesuit expulsion, in addition to Valdés, were Francisco Félix Romero and Juan Francisco Arce Rosales.

loss of thousands of souls of those poor natives. These proven truths, Señor, the curas themselves can judge, because they still live in the Real de Minas de Baroyeca in the Province of Ostimuri.

29

These, Señor, are the effects which the modification of the government have produced on the Mayo and Yaqui rivers. It will give rise to incomparably worse effects in the 14 Pima pueblos if it is established there, as we fear it may be. When the Indians have been removed (they are mostly neophytes) from the government of the religious, they will cease to receive any religious instruction and they will fail to become rooted in the Holy Faith. Because it is a common tendency of human beings to be bored with spiritual matters, they put them off in favor of perishable affairs. This infirmity is usually stronger in the Indians, and much more so even in recent converts whose tender status in religion makes them more vulnerable to the powerful influence of the Common Enemy. Libertinism, the insubordination in which they lived in the open, idleness, lack of foresight, distrust, and above all, instability, are characteristic of them. Now if at the very beginning of their conversion they are informed that the ministro has no authority to get them to church at the regular time, that they can wander where they wish, that they can decide all their own actions and movements — their perdition will follow beyond any doubt.

30

The Indians, Señor, are incapable of governing themselves for many years after their conversion. They are always children. Our missionaries have acquired this understanding through constant experience since the discovery of America, and we have become absolutely convinced of its truth. These missions, Señor, are not now the same ones which the regulars who have been expelled founded except for the material sites on which they are located. In everything else they are conversiones in the strictest sense. At present they are for the most part comprised (and some pueblos are entirely comprised) of gentiles who join the reducción every year. This can be demonstrated mathematically by the lists and books of baptisms. The old time Indians of these missions have died out due to the continual deaths caused by Apaches, sickness, and fighting when there is an uprising, as is clear from the reports that we can give concerning the reduction of some of them in modern times. Of what importance is it, then, that these missions have been here for more than a hundred years while their population has the characteristics of one that is barely ten years old? Should this date be reckoned from the days of their baptism? Consequently, it must be concluded that they are conversiones in the strict sense and should be governed as such.

31

If this type of government is started, there will be greater expenses for founding new missions. Experience shows that the temporal goods of the missions are dissipated very quickly when placed in charge of *comisarios*. As a result they will lack the resources necessary to provide for new foundations. Within a few years the Indians will find themselves in the ultimate wretchedness. They will be obliged to return to their freedom in the wilderness from which they were originally drawn with great effort.

It is, Señor, no doubt very difficult to get the Indians to like commerce, Christian doctrine, and industry, because all these are repugnant to them. Experience teaches that they must be ruled like children in a family if they are to have any happiness. If we reflect on all this we will have tangible proof of all these assertions.

32

When the Jesuits were expelled, the temporal goods of the missions were inventoried and put in charge of comisarios. The Indians were freed to conduct trade and to be absent from their pueblos. They were left free in all matters in which now they must obey orders. This rule had lasted hardly two years when the missions were given to us and we became witnesses of the results. Señor Gálvez was informed of the situation. He then requested inventories on a trial basis and he demanded an accounting for the goods. When the goods listed on the inventories were compared with the original amounts that were given into the charge of comisarios, he was horrified to see that from a third to a half had been lost in such a short time. He then ordered the comisarios to turn over to the missionaries whatever was left. He asked the missionaries to take charge of these goods (trusting in their love of country, obedience to the Sovereign, and purity of conscience) and at least to preserve them. His hope was not in vain, and the proof is evident.

33

Compare the pueblos which are now in existence under that sort of government with those which we have directed until the present according to the orders of Señor Gálvez, and there must be astonishment that ours, although on a hostile frontier ever under attack by the Apaches and far from communication with the province, still preserve their possessions with notable increase. The Indians are being assisted in all their necessities. The gentiles are favored. The churches have plenty of sacred vessels and vestments. Eight churches of lime and brick have been constructed. The rest have been completely repaired, even in pueblos where there were as few as seven Indian families.[26]

Among the missions otherwise administered there is rarely a church which is not threatened with ruin or which is not destitute of sacred vessels and vestments and whose Indians are not afflicted with misery.

34

These, Señor, are the benefits which the ancient government of our missionaries have produced. Consequently, in some missions that cédula real has been peacefully observed in which under date of September 24, 1668, one of our Catholic Kings says these words:

I beg and charge the Bishops in this Northeast to permit the missionaries the exercise of such powers in the missions in which they are active. The regular prelates may send them to any of their subjects without having to ask permission for it. They require neither appointment nor institution by the Bishop to administer the holy sacraments in the missions nor to do anything else which will contribute to the conversion of the unhappy Indians, nor for the instruction of converts. The Bishop should give them all the help they need. In the interim, when they cannot yet be brought together in regular pueblos and they are still not advanced enough for the founding of doctrinas in the missions — it is my will that they shall continue

---

26. It is too bad Father Bringas does not list the "eight churches of lime and brick." In September of 1797 Father Francisco Yturralde (1798) reported that Oquitoa was "sheathed on the outside with brick and lime mortar"; Saric, although of adobe, had a "vaulted roof," which suggests burned brick rather than sun-dried bricks; Cocóspera was under construction, being made of brick and mortar; Magdalena's wooden roof was "cemented," and its sacristy was under construction; and Pitiquito, San Xavier del Bac, San Ignacio, and Tubutama were "of lime and brick." That these were the eight churches referred to by Bringas is further borne out by the May 18, 1803, report of Father Francisco Moyano: "The churches of San Xavier del Bac, of Cocóspera, of San Ignacio, of Tubutama, of Saric, and of Pitic [Pitiquito] were acquired in a condition of disrepair; but now there are many structures of brick and mortar, having been built in the first instance [San Xavier] due to the zeal of the deceased Father Fray Juan Belderrain [Velderrain] who began the work, and to that of Father Fr. Juan Bauta. Llorens who finished it nearly six years ago; the second [Cocóspera] due to that of Father Juan de Santiesteban, three years ago; the third [San Ignacio] due to that of [Father Sánchez Zuñiga]; the fourth [Tubutama] due to that of the deceased R.P. Barbastro who initiated the work, and to that of Father Fr. Francisco Yturralde who finished it; the fifth [Saric] to that of Father Fr. Florencio Ibañez; and the sixth [Pitiquito] to that of the deceased Father Fr. Matías Moreno, and the deceased Father Font. The rest of them have been renovated and repaired, with the exception of that of Tumacácori which is currently being rebuilt anew, and that of Cavorca on which work is about to start" (Moyano 1803). Magdalena and Oquitoa were probably "renovated and repaired" with brick and lime mortar.

*in charge of regular prelates and their religious alone, without anyone interposing
any impediment or obstacle in any matter which concerns them.*[27]

The cédulas reales which we have already cited have expressed this command
many times. Included in it is the authority given to the religious to control the
excesses of the Indians. It has been ordered many times by the Councils of both
Americas. According to these orders the conversores should rule the Indians as
is on record in the Mexican Council, Book 3, Title 2, paragraph 7;[28] and in the
Council of Lima of 1582, Document 4, Chapters 7, 8, 28, 77, 80, and 83-88;[29]
finally, in addition, even the least details of the government which this college
maintains in its conversiones have been presented to Your Majesty for your approval
by the Discretorium of the College of Discalced Franciscans of Pachuca in the
Northeast.[30] Your Majesty, after hearing the opinion of the Supreme Council of
the Indies, deigned to issue a cédula real dated in Madrid, March 24, 1791, approv-
ing it and strictly commanding that no obstacle to its observance should be inter-

---

27. The cédula real of September 24, 1668, was issued by the seven-year-old Carlos II under
the tutelage of his mother, María Ana of Austria.

28. According to the *Catholic Encyclopedia,* "Councils are legally convened assemblies of
ecclesiastical dignitaries and theological experts for the purpose of discussing and regulating
matters of church doctrine and discipline" (Wilhelm 1908: IV: 423). There are seven kinds of
councils, including provincial councils which "bring together the suffragan bishops of the
metropolitan of an ecclesiastical province and other dignitaries entitled to participate" (p. 424).
Gómez Hoyos (1961: 198) says that, "The two councils of imperishable fame which attained
the sanction of the Popes and the royal approbation and which lived during more than two
centuries in all of America and the Philippine Islands, were those celebrated in Lima and in
Mexico in the years 1583 and 1585."
   Even though Bringas writes of the Council of Lima in 1582 (rather than 1583), these
are doubtless the councils to which Gómez Hoyos refers. The results of the Lima Council were
put into execution by a cédula real of Philip II in 1591, and those of the Mexican Council by
Philip III in 1621. Both were incorporated into the Indian Code (Gómez Hoyos 1961: 198-199).

29. See note 28.

30. The Discalced Friars Minor was a branch of the Franciscan Order which had its beginnings
in 1496 in the founding of a strict hermitage of six brothers in the district of Granada in Spain.
In 1559 their minister was Saint Peter of Alcantara, who "forbade even sandals to be worn
on the feet, prescribed complete abstinence from meat, prohibited libraries, in all of which
measures he far exceeded the intentions of St. Francis of Assisi. From him is derived the name
Alcantarines, which is often given to the Discalced Friars Minor" (Bihl n.d.: 13).
   The first Discalced Franciscans arrived in New Spain in 1580, and from 1596 on they
worked among the Indians laboring in the mines of Pachuca (Hidalgo). This branch of the
Order of Friars Minor was suppressed in 1897 (McCloskey 1955: 7; Bihl n.d.: 13).

posed by anyone.[31] In this royal order Your Majesty has expressed the agreement of his Royal Will with that of his august progenitors.

36

This form of government, Señor, whose good results have been proven by experience, is the only one capable of restoring the pueblos, ensuring their happiness, and bringing about the reduction of the gentiles. We have kept both objectives in mind from the time when we first returned to receive the missions after the dissolution of the Custodia. We arranged to make a visitation of the missions and aimed it especially at the achievement of these objectives. The representations made to the Comandante General of Chihuahua have the same end. Taking into account the fact that in order to govern better the missions it is indispensable to put into practice the orders contained in the previously cited cédulas reales of Don Felipe V and Don Fernando VI. In these there is contained an order doubling the number of ministros in every one of the missions of the Pimería Alta. In view of this fact the Procurator of the College presented the following request to the Comandante General of Chihuahua:

Señor Comandante General: from Friar Diego Bringas, Procurator of the College of Santa Cruz de Querétaro of the Propaganda, in charge of mission affairs.

With due submission I appear before Your Excellency and depose: since it is the duty of my College to achieve the best possible method of administration in the missions of the Pimería Alta cared for by our religious in the Province of Sonora as well as to carry out their ministry to the fullest extent and to achieve the ends for which His Majesty pays their expenses, I consider it necessary to inform Your Lordship that one of the means most conducive to those purposes is to double the number of ministros in each of the missions of the Pimería Alta. The Discretorium of my College, Señor, is convinced of this. However, the College is short of workers. Even so, it picked nine of them to set forth with me from the College on the 16th of April of last year, 1795, which they did.[32] After first presenting themselves to Your Lordship on the 26th of May of that year, in the Valley of San Bartolo, they left me in order to stay with the ministros of the aforesaid missions and to relieve those older missionaries who stood in need of it. Now that these religious, Señor, have been distributed among their various destinations, I should explain to Your Lordship the causes which make this duplication of ministros necessary. I should explain the proven fact that the religious cannot live without the stipend which the piety of the King, Our Lord, has given as an alms

---

31. We are unable to locate the text of this cédula real, one issued by Carlos IV.

32. Bringas, of course, is quoting himself here. And this 1795 journey of which he speaks is that to which he has already referred in his report to the king. See notes 9 and 10 regarding this trip.

in accordance with Law No. 25, Title 15, 1st Book of the Recopilada de Indias.[33]
It was intended that we support ourselves on it as befits our state. I hope the lofty understanding of Your Lordship will consider the reasons which I will here briefly expound to be sufficient for both the duplication of ministros and for the provision of the stipend.

These reasons, Señor, are of two kinds. Some deal with the persons of the ministros. Others concern our aim of establishing missions. As to the first: the canon law, the law governing the regular clergy, the law governing Indians and even the very Leyes de Partida command that the ministros should not live alone.[34] This is to avoid defects in the religious clergy which would have harmful effects on the public. It also makes it possible for the clergy to sustain each other mutually in conduct worthy of their ministry and in giving enlightenment to the pueblos. The observance of these very wise laws, Señor, is a necessity in that distant land where the ministros lack the assistance which may keep alive in them the sacred fire of the spirit which animates the Sovereign Ministry of the Propagation and Conservation of the Faith. Although it is purely a result of the Lord's mercy, we have not had the misfortune of knowing that any of our religious were worthy of correction for improper actions.

However, Señor, my College takes into account that its alumni are not mere stones separated by great distances from their center and which have been laboriously sculpted so as to provide spiritual improvement. It is not impossible in view of human frailty that one of them may turn out to be a stumbling block, and it is the duty of the good shepherds to provide the lands with remedies against evil. The College does it in this way. It takes for granted that the more worthily, faithfully, and fruitfully a religious serves his God and King, the more exact he should be in the observances of his institute. These can be better practiced when he is encouraged by a companion who will sustain him and be a witness to his actions.

But, Señor, if there were no other motive than the imminent danger which has been frequently experienced in those provinces of the priests' dying without the sacrament of confession — this alone would suffice to move the pious and royal spirit of His Majesty to pay the stipend for a companion for the ministro. In the course of my journey, Señor, I have been practically an eye-witness to the two most recent examples of this misfortune in the deaths of Father Oliva and Father Pamplona, both of whom died without the sacrament.[35] Not long ago in the Mission

---

33. This law, initially written in 1593, states that "Religious of the Order of Saint Francis, in accord with their Institute and Rule, can neither be proprietors nor have incomes. For the security of their consciences it is necessary to state that the stipend assigned to those who teach the doctrine to the Indians is given to these religious as an alms rather than as a stipend or income. . . ."

34. See *leyes de partida* in the Lexicon.

35. Friar Antonio Oliva was a blue-robed priest enrolled in the province of Santiago de Jalisco rather than a gray-robed Queretaran. He was serving at Opodepe in Sonora at least as early as 1784, and he was still assigned there in 1790 (Roca 1967: 139; Dobyns and Ezell 1959: 54). We can find no information concerning Father Pamplona.

of San Xavier del Bac there died in the same manner Padre Friar Juan Bautista Belderrain, a religious from our College.[36] The ministro from Tumacácori hastened to save him, hurrying fifteen leagues, but to no avail. It is a matter of great regret that this spiritual help should be lacking. Such help is a prime necessity for those whose duty it is in their turn to provide it for all the faithful. This danger is certainly one capable of holding any ministro back. The more useful he is the more virtuous and prudent such a ministro will be in a matter so decisive for one's eternal destiny. The law is intended to avoid all these ills, Señor, in giving the command that religious should live with companions: thus the canon law in the second Chapter, entitled "Monks," Title 35, concerning the monastic status. The 3rd Book decrees thus concerning the law governing the regular clergy in Chapter 5 of our general laws. The "Indian" in Book I, Title 7, section 1, says: "They should not let any religious die alone in a villa nor a fort nor in the parish church; but he should be placed in a major convent. However, if it should happen that they had to put him somewhere else this should be with other friars. Holy Church commands this to bring it about and to give him strength to be able to fight with the devil and the world and the flesh, which are enemies to the soul." As Solomon said, "Woe to him who is alone, for if he falls into sin, there is none to help him rise out of it."[37]

I overlook, Señor, those material needs which would be quite tolerable for any true religious. Such a one would suffer them even to the ultimate extreme, since he is sheltered by the spirit which caused him to leave the world in the first place. However, Señor, if we are considering the reasons why this doubling of ministros will contribute to the attainment of our purposes, then our missions are

---

36. Juan Bautista Velderrain was stationed at Mission San Francisco de Borja de Tecoripa in June 1775, where he was involved with the local Nevome Indians — a group of Piman-speakers — in the construction of a new church (Ahlborn 1974: 9; Roca 1967: 247-248). Tecoripa was ceded to the Jaliscan friars in September of 1776, and, according to Father Pedro Font (1776), Father Velderrain transferred to Tumacácori where he was *compañero* to Father Pedro de Arriquibar (Kessell 1965: 81). On Christmas Day, in 1776, he was at San Xavier del Bac (Garcés 1776). He and Father Joaquín Velarde were both at San Xavier in mid-1777 (Garcés 1777). Father Velderrain served with the roving minister of San Xavier, Francisco Garcés, until the latter's permanent departure on August 1, 1779, for the Yuma missions and a rendezvous with martyrdom (Forbes 1965: 182; Garcés 1778). Velderrain remained at Bac until his death on May 2, 1790, "from a vomiting of blood" (Querétaro 1776–1852; Entry No. 203). As Father Bringas complains, Father Baltasar Carrillo, who was at Tumacácori (Jackson 1951: 39), arrived too late to attend him. Father Velderrain's remains doubtless lie buried somewhere at San Xavier.

It was Velderrain who began construction on the church of San Xavier del Bac, perhaps the best known Spanish mission structure in the United States. He probably started work on the building in 1779 or in 1780 after Father Garcés' departure for the Yuma missions.

37. The quote from Solomon is found in the Holy Bible in the Book of Ecclesiastes, chapter 4, verse 10: "For if they fall, the one will lift up his fellow; but woe to him that is alone when he falleth; for he hath not another to help him up." The term "our general laws" refers to the laws of the Franciscan Order. The remaining citations are neither to the *Recopilación de Leyes de las Indias* nor to the *Siete Partidas*, both of which are arranged by book, title, and law rather than by book, section, and chapter. The original Spanish reads: *Así el derecho Canónico en el Capítulo Monachi 2° Tít. 35 de Statu Monacor. Libro 3° decrétalo así el derecho Regular en el Cap. 5 de nuestras Leyes generales. El Indiano en el Lib. 1° Tít. 7, partida 1° por estas palabras. . . .*

still in the first stage. They are on the frontier of a numerous group of gentiles. Their reduction to the sheepfold of the Church is the primary object of our Sovereign's piety. It is necessary that the Indians of those pueblos should never be without the assistance of a pastor. But the ministros, in their turn, are left with no proper attention paid them. When the missionary goes out to round up those wild lambs which wander through the fields, he is unable to keep watch over those left in the flock. The places inhabited by the gentile Papagos, Señor, can be allocated to the various missions. The propagation of the faith, however, is a delicate matter which must be built on solid foundations. The ministros must go at times into the wilderness and live with the barbarians in their huts for from eight to fifteen days. During this time they are able to speak to the Indians of religion and civilized life. They can convince the Indians that their sole object in making such journeys is to attain the true happiness of the natives.

If the arrangement described above is made in order to facilitate the trips of the missionaries, then this serves as a preparation for the foundation of other missions when the Indians whom we visit are sufficiently advanced to request them of their own accord. The missionaries work to teach them these things in their own country and thus gradually prepare them to receive Holy Baptism. With your great understanding, Señor, you will see that one missionary alone cannot carry on this sweet and useful labor. To put an inexperienced man in charge of the propagation of the faith on an 80-league frontier requires that we also have another man of experience in order to continue the visitas. This is for the benefit of more than 7,000 souls of the gentile nations of the Papagos, the Pimas Gileños, and the Cocomaricopas. No guards are necessary because the solitary missionary, in poverty and unarmed, causes no suspicion. Living in their midst the ministros transform those barbarians into Christians for the Church, vassals for the Sovereign, and useful members of society. These are the purposes for which missions are founded, but to attain them, the ministros must be doubled in every reducción.

But our feeble efforts, Señor, our thoughts (if the kindness of Your Lordship will permit me to say so) have as their object not only the propagation of the faith but also the conservation of the faith already implanted. This latter is the main object on which the resources which His Majesty spends on the missions in our charge as is also the well-being of the province in which we live insofar as is compatible with the sanctity of our ministry.

This, Señor, is the spirit of our Order and the special spirit of our apostolic ministry. Our Holy Patriarch [Saint Francis of Assisi] thought, and for the same reason, that he should live with his family, not living thus for himself alone but for the happiness of all.

These purposes and these alone are the spring which motivate the zeal of my·College. It never loses sight of them and it implores the kind protection of Your Lordship in their achievement.

I propose to Your Lordship a method which probably would cut in half the stipends which are necessary for the eight companions, thus making this project less expensive. Each of the missions of San Xavier del Bac, Tumacácori, Ati and Cocóspera is near a presidio. San Xavier has a pueblo de visita *located one-quarter of a league from the Presidio de Tucson. Tumacácori is two leagues from the Pre-*

*sidio de Tubac. Ati is a like distance from the Presidio de Altar. Cocóspera is
ten-leagues from the Presidio de Santa María. His Majesty pays each presidial
chaplain a salary of 480 pesos [per year]. If it so pleases Your Lordship, these four*
*presidios should be placed under the spiritual jurisdiction of their corresponding
missions. The missions will give them great spiritual assistance as can be easily
proven from past occasions when this assignment has been given them. In the past
the missions have served the presidios gratis, with the exception of Santa María.
We also beg Your Lordship to assign a stipend for these ministros. If this is done
it will only be necessary to provide support for the five regulars in the four remaining missions in whatsoever way is pleasing to Your Lordship.*

*It is not my business, Señor, to evaluate this idea. Certain advantages result-
ing from such an arrangement will not escape your keen understanding. I should,
however, in my own native simplicity and loyalty, explain to Your Lordship that
if this measure is put into effect, then, even though the ministros will be serving
the presidios frequently and punctually, they still should not be considered chaplains in the strict sense. The office of chaplain is not proper to our institute.*

*The measure, Señor, of doubling the number of ministros was ordered by
the Catholic Kings Don Felipe V and Don Fernando VI. They made special men-
tion of these same missions of the Pimería Alta in their cédulas reales. The first
of these was dated November 13, 1744, and was directed to the most excellent
Conde de Fuenclara, Viceroy of México. The second was dated December 4, 1747,
in Buen Retiro, and directed to the Most Excellent Don Juan Francisco de Huemes
y Horcasitas, the successor of the preceding.[38] They wrote as follows:*

*"It is assumed that it is very important in all the frontier reducciones that
one of the missionaries should be able to make* entradas *into the lands of the infidel
in order to attract them and win them over without, however, leaving the mission
population bereft of religious instruction and needed supervision. The religious
who remains [at the mission] will provide them."*

*That this duplication refers to our missions of the Pimería Alta is evident,
Señor, in these words: "The methods described above can be put into practice in
the missions which belong to the same religious order (it speaks, Señor, of the
expelled order) in the Pimas Altos or in the Province of Sonora placing two missionaries in every frontier reducción of pagan Indians."*

*That the corresponding stipend should be given to those religious who have
companions, Señor, is commanded in the cédulas reales in this manner: "To those
who are added for this reason shall be paid an additional stipend equal to the one
paid to the other missionaries in these provinces. This duplication will be for the
missions of Sonora as well as those of the Pimas Altos."*

*At present, Señor, the same causes still exist which motivated the royal spirit
of the Catholic Kings to order the duplication of ministros. There is no mission
in the Pimería Alta which is not located on an active frontier and whose ministro
cannot visit, attract, and catechize the gentiles. This is done every year. As a result
of these measures and those which were put into practice by the Captain of the*

---

38. See note 19 for the term of this viceroy.

Presidio de Tucson in accordance with the order of Your Lordship of July 6 of last year, 1795, the Papagos of the ranchería of Aquistuni were offered certain privileges if they would join the pueblo de visita of the mission of San Xavier del Bac. As a result, 134 Papagos of both sexes came to the pueblo. They have remained there since January 19 of the present year. They received instruction in the catechism with proper submission and understanding. Fifty-one of the children have already been baptized. For this reason as well as on account of the favorable results of Your Lordship's order, I humbly request you to command that the needed oxen and tools be given these Indians so that they will see what advantages come to them from their union with the pueblo. This will strengthen it, and when they begin to improve their crops their example will motivate others of their nation to become civilized Christians.

One of the first things to be done is to put them to work in agriculture. And so I must inform Your Lordship that since the presidio is so near the pueblo the farming practiced by the inhabitants and the soldiers causes a scarcity of water for the Indians. The Indians' crops are also badly damaged by the cattle and other animals belonging to the inhabitants of our presidio. For this reason, I humbly beg Your Lordship to order that the damage be repaired and that the Indians be permitted to use the water they need. This seems to be in accord with the laws of the Recopilación de Indias, *Law 1, Title 17, Book 4, and Law 2, Title 3, Book 6.*[39]

I must also explain to Your Lordship that the ministro of San Xavier del Bac, taking into account the extreme poverty of these Indians and not wishing them to have an excuse for returning to the wilderness, saw himself forced to give them food and clothing.[40] *He kept a precise account so that when it should come to Your Lordship's attention you might be willing to command that the cost, which is at present borne by the Mission of San Xavier del Bac, should be paid.*

---

39. Bringas seems to be stretching a legal point in citing Book 4, Title 17, Law 1 in support of giving the 134 Papagos oxen, tools, and water. The signs a modern traveler finds posted on the doors of hotels and motels in both Mexico and the United States are analogous to this law, which dates from 1538 and 1550: "We order the viceroys, presidents, governors and magistrates that they should give proper orders that supplies and necessary provisions be given travelers in inns and hostelries; that a just price should be paid; that there shall be neither extortion nor other poor treatment; and that there shall be available lists indicating the fair prices to be charged for traffic and commerce."

Law 2 of Title 3, Book 6, dating from 1604, simply states that the prelates of the Church should help to facilitate reducciones.

40. The minister of San Xavier del Bac to whom Bringas refers was Father Juan Bautista Llorens. Father Llorens, from the province of Valencia in Spain, was one of nineteen Franciscans brought to Sonora from Spain by newly appointed Bishop Antonio Reyes in 1782. He served in the Custodia de San Carlos de Sonora from its inception in 1783 until its demise in 1791, spending most of his time from 1787 through 1790 at Ati on the Altar River in Pimería Alta. He then became affiliated with the College of Santa Cruz de Querétaro, and was sent to Mission San Xavier del Bac in 1791 to replace the deceased Father Velderrain. In 1797 Father Llorens completed the work begun on the church by his predecessor, and he continued to serve at San Xavier until shortly before his violent death in the Presidio of Santa Cruz, Sonora, on July 4, 1815. Before leaving San Xavier he had been separated from the Queretaran college in September 1814 (Fontana 1963: 9, 11; Geiger 1959: II: 343, 358; Querétaro 1776–1856: Entry No. 260; Roca 1967: 110).

The justice of Your Lordship and considerations of humanity and religion encourage me humbly to ask for the remedy of an evil which could have dire consequences. As a result of the frequent campaigns they carry out against Apaches, the Gileño Pimas take their captives, both women and children, to the pueblo of Tucson.[41] There they turn them over to the Indians and inhabitants at low prices. These captives are then taught the catechism and serve to increase the population of the pueblo. Last October they brought some prisoners to the pueblo of Tucson and gave some of them to their relatives and sold some of them. There were present ten gentiles from the Gila who had come to lead us to their country. These gentiles saw one of the Spanish officials of the province take possession of some of the captives, and without the slightest recompense for their captors, carry them off to Arizpe. I am a witness, Señor, to this deed, and I can prove it should Your Lordship so demand.

The least harmful consequence which will follow from all this will be a painful wound to the most sacred elements of religion and the most sensitive part of humanity, because after this the Gileños will kill the adult women for whom they can expect no payment. This will cause the loss of those souls (who formerly were made safe at a low cost) and will offend religion and humanity. What I have said is more than enough to get Your Lordship's attention since you so nobly insist on keeping good faith with the barbarians, even when they least deserve it, in order to touch them by the force of example.

In virtue of what I have expounded thus far, I humbly beg and request Your Lordship in the name of my College of Santa Cruz de Querétaro to deign to act in accordance with my petition, or as may be more to the pleasure of Your Lordship.

Chihuahua, March 15, 1796
Friar Diego Bringas

To explain fully the effect produced on the office of the Comandante General by such weighty considerations as those given above — we deem it indispensable to tell Your Majesty of the opinion of the Asesor and the Comandante given in a letter of December 20 of the last year, 1796, which runs as follows:

Opinion

Señor Comandante General:

The Reverend Father Friar Diego Bringas, in his capacity as visitador of the missions of Sonora and as delegate of the Apostolic College of Santa Cruz de Querétaro, made a plea on the 15th of last March in which he touched on particular points which should be treated individually for the sake of greater clarity.

---

41. The matter of Indian captives and their sale into servitude or slavery has been discussed at length by Dobyns, Ezell, and others (1960) and by Bailey (1966). Such captives were commonly called *Nixoras* (*Nijoras; Niforas;* etc.), although other terms were used to describe them as well (see note 111).

1st Point. Since he had brought with him nine religious who have no place to which they can be assigned, he proposes first that for the better rule and administration (both spiritual and temporal) of the missions, two religious should be placed in each mission and each should receive a stipend.

2nd Point. In order to provide some relief for the Royal Treasury from this new burden which the payment of two stipends would bring, the administration of the presidios of Tucson, Tubac, Altar, and Santa María de Suamca should be assigned to the ministros of the neighboring missions of San Xavier del Bac, Tumacácori, Ati and Cocóspera. To them would be assigned the 480 pesos which their present chaplains receive as salary. It is stipulated that they are not to be given the title of chaplain, as this is not proper to their religious order.

The cédulas reales of November 13, 1744, and that of December, 1747, which support this doubling up of ministros are not to be found in the archives of this comandancia *as they are dated long before it was established and are not available for reference. However, even assuming that Father Bringas has quoted the content of these cédulas correctly, they seem to be limited to the new reducciones or conversiones on the frontier of new Indian country. It is well known that for these it is useful and fitting to have two ministros, so that while one is busy making entradas into the country of the infidels to attract and win them over, the other may remain at the mission to teach the doctrine. The mission, of course, is already populated and has good rules and established government. The misiones of Sonora are so old that if we are to judge by the length of time already gone by since their establishment they should by now have been made into curatos or doctrinas in a formal sense. Therefore, it so happens that we are no longer dealing with those new reducciones to which the cédulas reales refer. The present ministros of the Sonora missions can visit the rancherías of infidels in the vicinity without running the risk that in their absence from the mission their parishioners would flee or change their beliefs. The most excellent Father Friar Manuel de la Vega, Commissary General of the Indies, made use of the faculties which had been conferred on him in a Pontifical Brief of November 17, 1779, and set up on December 14 of the succeeding year, 1780, General Statutes for the founding and rule of the new custodias of these provinces.[42] The Supreme Council of the Indies approved them*

---

42. Father Manuel de la Vega, O.F.M., as commissary general of the Indies, had jurisdiction over all Franciscans in Spain's New World possessions. The Franciscan commissaries general of Peru and New Spain were under him, and he had authority to communicate directly with the crown (McCloskey 1955: 25-26 n. 33). As early as 1776 José de Gálvez, who was then governor pro tempore of the Council of the Indies (Priestly 1916: 7), asked Father de la Vega to look into the possibility of creating custodias in New Spain. The plan for custodias, a brainchild of Father Antonio de los Reyes, was approved by the king on June 30, 1777.

"The next step was to seek papal approval. The plan was sent to the Spanish ambassador at Rome, the duke of Grimaldi, who submitted it to the Holy See. Rome approved it on November 17, 1779, six months after the erection of the diocese of Sonora and a year and a month before the appointment of Reyes as its first bishop. The Franciscan commissary general was asked to draw up more detailed statutes for the government of the custodies, and Rome approved the statutes. The Apostolic Brief of Pope Pius VI on the custodies and statutes, a document of forty-two pages, was printed and published at Madrid in 1781" (Geiger 1959: II: 347).

on February 19, 1781, with the express stipulation that they should in no way infringe on the royal prerogatives or orders of His Majesty or those of the bearers of ordinary diocesan jurisdiction. This stipulation is found in the real cédula which was issued on May 20, 1782, after consultation with the same Supreme Council.[43] Copies were sent to this office of Comandante General, to the Most Illustrious Archbishops and Bishops, and to the Reverend Provincials and Guardians of the Province and the Colleges of Saint Francis, for observance and compliance.

In paragraph 6, Article 3, of the above-mentioned cédula real it is forbidden for any missionary to reside or live alone in the pueblos, misiones, and new conversiones. The Reverend Father Friar Sebastián Flores, who was the first custodio of San Carlos de Sonora, had moved for compliance with this provision in a petition dated December 4, 1783.[44] He received a reply on the 24th of that same month and year, which stated that there was no objection to stationing two ministros in each mission as long as it would not be an expense to the Royal Treasury, but that at that time only one stipend had been assigned to the religious in charge of the eight missions of the Pimería Alta as was the case with the others in Sonora. It also stated that there was neither order nor permit in existence to allow the imposition of a double stipend on the Royal Treasury. This would amount to a great sum if it were applied to all the missions of the province. This is found in Book 9 of the file on custodias under number 445 of the 3rd Book of Sonora.[45] The fact that the Reverend Father Flores was silenced and did not repeat his petition proves clearly that before and after the founding of the custodia of San Carlos of Sonora, those missions had only one ministro each, and the addition of another would have been an innovation which would have doubled the burden on the Royal Treasury compared to that imposed by the present stipends. It might also serve as an example for other provinces and missions to make similar requests.

It is asserted that the presence of two ministros in every mission would be useful and fitting for their better government. On the contrary, however, it would be considered injurious by those religious who are oldest and most experienced in mission management. Their opinion is based on their experience and on the strife and great inconveniences which arose naturally due to the diversity of their personalities.

The Reverend Father Friar Francisco Antonio Barbastro made this statement in number 78 of his petition which he made acting both for himself as well as

---

43. This is the cédula which ordered the erection of four new custodias in northern New Spain. See note 2 for details.

44. Friar Sebastián Flores had twice been guardian of the College of Santa Cruz de Querétaro, serving his first term from 1778–81, when in October 1783, he was appointed by Bishop Antonio de los Reyes to become the first custos of the new Custodia of San Carlos de Sonora. The headquarters for the custodia were situated at Banámichi on the Sonora River, and it was here that Father Flores died on January 1, 1784, barely two months after his appointment. A Spaniard, he had come to the New World from the Holy Province of San Miguel (Geiger 1959: II: 358; Querétaro 1776–1856: Entry No. 173; Roca 1967: 160, 378).

45. This probably refers to an unpublished file of documents. We have been unable to locate them.

representing his College of Santa Cruz de Querétaro.[46] He sent the petition from the Mission of Tubutama on December 24, 1783, and he repeated this in the 5th point and others which he later wrote in Aconchi on July 9, 1788. He repeated it again to the Supreme Government so that it might be forwarded to His Majesty. The College followed this well-based judgment which had been drawn up in its name, and supported by a prelate as irreproachable, old and experienced as the Reverend Father Barbastro. From all this it must be inferred that when Father Bringas drew up his plea of March 15 he was not aware of these antecedents, and so adopted the opposite opinion since it was more favorable to his main purpose of getting a stipend for the religious who had come with him and who now found themselves in Sonora without any proper destination, since there were not enough missions to which to assign them.

The cédulas reales of July 16, 1790, and August 17, 1791, which were drawn up in consultation with the Council [of the Indies] ordered this office that the missions should continue to receive help as formerly with the condition that a definite change may be made when information which has already been requested makes it possible to decide what is best for the four new custodias.[47] This is the most recent ruling made concerning this matter, and orders have been given that it be observed and complied with. Consequently, the missions should continue in the care of only one ministro in accordance with both ancient and modern practice which has been observed without interruption.

When His Majesty had been informed of the scarcity of clergy in these provinces to serve in the important position of presidio chaplain, he condescended to command in the Royal Order of October 16, 1778, that the chaplaincies should be temporarily assigned to religious of the Order of Saint Francis.[48] In another Order of February 8, 1782, he approved the appointment of Friar Juan Bermejo

---

46. Francisco Antonio Barbastro was born in the Villa de Cariñena in Aragón, Spain, in the Bishopric of Zaragosa in 1735. He arrived in 1770 at the College of Santa Cruz de Querétaro to take up missionary duties, and for the next thirty years, until his death at Aconchi on June 22, 1800, he worked among the Indians of Sonora. He was in charge of the mission at Ures by 1775; he served at Tubutama in 1776 and again from 1778 to 1783; he was at Banámichi in 1784, and at Aconchi, with its visita of Baviácora, by 1787 (Bringas 1960: 22-24; Gómez Canedo 1971: 9-18; Roca 1967: 378 n. 100).

A religious for all but twenty of his sixty-six years, Father Barbastro was a prolific writer concerning the history of Sonora and of the Franciscans, although his many manuscripts in the Civezza collection in Rome await publication. He succeeded Sebastián Flores in 1784 as the only other custodian of the Custodia of San Carlos de Sonora, and it was largely due to his efforts that the custodia was finally abolished in 1791. He was president of the missions of Pimería Alta from 1777 to 1783 and again from 1791 to 1795; he was fluent in both the Opata and Pima Indian languages; and it was he who started construction of the Franciscan mission at Tubutama, a structure which has continued in use as the church of that village (Bringas 1960: 22-24; Geiger 1959: II: 358, 362-364; Gómez Canedo 1971: 13, 17 n. 12; Moyano 1803; Roca 1967: 378 n. 100).

47. See notes 3 and 4 for quotes from these cédulas reales.

48. We have been unable to locate the text of this royal order of Carlos III.

as Chaplain of Santa Fe, New Mexico.[49] He was a religious of the same order, and a missionary of the custodia of that Province. His Majesty further ordered that Friar Juan and the other religious who were employed as chaplains of presidios should enjoy the same privileges and exemptions which belong to others in their respective provinces who have administered missions for a period of ten years. As soon as the custodia of San Carlos of Sonora was erected its prelate and definitors contended that its religious were neither compelled by the Most Illustrious Bishop nor by the Comandancias Generales to serve in curatos nor as chaplains of presidios. His Majesty deigned to command in a real cédula issued in consultation with the Council of the Indies on January 20, 1785, that only in case of a total lack of secular priests or suitable regulars should curatos and presidios be entrusted to missionaries.[50] As soon as this lack should have been remedied by any means possible, they should be relieved of this temporary burden so they might freely and zealously apply themselves to the punctual discharge of the obligations attached to their apostolic office, i.e., the conversion of the gentiles.

In another cédula real of August 20, 1793, he commanded that secular or religious priests who serve as chaplains of presidios should be paid the stipend from the day they set out from their destination just as had previously been ordered with regard to the religious who set out for the missions.[51]

This was also ordered in the Pontifical Brief of October 11, 1795, which was approved by the Council on February 4.[52] It was sent to this Comandancia General for observance in compliance with the Royal Order of June 23 of the current year.[53] The faculties previously granted to the Vicar General of the Army and Navy had been published elsewhere. This order is to the effect that the Vicar General might exercise any ecclesiastical jurisdiction either personally or through other priests sub-delegated ad hoc, over those who should at any time be employed in the administration of the sacraments and the spiritual direction of souls be they clerics or priests, seculars or regulars, even though they belong to mendicant orders. Those so delegated may exercise this jurisdiction in the same way as if they were the true prelates and pastors of secular clerics and Superiors General of Regulars. They could act as judges in all ecclesiastical and civil legal cases — civil, criminal,

---

49. We have been unable to locate the text of the Royal Order of February 8, 1782, issued by Carlos III. Friar Juan Bermejo, O.F.M., was appointed custos, i.e., head of the Custodia de la Concepción in New Mexico in 1782, although this custody was never actually implemented (Domínguez 1956: 244 n. 3). His tenure as chaplain at Santa Fe was apparently impermanent, because in January 1789 he was requesting to be returned to that post. In November 1791, the Tiwa Indians of Isleta Pueblo, New Mexico, were asking that Father Bermejo be assigned as their missionary (Twitchell 1914: II: 306, 339).

50. We have been unable to locate the text of this cédula real of Carlos III.

51. We have been unable to locate the text of this cédula real of Carlos IV.

52. We have been unable to locate the text of this pontifical brief of Pius VI.

53. We have been unable to locate the text of this royal order issued by Carlos IV.

and mixed — which might occur among or against the aforementioned persons as well as any other persons whose residence is with the Army and who in any way are subject to the ecclesiastical forum.

The conclusion to be drawn from these pontifical and sovereign regulations is that when there are no secular or regular priests the curatos and presidios may be entrusted to the missionary religious of the Apostolic Colleges of the Propaganda Fide. These missionaries could be compelled to provide priestly services until the lack of proper clergy has somehow been remedied. They may then be relieved of this duty so as to apply themselves zealously to the punctual fulfillment of their apostolate, that of converting the infidels.

The lack of secular or regular priests suited to this work is so well known in Sonora that in the absence of any other remedy this Comandancia General was forced to request the Most Excellent Viceroy for religious of the Provincia de San Diego. They came at the expense of the Hacienda Real *and at present are fulfilling the above-described needs. However, when they die, we will find ourselves still having to request the assistance of their Order and having to bring them here at Royal expense. The presidios must get along without them until the arrival of pastors who can administer the sacraments and provide spiritual nourishment. Now, since this is precisely the situation in which the apostolic missionaries may be compelled to serve them, it seems to me that Your Lordship should agree with me in declaring that there are neither regulation nor just motive for burdening the Hacienda Real with this new expenditure for two stipends in each mission.*

In order to provide fitting employment for the religious of the Apostolic College of Santa Cruz de Querétaro who were brought to Sonora by the Padre Visitador, Friar Diego Bringas, an official petition should be made to the Most Illustrious Bishop of that diocese as military sub-delegate to keep them in mind. He should be asked to nominate them as presidial chaplains for present and future vacancies. He should inform the Reverend Father Guardian and the Definitorium [governing council] of the College of this step for their information and guidance.

3rd Point. Father Bringas states that as a result of the orders of this Comandancia General and the measures which were taken by the Captain of the Presidio of Tucson to comply with it, all the people of the pueblo of Tucson were assembled. There were 134 gentiles of both sexes from the ranchería of Aquituni.[54] In accordance with the third, fourth and fifth points of his petition, he requests that they be given oxen and tools for sowing crops so that when they see the advantages that they derive from the reducción, their example would inspire others of their nation to embrace civilized and Christian life.

4th Point. Measures should be adopted to keep the cattle of the soldiers and residents of the Presidio of Tucson from damaging the crops of the natives who live in the nearby pueblo of that same name.[55]

---

54. Aquituni, which would be rendered Ak Chin (Arroyo Mouth) in modern Piman, was a Papago farming village on the lower Santa Cruz River between Tucson and the Gila River.

55. The "nearby pueblo" of Tucson was an Indian settlement on the west bank of the Santa Cruz River, immediately opposite the presidio of Tucson, which was on the east bank.

5th Point. They should be permitted the use of the water they need.

And lastly, the Mission of San Xavier del Bac should be reimbursed for the cost of the food and clothing which they furnished the extremely poor Indians who had been most recently reduced so as to avoid their return to the wilderness. The *ministro* is supposed to have kept an exact account of this and will present it to Your Lordship upon demand.

In the separate papers, under number 57, Book 3 of Sonora, concerning the division of lands and waters between the natives of the Pueblo of Tucson and the troops and the residents of the presidio of that name, measures have been taken to avoid disputes between the parties and to apportion the use of the land and the water without wasting them as has happened before.[56] For this reason no new measures are needed in addition to the other two, which concern furnishing oxen and tools so that the newly reduced Indians can sow their fields and the reimbursement of the food and clothing with which they were assisted by the Mission of San Xavier del Bac to which they have been joined.

It should be kept in mind that in Article 2 and following of Title 15 of the *Regulations for the Peninsula of California,* which were approved and ordered to be obeyed by the *cédula real* of October 24, 1781, it is expressly provided that in the 1,000 pesos granted to each foundation all the needs of its farm work and tillage are included.[57] For the progress of the new foundations, the old ones were permitted to help out with seed and cattle insofar as they could without themselves suffering a lack of these things. The old missions ought thus to help and contribute to the foundation and establishment of new ones. With much greater reason should the Mission of San Xavier del Bac do this, just as it has actually done, to assist in its own repopulation and growth. It has the obligation, so far as its funds permit, to help the families of gentiles who have recently been joined to it. It is natural that at the time of their foundation, the 1,000 pesos should have been supplied from the Royal Treasury for their material outfitting and tillage. There is no reason to burden it with the proposed new expenditure. Even if this should be done, it would be exclusively up to the higher authorities of the Royal Treasury. For these reasons, it seems to me that Your Lordship should, if you are willing, declare that there is no authority to provide oxen and tools. Neither is there authority to repay the Mission of San Xavier del Bac for the cost of food and clothing provided from its funds for the gentiles who were recently reduced and joined to the Pueblo of Tucson, its *visita.*

6th Point. In order to spread the sentiments of humanity among the hostile Indians; to cause them to know and to appreciate the advantages of the exchange of prisoners; and to abolish the barbarous cruelty with which they have so often

---

56. This citation is probably to unpublished documents in a legal archive. We have been unable to locate them.

57. The regulation of Baja California of which Galindo Navarro speaks was issued by Don Felipe de Neve, governor of both Californias, in June 1779. And as Bringas notes, this regulation received royal approval through the *cédula* of October 24, 1781. The provisions of the regulation, including those alluded to here, are summarized by Bancroft (1884a: 339-341).

killed their prisoners, it is provided in various articles of Title 10 of the Regulations for Presidios, that booty taken from them consisting of horses, mules, cattle, food and other of their few possessions, should be distributed solely among the soldiers and Indian scouts who took part in the action as a reward for their efforts.[58] *In no case, however, should this apply to the human captives. They should be well treated and assisted. They should be converted and instructed. This applies especially to the women and children. They should try to arrange for an exchange of prisoners. All mistreatment of captives should be prohibited. The pain of death should be inflicted on those who kill prisoners in cold blood.*

All vassals of His Majesty, without distinction, are obligated to obey strictly these just rules. This obligation, however, should not be extended indiscriminately to those groups of friendly gentiles or allies of our arms who are not subject to his sovereign rule. These latter should be governed solely by their own traditions. This type of warfare [i.e., the humane regulations cited here], far from contributing to the pious purpose of saving the lives of prisoners, and the prohibition of their sale or ransom, would have exactly the opposite effect and would cause them to kill their captives in cold blood. This is because the only reason they have for letting them continue to live is their own profit. If they are deprived of the hope of making a profit due to the prohibition of the sale of captives they would kill them at once to be rid of the burden of guarding them as well as to prevent their escape.

The Apache nation, which wages a cruel war on our own populations and territories, also persecutes the Papagos and the Gila Pimas who are our friends and allies. It is just and fitting that we assist them so far as possible against our common enemy. Since there are no means more adequate for so doing than permitting and even helping them in the sale and barter of their prisoners, it consequently follows that instead of forbidding this it is proper to tolerate and even to encourage it in the future. Far from being in opposition to the sovereign decisions of His Majesty, on the contrary it is in accord with his pious and Christian intentions, as there is absolutely no other way to save these captives from inevitable death if there's no profit to their captors.

For these reasons, as well as because we have learned from experience that barbarous Indians and their women who are left on or near the frontier readily flee and go back to their rancherías, it seems to me that with regard to the 6th point of Father Bringas Your Lordship might be pleased to agree. Orders should be given to the military commander of Sonora that the frontier captains should

---

58. Title 10 of the Royal Regulations of 1772, promulgated by the cédula real of September 10, 1772, pertains to the "Treatment of Enemy or Indifferent Indians." These regulations, which concern the presidios forming the frontier line of defense for New Spain, have been published in full in Spanish and English translation (Brinckerhoff and Faulk 1965). Section 5 of Title 10 says specifically: "The spoils that are taken from enemies, whether of horses, mules, cattle, provisions, or other effects of the little that they possess, are to be divided solely between the soldiers and Indian scouts and auxiliaries that took part in the action as a reward for their struggles; but in no case is this to apply to the persons to whom the preceding instructions apply" (Brinckerhoff and Faulk 1965: 33). The latter reference is to Indian prisoners who are to be set free. The "preceding instructions" specify that spoils are not to be taken from the freed prisoners in hopes that they will tell their tribesmen about the humane treatment they received from the Spaniards.

not prevent the Papagos and Gila Pimas, our friends and allies, from selling or trading so many head of hostile Apaches who are taken captive and brought to our presidios and towns. If there are among the barbarians any adult males or women, they should arrange to acquire them at the lowest price possible. They should then be sent to Mexico City to prevent their escape. In any case, Your Lordship should act as he pleases.

Chihuahua, December 9, 1796
Galindo Navarro[59]

[❃ ❃ ❃]

In accordance with the opinion of the Asesor on the first point, the Bishop of Sonora should not be given the right to use as chaplains those religious of the College of Santa Cruz de Querétaro who were brought here by the Reverend Father Friar Diego Bringas, since they are actually stationed in the missions. Orders should be issued that the Indians of Tucson are not to be discriminated against in the use of the lands and waters that belong to them; and that in the ransom of the captured head of Apaches whom the Gila Pimas bring to the missions of the Pimería, only childless adult women and the adult males shall be taken owing to the danger of their fleeing; but those who turn them over shall be recompensed. As far as providing assistance is concerned in settling the 134 persons from the ranchería of Aquituni in the mission of Tucson, you shall continue to observe the provisions of the order of last August 12 which have been added to the file together with the antecedents to which I refer, as well as others relative to the religious whom the Reverend Father Bringas brought in his charge.

Nava[60]
This is a copy.
Chihuahua, December 20, 1796
Manuel Merino[61]

---

59. Pedro Galindo Navarro was appointed by Teodoro de Croix as his assessor (i.e., his auditor or his lawyer) when he became the first comandante general of the Comandancia General of the Provincias Internas in 1777 (Thomas 1941: 20). It is clear from this report that Galindo Navarro held the same position at least until 1797 under Pedro de Nava (Castañeda 1942: 194).

60. Pedro de Nava became comandante general of the Western Provinces of the Comandancia General of the Provincias Internas on March 12, 1790. He was ad interim comandante of the Eastern Provinces as well. By a royal order of November 23-24, 1792, the two provinces were again made one and the comandancia general of the Provincias Internas was made independent of the viceroy of New Spain.

As comandante general, Nava, whose capital was at Chihuahua City, was responsible for Texas, New Mexico, Coahuila, Nueva Viscaya, and Sonora and Sinaloa. He remained in office until August of 1800 (Loomis 1969: 266-267; Simmons 1968: 42).

61. Don Manuel Merino y Merino was a lieutenant in one of the five companies of troops accompanying Teodoro de Croix's 1777–78 inspection tour of the Provincias Internas. He was secretary of the council of war held at Monclova in December of 1777, and he eventually became secretary of the Comandancia General of the Provincias Internas (Bolton 1914: II: 147-149; Morfi 1935: 19; 1967: 389 n. 4).

 **38**

This judgment, Señor, with the decree of the Comandante, is the first formal measure we have seen taken in regard to the many pleas we have presented up to the present time. They made necessary a long explanation of the way in which they altered many points of the order and substance of our own expositions. This was because he omitted the first point and failed to reply to the first request made by the Procurator of this College on March 7 of that same year, and which related to new foundations. He only replies to the second point. It is worth noting that the Asesor makes certain assumptions which we do not. He suppresses some reasons (and those may be of greater weight and quantity) which we allege with regard to the doubling up of many ministros. He also cites a cédula real without stating any other reason for doing so except that it was necessary. All this we shall discuss concisely and accurately.

 **39**

In the first point of this decree, the Asesor assumes that the new religious who came with the Visitor of the Missions and Procurator of this College had no assigned destination. That the contrary is true is clear from part 2 of the petition. He says that he presented them personally to the Comandante; that he informed him of their destinations, which was to serve as companions to the missionaries. The Comandante did not object to their continuing on their journey to the missions.

40

In the second point either the Asesor contradicts himself or he gives clear proof that he is uninformed about the situation of the missions of the Pimería Alta. Without referring to the authority of the cédulas reales of November 13, 1744, and December 4, 1747, he asserts that they do not exist in the archives of the office of the Comandante General (this lack is not our fault).[62] He adds that even if these cédulas, which were quoted literally by the Procurator, actually existed they seem to be limited to the new reducciones or frontier conversiones which had been instituted for Indians who have as yet not been reduced. The Asesor agrees that the ministros should be doubled up in the frontier missions to the infidels if the two cédulas cited should actually exist. We say, then, that he either contradicts himself or else he does not know where our missions are. When the map [p. 98] shows their location on a wild frontier of infidels and enemies, either the Asesor does not know or he is contradicting himself. But this is not the only objec-

---

62. See note 19 for discussion of these two cédulas reales.

tionable matter. There is also the fact that the Asesor says (seemingly in arbitrary fashion) that when the cédulas reales speak of the fitness of doubling up of ministros in all the Indian reducciones, they refer only to the frontier reducciones. For these the cédulas reales which have been cited consider this doubling up to be not only fitting, but absolutely necessary. However, we are still more astonished that the Asesor did not take into consideration the next clause referred to by the Procurator, for it removes all doubt. It says, with no ambiguity at all, that the ministros should be doubled up in the frontier missions of the Pimas Altos — and they are precisely these which are the object of our petition.

In the same second point of the decree, the Asesor makes the assumption that there are neither danger nor risk involved when the missionaries visit the infidels and leave their missions unattended. However, we find there are many dangers. We do not believe it is in conformity with the mind of Your Majesty, nor is it in conformity with the duties of the good shepherds to abandon their own flock in order to seek out another which has not yet been placed in their care. We further point out that the Asesor assumes that our missionaries have frequently abandoned their flocks in this way. He can never prove this assertion. On the contrary, they have always left their missions in charge of another ministro when they left to visit the gentiles. This shows even more the need of having two missionaries.

In the third paragraph the Asesor says that the oldest missionaries who have had the most experience in the management of missions are opposed to the doubling up of ministros. They base this on their own experience, which shows that diversity of character would naturally produce discord and serious inconvenience. He further says that the Reverend Father Friar Francisco Barbastro made this statement in his petition dated December 24, 1783, and that he repeated it in that of July 9, 1788. He infers from this that at the time the Procurator made his petition, which was March 15, 1796, he had not been informed of these antecedents, and was only trying to place the religious he had brought with him and who had no definite assignment.

We reply, Señor, that this College, since the time it has had a sufficient number of workers, has constantly emphasized and practiced having men doubled up. This was done in the Province of Texas until the time it surrendered those missions.

As soon as the Province of Sonora received them, it made a petition to the Viceroy of Mexico to be able to do the same thing. Furthermore, this Discretorium and College are comprised of religious who are quite sufficiently experienced, some of whom are older than Father Barbastro, and they have always been of this opinion. They had many reasons for this which are of much greater weight than the mere risk of dissensions based on conflicting personalities.

As far as the judgments of Father Barbastro are concerned, which are expressed in the quotations of the Asesor, we say: That if he had remembered that the *custodia* of San Carlos of Sonora was founded on October 23, 1783, he would not cite as decisions of this College those which were made by a single religious who was only an individual member of the Custodia over whose missions this seminary had no influence at all and on a date so long after the creation of our Custodia as December 24, 1783. Without any doubt, if on that date the missions had actually been within the effective care of this College, it would never have permitted such a decision to be sent to the government, one which it has always considered to be notably injurious.

But if at any time Father Barbastro, being Custodian, expressed this opinion to the government, he saw himself forced to do so because at the time he was prelate of a Custodia composed of religious who had for the most part been collected at random from at least four different Provinces. However, at this time the sons of this College alone are occupying those missions, and they are used to its strict observance. They are pleading for companions, and as experience has shown, it is only the lack of these which can keep them from beginning their ministry. The constant attitude and desire of this College were presented to the Procurator when the College made the aforementioned petition. The College was not motivated to station its religious as the Asesor supposes. It was also moved by the powerful reasons and authorities which it cites, and from which the Asesor disassociates himself. We believe that even only one of the reasons which he omits would move the pious and royal heart of Your Majesty, namely, the consideration that the religious die without confession after having spent their lives in the service of God and Your Majesty.

We recognize, Señor, the authority possessed by the Asesor in virtue of which he can make decisions contrary to the cédulas reales. We refer to the cédula real of Don Carlos III, glorious father of Your Majesty, dated January 20, 1785.[63] In this instance His Majesty orders that only when there are no other priests should the curatos and presidios be turned over to the missionaries. However, as soon as other priests were available, missionaries should be relieved of this interim burden. In spite of this the Asesor decided that by virtue of the cédula real the missionaries could be forced to care for the curatos. In doing this he presupposes one thing, invents another, and attacks the Apostolic Institute.

 79

He assumes that the missionaries must be forced to serve Your Majesty in the presidios. On the contrary, it is proved that they have always served in them faithfully and without recompense. He invents a use of force which the cédula real does not order. He attacks the Apostolic Institute by giving the order that (as may be inferred from the spirit of his statements) the missionaries are to be installed officially as chaplains with presentation, confirmation, and title. This is contrary to our apostolate and to that which I. have requested the Procurator to obtain for us.

It is equally strange that the Asesor finds a difficulty in the fact that the Discalced Fathers should not be able to continue the administration of the presidios and that as a result the Comandancia would find itself forced to bring in chaplains at the expense of the Royal Exchequer.[64] Thus the presidios would be forced to get along without regular pastors to administer the sacraments until the chaplains arrived. This is strange because, first of all, it can never be proved that the missionaries have ever made any difficulty whatsoever about administering the sacraments gratis in the interim, just as they are doing at present for the presidio at Tubac, when proper chaplains have been lacking in the presidios of the Pimería. Secondly, there is no impropriety about the faithful receiving spiritual aid from an interim chaplain. He administers the same sacraments to them as does their own chaplain. He preaches the same Gospel. He buries them with the same rites of the Roman Catholic Church. Finally, the expense of bringing the chaplains doesn't seem to be a demand which is contrary to the Royal will. Your Majesty has ordered that the religious who make trips in your service should travel at the expense of the Royal Hacienda. This expense which the Asesor mentions is not incurred by the missionaries of this College when they serve a presidio which has no chaplain. They cause no expense at all to the Royal Hacienda. It is easy to present many sworn statements as to the truth of this, and as to the frequent occasions on which the missionaries have acted thus in the two Pimerías during the period of 29 years.

---

63. This is the same cédula real referred to by Bringas in section 37, the text of which we have been unable to locate, as mentioned in note 50.

64. See note 30 for discussion of the Discalced Friars Minor.

48

On the fifth point, the Asesor determines with regard to the complaints about injuries suffered by the Indians of Tucson at the hands of soldiers and other residents in the use of their water that fitting provisions have already been made in File Number 570, Third Book of Sonora.[65] It seems to us that it would have been more fitting to have decreed that they should have been ordered to put the aforementioned provisions into effect. If that sort of decision should be made in all cases of infraction of the laws, protests would be useless, for everyone knows that there are laws, but many do not respect them. It is not enough simply to tell them that laws exist. They must be compelled to obey them.

49

As to the third and fifth points, the Asesor decides that tools cannot be given to the gentiles who live in Tucson, and that no repayment may be made to Mission San Xavier del Bac for what it has spent in supporting and helping these gentiles. His reason is that in Title 15 of the Regulations for the Peninsula of California it says that all the needs of cultivation and tillage are included in the 1,000 pesos granted to each foundation.[66] For the more rapid growth of the new missions the old ones are allowed to assist with seeds and cattle insofar as they are able. The Asesor concludes that it is natural that since at the time of its foundation 2,000 pesos were given to Mission San Xavier, there is no need for this new expenditure.

50

We shall explain to Your Majesty, Señor, only the most obvious points of this decree in order not to weary you.

We have not seen the regulation mentioned. We suppose, however, that it was composed in accordance with the ancient and constant practice of the missions. But it does seem strange to us that the 1,000 pesos with which the mission was founded are supposed to be of a different nature from all other material things; that is, permanent. It is now a century since the Mission of San Xavier was founded. The Apaches have been attacking it for more than 40 years. In spite of this, the Asesor decides that those original 1,000 pesos still remain either in themselves or in

---

65. Like "number 57, Book 3 of Sonora," cited in note 56, this is another reference to what is in all probability an unpublished legal archive, one we have been unable to locate.

66. See note 57 for discussion of this provision.

their products even though such an amount would never be enough to pay for everything that the barbarians have stolen there. As for these missions' lending to others those things which they do not need for themselves, that cannot fit San Xavier either. It is in debt for finishing the construction of its church, and it has no superfluous goods (although much is owed it).[67] Furthermore, it has always been the practice to make such loans regardless, with the understanding that they would be repaid.

51

This, Señor, is the reason why we never dare to arouse in the gentiles the slightest interest in being reduced. They have learned by experience that afterwards it is impossible for us to keep our word to them and to provide them with various advantages at very low cost. This is the first and chief reason for the loss of the two missions founded for the Yumas on the Colorado River in the year 1780. Much was promised them, and later on, the promises were not fulfilled. The final proof of this truth is the sad news which the President of our Missions of the Pimería Alta gives us in a letter of December 4 of the last year, 1796, concerning the order which he had been commanded to communicate to the then ministro of San Xavier to the effect that he was not to admit any more gentiles into his mission. The result was that those who had entered it a short time before returned to the wilderness. This gave rise to the request made by the Procurator that in spite of this occurrence the minister should try to persuade those very same gentiles to return and live peacefully at San Xavier. If this order agrees with the Catholic zeal of Your Majesty, although being at the same time contrary to the spirit of the Laws of the Indies (which we cannot possibly imagine), from now on Your Majesty's expenditures to bring a larger number of workers for the reduction of the gentiles will be useless.

52

As to the sixth and last point, we are much surprised that the Asesor decrees something which we didn't ask for, and at the same time passes over in silence

---

67. The debt referred to was what was owed on 7,000 pesos borrowed by Father Velderrain from Don Antonio Herreros. Señor Herreros extended the credit, believing he would be repaid through the sale of San Xavier's wheat crops, which had not been planted. He had not received his money by the end of 1795, when he was "clucking like a chicken" for its payment (Yturralde 1795). It is clear from what Father Bringas says that he still had not been paid by the end of 1796.

A situation in reverse arose in 1821 when Father Juan Bautista Estelric sold Lieutenant Don Ignacio Pérez 4,000 head of Tumacácori's cattle on credit, hoping to get money with which to finish a new church. It took Father Ramón Liberos, Estelric's successor at Tumacácori, more than two years to collect (Kessell 1969).

that which we're really asking for. And this is a very grave evil. In the second from last point of his disquisition, the Procurator of this College asks that reparation be made for the prisoners taken from the Indians. He says he is a witness to the fact that they were taken away without paying for them and he warns that the Gileños brought them to sell and did, in fact, sell some of them. It seems that in accordance with justice and the request that was made the decree ought to state that the price of those prisoners would be repaid and that in the future justice should not be violated. Indeed, the Asesor decrees that the gentiles should not be prevented from bringing prisoners to sell, and we, for our part, have not objected to this. But he says nothing about justice and restitution, and these are the very objects of the plea.

Finally, Señor, the decree of the General itself testifies to the justice of our petition. Even though it does not agree with the doubling up of our ministros, we leave this very grave need to the Royal clemency of Your Majesty. The same causes, Señor, which moved the Royal spirit to issue those regulations still exist today. The needs which occasion them are the same. The effects they should produce will be even greater and more arresting now. The only thing lacking is that these regulations should be put into effect.

53

We have now clearly proved, Señor, that our eight missions in the Pimería Alta are conversiones in the strictest sense as far as actual practice is concerned. They have been such without interruption from the year 1768, when we received them, up to the present day. The only way in which they are the same missions that were founded by the now-expelled regulars is that they are on the same ground. We have also proved that their Indians are incapable of being governed in any other way than that which is peculiar to conversiones. To change this would be an obstacle to their conversion and to the propagation of the faith. It only remains for this government to fix its attention, as is so needful, on the goals which we will respectfully request of Your Majesty after we have explained the third object of this, our plea. I refer to the conversion of more than 25,000 poor gentile Indians who are on the frontier beyond the aforementioned eight missions. The majority of them are in a most advantageous state for receiving the Gospel and becoming subject to the rule of Your Majesty.

54

No doubt, Señor, that a major part of our explanation, and even more which should be said concerning the third point, would arouse Your Majesty's astonishment and grief. We have the satisfaction of knowing that it is grounded on truth. Persons will testify to this — persons who are not animated by a spirit of partisanship and who are not forced to give a different slant to matters due to the fact that they themselves are responsible for the facts and misfortunes. This College has never failed to make all the pleas and petitions which might be conducive to the proper discharge of its ministry. To this the many legal documents and memorials are a testimony. We keep them all in these archives, even though there have very rarely been any occasions on which we have obtained any decision or formal reply from the year 1781, after the government of the Provincias Internas was initially separated from the authority of the Viceroy. There have been many petitions to which either no reply was received at all or to which a reply was made but only in vague and indefinite terms.

It would be easy for us, Señor, to prove this truth if we could only send to Your Majesty's royal presence a file which exists in the Comandancia General of Chihuahua. It is, we suppose, very large. In it are submerged the petitions which have been made in this affair from the year 1781 to the present. That dated March 7 of last year, 1796, which was made in that very town by our Procurator himself, suffered the same fate. In this manner the resolution of affairs which is so important for the service of God and of Your Majesty has been delayed for an indeterminate number of years. In the meanwhile, however, we have had the grief of recovering the remains of the cadavers of six religious youths who were true and zealous ministers of God and faithful vassals of Your Majesty.[68] They spurned death and danger and finally died, torn to pieces by the barbarians. They had not yet cut the ears of those harvests which they left and which were just at the point of being added to the granary of Holy Church. The temporal evil of abandonment prevented the harvest, and we now must work again making the same efforts which we confidently hope that Catholic zeal of Your Majesty will multiply by protecting a cause which is all for God and your royal service.

This College had hardly more than taken charge of the missions of Sonora when after only two months of residence in the Mission of San Xavier del Bac it fell to the lot of the Venerable Father Friar Francisco Garcés, son of this Seminary, urged on by the information received from the numerous gentiles nearby, to

---

68. The six Queretaran friars were Fray Juan Crisóstomo Gil de Bernabé, martyred at Carrizal, Sonora, by the Seri Indians on March 7, 1773 (Roca 1967: 174); the four martyrs who died at the hands of the Yuma Indians on the lower Colorado River in July 1781 — Francisco Garcés, Juan Díaz, Juan Barreneche, and José Matías Moreno (Roca 1967: 345 n.n. 24-27); and Friar Felipe Guillén. Father Guillén, from Piles in the province of Valencia in Spain, arrived at Querétaro in 1770. He served two years in Texas and six in Sonora, where he was lanced in the chest by "barbarians" on April 27, 1778, on the road between missions Santa Teresa and Ati. He was forty-one years old at the time (Bringas 1960: 62; Ocaranza 1933: 15; Roca 1967: 354 n. 23). Also see notes 69, 72, 73, 88, and 90.

set out for the first time to reconnoiter their situation.[69] He continued these apostolic journeys until the year 1776, making six trips in all in various directions and always accompanied by gentiles. He found up to 25,000 Indians on the banks of the Gila, Colorado, and other rivers. He cleansed them, disposing them to receive the Gospel and vassalage. All this is proved in detail in the data which were sent to our Catholic Monarch, Don Carlos III, august father of Your Majesty. He deigned to command that thanks should be given to this ministro in his royal name for his zeal. He also gave orders that provisions should be made in orders to the Viceroy of Mexico for founding missions on the above-mentioned rivers.

But when due to his interest in these new foundations His Majesty ordered that the Comandancia of the Provincias Internas in charge of Don Teodoro de Croix should be made independent of the Viceroy of Mexico, this College, through its ministros approached this Caballero asking support for the erection of two missions in the nation of the gentile Yumas who live on the banks of the Colorado.[70]

---

69. Father Francisco Tomás Hermenegildo Garcés was born in the town of Morata del Conde in Aragón on April 12, 1738. In 1768 he became the first Franciscan to be assigned at Mission San Xavier del Bac, coming there directly from the College of Santa Cruz de Querétaro.

"From Bac, Garcés made a number of journeys into the lands of the Indians to the west and north: in 1768 he visited the Papagos, nearest west, and went up to the Gila River, and while he was away and stricken with a sudden illness the Apaches plundered his mission; in 1770 he went again to the Gila River and to the Opas; in 1771 he went further west and reached the Colorado, which he followed to its mouth on the Gulf of California; early in 1774 he accompanied a small expedition under Captain Juan Bautista de Anza to San Gabriel Mission in southern California; the next year, starting with the second and much larger expedition led by Anza, who was now promoted lieutenant-colonel, he branched off by himself and made the extensive travels described in the present day-to-day Record; and in 1779 he visited his old friends the Yumas, who lived at the confluence of the Gila and Colorado rivers. He was a memorable traveller in the interest of both church and state" (Garcés 1965: v). His travels came to an end among the Quechan Indians on July 19, 1781, when he was martyred at his mission of La Purísima Concepción on the lower Colorado River (see note 68).

Although by far the best-known Franciscan to serve in Pimería Alta in the Spanish period, Garcés' biography has not yet been written. His diary of his 1774 journey to California has been published in English translation, as well as his brief summary of that trip and the diary of his 1774 return to San Xavier (Garcés 1930a, b, c). Five of his letters have also been published in English translation, as have two versions of the diary of his 1775–76 expedition (Bolton 1930: 68-76, 143-147, 276-290, 314-315, 319-320; Garcés 1900, 1965).

70. "Don Teodoro de Croix, Caballero of the Teutonic Order, was born on June 20, 1730, in the castle of Prévoté, near Lille, France, the ancestral home. At the age of seventeen he entered the Spanish army and went to Italy as an ensign of Grenadiers of the Royal Guard. In 1750 he transferred to the Walloon Guard, ranking a lieutenant in 1756. In the same year he was decorated in Flanders with the Cross of the Teutonic Order, which gave him the title Caballero. In 1760 he was made a colonel in the Walloon Guards; by 1765 he had become a captain in the Viceregal Guard. As such, he accompanied his uncle, the Marqués de Croix, viceroy of New Spain, to Mexico in 1766. In the same year the viceroy appointed him governor of Acapulco. Between December 1766 and 1770 he served as inspector of the troops of the kingdom of New Spain with the rank of brigadier. In 1771 Croix left Mexico with his uncle, arriving in Spain in 1772 after a five months' stay in Havana. Here he remained until 1776" (Thomas 1941: 17-18).

The office of the Comandancia General of the Provincias Internas was created by an order of the king to Croix dated August 22, 1776. The authority of that office, for all practical purposes,

We informed him about everything needed for their proper establishment. The new Comandante had received an order from His Majesty issued in El Pardo on February 14, 1777. In it he was ordered to grant the request of the Captain of the Yumas and give him the missions and presidios and whatever was needed for their establishment.[71] The Comandante offered to go personally to the Gila and Colorado rivers in order to manage everything better. The illness which he suffered, however, as well as other incidents, slowed down these negotiations until February 5, 1779. The Caballero, seeing the persistence of the Yumas in requesting that missions be founded, wrote on this date to the President of the Pimería ordering the Venerable Father Garcés to go to the Colorado River to console the Yumas, taking along another ministro for company. He should begin the catechism and start to baptize the gentiles. The political governors and the military would promptly supply their needs.

58

The missionaries went to work to carry out these provincial orders for the foundations. They approached the governor, who then authorized the necessary expenditures. The military, however, assigned only 12 soldiers as guards in a country where there are 3,000 Yumas and where the nearest help is 90 leagues away. However, Father Garcés arrived at the Colorado with only two soldiers and a scout at the end of August 1779, with no funds at all. His companion, who was the Venerable Father Friar Juan Díaz, arrived with the rest at the beginning of October.[72] At that point Father Garcés noticed some new events of importance

---

70. (cont'd)
was separated from that of the viceroyalty of New Spain (Loomis 1969: 261-264; Thomas 1941: 18-19).

The friars who seem to have exerted most pressure toward the establishment of missions among the Yumas were Francisco Garcés and Juan Díaz. Both wrote a report to Viceroy Bucareli on March 21, 1775, urging their establishment, and Teodoro de Croix was made aware of their urgings (Bolton 1930: 276-290; Thomas 1941: 175-176, 213, 219).

71. This order to Croix from the king was issued through José de Gálvez, who was then in the royal court. Bringas exaggerates slightly when he says Croix was ordered to grant the Yumas the missions, presidios and everything needed to support them. The order actually says, " . . . and in due time given the missions and presidios which they request" (Bolton 1930: 409). El Pardo is the name of the royal palace in the province of Madrid which was built by Carlos I and Carlos III (Toro y Gisbert 1948: 1384).

72. Juan Marcelo Díaz was born in the Villa Alaxar in the Archbishopric of Seville in May 1736. He "sacrificed his liberty to the yoke of our religion" in the Province of San Miguel of Estremadura when he was eighteen years old; he traveled to Querétaro in 1763; and in 1768 he became the first Franciscan to be sent to Caborca, where he began thirteen years "spent among the barbarous infidels" (Bringas 1960: 111-112; Roca 1967: 119, 354 n. 27).

In 1774 Díaz accompanied Juan Bautista de Anza on the latter's first expedition to California, keeping a diary of the round trip and writing a letter along the way (Bolton 1930: 128-129; Díaz 1930a, b). On his return to southern Arizona in June 1774, he learned he had been appointed president of the Missions of Pimería Baja by the College of Querétaro (Bolton 1930: 153-154).

In 1779 Díaz and Garcés went to the lower Colorado to establish a mission among the Yumas. By 1781 two mission colonies and four friars were in operation here: San Pedro y San Pablo de Bicuñer, with Díaz and José Matías Moreno; and La Purísima Concepción, with Garcés and Juan Barreneche. On July 17, 1781, the Yumas attacked Bicuñer, and Díaz and Moreno were dispatched to martyrdom (Ives 1966: 50-53).

as well as some restlessness among the Yumas. On September 3 he wrote to the Comandante General, giving an account of everything. He told him he needed help at once in order not to place the entire operation in danger. Father Díaz sent exactly the same news and the same request from the river in a letter dated November 5 of that year.

When the ministros were together in the midst of that numerous nation, they decided it was necessary for one of them to go back to inform their jefe personally regarding the necessity of having help promptly if they were to avoid the loss of everything. Father Díaz went back. With a great deal of exhausting effort, his place was taken by the Venerable Father Friar Juan Barreneche.[73] The former came to the capital, Arizpe, and as a result of his report he obtained a decree for the founding of two missions in the Yuma nation. However, the Asesor dictated the conditions and method of setting them up. This was against the laws, against custom, against experience. Paying no attention to the wise arrangements which had been made by the Viceroy for the foundation, the two missions were founded

---

73. Juan Antonio de Barreneche was born in 1749 in the village of Lacazor in Navarra. He went to Havana, Cuba, as a youth, and at the age of seventeen he "abandoned business in the city" to prepare himself to enter studies for the priesthood. In 1768 he enrolled in the Convent of Havana, and three years later he went to the College of Santa Cruz de Querétaro. In 1779 he was sent to the Yuma Indians as a replacement for Juan Díaz, who had to make a trip to Arizpe, and he was serving at the mission of La Purísima Concepción on July 19, 1781, when he and Father Garcés were martyred there (Bringas 1960: 115-116; Ives 1966: 51-53; Roca 1967: 354 n. 25).

Elsewhere, Father Bringas (1960: 116-118) gives us considerable insight into the character of Father Barreneche: "He was, as his venerable companion F. Francisco Garcés once wrote, another Saint Patrick. As soon as he professed our religion he realized that a professed religious should consider himself as a reformed novice. His dwelling was the choir. His fasting was his abstinence. His rest was the vigil in prayer. His delights were the regular bloody scourgings which left his strictures written with the ink of his blood in the convent of that isle. His conversation was his continuous visits to the Most Holy Sacrament. His care was not to omit a single act of the novitiate after being professed. He continued this life with considerable augmentation in this seminary [Querétaro], where he arrived after a trip, mostly on foot, of almost 200 leagues from the coasts of Tampico, on the day after he arrived in the community.

"He fasted constantly during the Lents that our seraphic patriarch observed, but did so with such rigor that his food at midday was a little soup and garbanzos without any meat except when he was otherwise ordered by his confessor. In the evening he ate only herbs. Even this austerity seemed too little for him, and he demanded permission to fast on bread and water five days a week. He sacrificed himself, however, to the orders of the Superior, who would not permit it with such frequency. In addition to the common observances of this seminary, he took the discipline daily. He slept on bare boards without taking off his religious habit. Ordinarily he did not sleep after matins and kept on praying until the first Masses in the morning, even when he was a priest. His body was the victim of harsh and continuously worn hair shirts, which he continued to wear to his grave, taking them off only to sleep. His constance in the confession kept him there in the mornings and whole afternoons. His humility transcended all his works, and, in a word, what I have told you is only an incomplete indication of the exemplary life of this illustrious youth."

on the banks of the Colorado at the end of the year 1780 in spite of the protests of the missionaries. We shall explain the manner of doing this to Your Majesty when we insert the decree and its stipulations. The result, however, was a testimonial to all this. After seven months, on the 17th and 19th respectively, of July 1781, the barbarians ruined the two pueblos, cruelly beating the two missionaries to death with clubs, as well as many other persons.[74] The rest were taken captive. Thus the government discovered how important it was to take the advice of practical missionaries.

This was the status of the new conversiones when Our Catholic Majesty, Don Carlos III, was moved by the reports of Friar Antonio de los Reyes to expedite a cédula real. In it, dated May 20, 1782, he ordered us to turn over the missions of the Pimería Alta for the erection of the custodia of Sonora. Thus the Propagation of the Faith in those many nations who were disposed to receive it was halted for the space of nine years, when a new order of Your Royal Majesty dated August 17, 1791, commanded us to dissolve the custodia and again take charge of the aforementioned missions. So we began at once to take charge of them and to operate them again, and to take up the forgotten work of spreading the faith. In truth, Señor, the President of those missions has made repeated representations to the Comandante General concerning new foundations, especially in April 1793, on August 1 of the same year, on December 29 of the same year, and on February 2, 1795, without any results other than those mentioned in section 37.

Recently this College attempted a new entrada into gentile country, as we have already explained to Your Royal Majesty. We found they had the same desire to receive the Gospel. The Procurator of this College informed the Comandante as follows:

Friar Diego Bringas, of the Regular Observance of Our Holy Father Francis, authorized Procurator of the Apostolic College of the Propagation of the Faith

---

74. There were actually four missionaries killed in the Yuma uprising: fathers Francisco Garcés, Juan Barreneche, Juan Díaz, and José Matías Moreno. The best guess is that "other persons" included 31 soldiers, 20 male settlers, and perhaps as many as 20 women and 20 children, although some of the latter may have simply become captives and were never recovered (Forbes 1965: 204). A good first-hand account of the so-called "Yuma uprising" appears in McCarty (1975).

of Santa Cruz de Querétaro for Mission Affairs, appears before Your Lordship and with proper formality states:

That my College again took charge of the administration of the missions of the Pimería Alta in the Province of Sonora by decision of the King, Our Lord, whom God preserve. It desired in accordance with the confidence reposed in it, to promote the growth of the older missions and their welfare with the greatest zeal. In orderly fashion it also desired to promote the spreading of our Holy Faith and of his Majesty's dominions among the gentile nations on our frontiers. In order to obtain the desired results, my College considered it necessary to commission me officially to make a visitation of all its missions, through a new reconnaissance of those areas to obtain information on the present status of the nations who live there. I was to examine the condition of the gentiles by reconnoitering their location, number, relationships, industries, characteristics of the land, and related circumstances. I was then to make a complete report to Your Lordship, so that if you approved you might consent to order that whatever is necessary for the greater welfare of the old missions be furnished them. You might also command the founding of others in order to broaden the dominions of Our Sovereign and spread the knowledge and practice of the true faith. After having done all these things, Señor, as far as the weakness of my spirit permitted I must explain to Your Lordship what I found worthy of attention and capable of fulfilling the expectations of our Royal Majesty. That you may make a judgment concerning the particular objects on which I will report, I present Your Lordship, with proper humility, the map I made of those lands through which I passed.[75] [See p. 98 of this book.] I took the latitudes as accurately as possible. The report which I shall make to Your Lordship as briefly as possible rests solely upon the truth. It gives a practical knowledge of the receptive state in which the nations of the Papagos and the Gila Pimas, as well as the Cocomaricopas, presently find themselves for the acceptance of the Gospel and vassalage. This will result in a growth of religion and of the State and a considerable diminution in the expenses of the Royal Treasury for other foundations which are in less favorable condition than these of which I am speaking.

The first condition to be considered is that the best sites for the new foundations planned by my College are at a distance from the frontier which permits them communication with the old ones. These Indians for the most part speak the same language and are constant enemies of the Apaches. This gives a reasonable hope that they will help to strengthen the peace which those provinces presently enjoy. They will also be more quickly instructed in dogma and will cultivate the principles already planted as to social, rational, and political life.

At a distance of 25 common leagues to the northwest of the Presidio of San Agustín del Tucson at a minimum of 33 degrees north latitude is found the first pueblo of Gila Pimas which is known by the name of Vehurichuc. Almost due west of it, at a distance of three leagues, are located two other pueblos, the first known by the name of Chuburrcabon, and the latter by that of Sutacsonc, vul-

---

75. That is, from Cucurpe to the Gila River and return via Bísanig — the Pimería Alta.

garly Sutaquison. The number of souls which I personally counted in the three pueblos mentioned (with the addition of two small rancherías which are in between them and whose population is only estimated) amounts to 1500 persons of both sexes. There are 500 men capable of bearing arms, and the rest are youths, women and children.

Informed of the object of my journey, they expressed a constant love for our nation and long-held desires of receiving the Gospel and vassalage. They offered their children for baptism. Although it pained me, I did not consider it proper to baptize them. The Gileños, Señor, are not of those gentiles who barely have the use of reason. They are diligent, like to work, live from their own industry, and cultivate their fields. Although they work the soil crudely with sticks, they produce crops of a variety of seeds. They sow maize, wheat, beans and the other legumes that the Spaniards cultivate. The cultivation of cotton, which they know how to spin and weave, helps them out to the extent that many of them are partially clothed. The gamuza [antelope], which they know how to tan skillfully, the cotton fabrics, and the grain crop make up the bulk of their commerce with our pueblos and with some of the gentiles in the area. They have another activity which is all the more necessary in that it consists in the diminution of our enemies, the Apache. They take Apache prisoners to the nearby missions. These principles of economy, of industry and of commerce, proportionate to their rude mentality, as of now are precious seeds which protected and encouraged by the beneficent warmth of the Sovereign's protection promise abundant fruit in the future. Their frugality and their care for the increase of their few interests have made it possible for them to raise some horses and some kine, both large and small, although in small numbers. Under better guidance, however, these may increase so far as land will permit. Providence, Señor, has doubtless placed this nation at the doors of a large gentile population so that, blessed by religion and the rule of His Majesty, they might give to those barbarous peoples proofs which are unmistakable that they, too, may share in this happiness by following their example. Señor, this is not a nomadic nation. At present we have found them at peace and calm in those same places where the religious of my College and the Reverend Father Apostolic Visitor, Friar Francisco Garcés, now deceased, had visited them so frequently between the years 1768 and 1775. Their pueblos are solidly built, and in some of them I have seen houses with brick [or stone] walls [casas formadas de pared].[76] Their fields are solidly and cleverly fenced and diligently worked. They know how to make use of the advantages offered them by the Gila River near whose banks they live. It covers the fields at flood season. This is one of the factors which promises a successful foundation in a terrain which with the assistance of improved

---

76. The aboriginal house of the Gila River Pimas was a dome-shaped hut constructed of poles covered with mats woven from carrizo. There were a few flat-roofed structures reported for Upper Pimans in the late seventeenth century, but these were very rare (Ezell 1961: 49). Bringas' remark makes it appear that by the late eighteenth century Spanish influence had made itself felt among the Gila River Pimas to such an extent that a few of them were building flat-roofed houses of stone or, more likely, of sun-baked adobe bricks.

methods will yield an abundant harvest. This land is good for all kinds of seeds and plantings.

The careful and attentive inspection which I have made of all things in that country, including its inhabitants, stimulates me to say that one can count on the loyalty of this nation which has now for almost half a century been asking for the Gospel and for vassalage. It is easy to prove that during these years they have never joined hands with our enemies to attack the province. Instead they have acted as faithful allies. They have conducted their own campaigns against the barbarous Apaches. They had just done this at about the same time I visited their country. From it they obtained the profit of 18 head [of Apaches], including Apache dead and prisoners. It is incredible that they would ever think of insurrection once they were reduced in missions. Besides, with the hostile Apaches on their east, north and northwest, and with the Yumas on the west, even though their allies the Cocomaricopas are in between, they have nowhere else to go without the disadvantage of finding a number of enemies and of abandoning their homes, pueblos, crops, and other interests. They are thoroughly acquainted with our customs. They are within sight of our most remote missions, which they have the habit of frequenting. There seems to be no well-founded reason to suspect that they would turn against a rule which they themselves recognize as beneficial to them, or that they would turn against customs, law enforcement, and government which they are trying to imitate. They have been asking this of us for such a long time that it's a mystery that a nation with so many things to recommend it does not at once receive the benefit of the laws of both Majesties.

To inform Your Lordship as exactly as possible and yet be brief, I must describe concisely the qualities of the terrain — its natural products and those which with proper care it may bring forth. When one travels from the presidio of San Agustín del Tucson to the first pueblo of Gileños, it is level terrain suitable for the construction of a straight road for the entire distance of 20 common leagues, or 5,000 Castilian varas. In this whole distance only 13 leagues are without permanent water, even during the driest season.

The natural products of the country as far as to the banks of the Gila are kinds of bushes: chamizo [fourwing saltbush], ocotillo, hediondilla [creosote], and others which are unknown. Pasturage is scarce except for some points right beside the river, and in a cienega which is to the west of the pueblos. As for trees, the banks of the river are covered with cottonwoods and willows which are the only timber for construction, although at a distance of 25 leagues almost directly north there is an abundance of pine. Mesquites, creosote bushes, and saguaros are found in the open country, as well as quail, rabbits, hares, and deer. The river abounds in fish of various species. As for harmful animals, none are seen but the coyote. The fruits which are actually grown and cultivated by the inhabitants are various: beans, maize, wheat, watermelons, melons, squash, and cotton. If you wish to consider others which can be grown there, every species of grain, tree, and legume would do well because of the mild climate and even temperature. The river can fertilize these beautiful tracts of land with its waters. These can easily be conducted anywhere for farming. Even the gentiles steal a portion of its water by means of a poorly built dam which feeds a main ditch along their fields and distributes the water to small fields cultivated by each family.[77] If I did not fear to bore Your Lordship, I would linger on the exposition of all these particulars. However, there are additional matters to be treated.

What I have said shows that this area satisfies the requirements for new settlements, as indicated in the First Law of Don Felipe II, registered in Book 4, Title 5, of the Laws of the Indies.[78]

Ten leagues to the west of Sutaquison, the Gila joins its waters with those of the river of the Asunción [Salt River], which comes from the north from the land of the Yumas and Comanches. It bathes the land of the Moquinos and brings to the Gila more water than the Gila itself has.

Going almost 15 leagues to the west of this pueblo one encounters the first of the gentiles of the Cocomaricopa nation. They are allies of the Gileños and the Papagos, and are enemies of the Apaches and Yumas. Their land is rich and has almost the same qualities as that of the Gileño Pimas. They, too, are inclined to receive the Gospel and vassalage. I have dealt with a considerable number of them and hopes are well founded that they will easily reduce to missions after missions have been established for their allies, the Pimas. They exceed the Pimas in number. If Your Lordship will fix your lofty attention on the map which I insert, you will find leagues of terrain almost in the form of a square in which more than 15 rancherías are located in southeast to northwest direction from the vicinity of the mission of Caborca and running almost parallel to it are 18 other settlements which, with the exception of the presidios, are in charge of my College. They come to an end near the banks of the Gila to the west of the Gileño Pimas. This nation, which approaches the number of 4,000 souls, always allied to the Gileños, constantly hostile to the Apaches, continuously familiar with our towns, peaceful, obedient to the orders of the captains of the presidios of Altar, Tubac, and Tucson, yearly — although in very small numbers — join the flock of the church in our missions. This nation, which subjects itself to the direction of the judges who are picked from among them by the captains previously referred to, is one of those which are in need of the benign protection of the Sovereign and which when reduced to missions would strengthen the passage to those of the Gila and would form a double line of communication between our old missions and the new ones. In this way the progress of both pacifications would be achieved without leaving at our backs any nation which does not recognize the law and vassalage.

It seems in no way fitting, Señor, to try to force the Papagos to abandon their land and become incorporated in our pueblos. Constant experience has taught us and has made them feel that the climate of the Pimería takes away their health and life in a very short time. All this aside from the fact that Señor Mendoza, Governor of the Province of Sonora, already tried this incorporation, and they rose

---

77. The evidence is equivocal as to whether the Gila River Pimas used ditch irrigation before the coming of the Spaniards. A discussion of aboriginal techniques and of the history of Pima farming is found in Ezell (1961: 36-38).

78. Law 1 of Book 4, Title 5 of the Laws of the Indies is entitled, "That the lands and provinces which are chosen to be populated should have the qualities stated."

up to prevent it.[79] Whenever since then it has been proposed to them, they have looked at it with aversion. It will never be useful to depopulate a country with 80 leagues of frontier almost in the shape of a square merely in order that after a peaceful nation has been thus dispossessed this broad area should perhaps be opened to a numerous population of gentiles of different nations who might simply desire to start a new war with us. Also, in the absence of missions which could be founded in their countries, we will be lacking supply points for the propagation of the faith and for further pacifications. This is what I understand to be the substance of the judgment of the captains of those presidios, and there is no doubt that it is the judgment of the deceased R. P. [Reverend Father] Apostólico Friar Francisco Garcés. His practical knowledge in this field is vouched for by seven expeditions during the space of thirteen years through the midst of these and many other nations. Lastly, Señor, this is a step which it seems is rigorously prohibited by the Laws of the Indies 12, 13, 14, 15, and 16 of Title 1, Book 6, of the collection.[80]

In spite of the fact, Señor, that the land of the Papagos is mostly lacking in water, there are some places suitable for foundations. Only a little more than 20 leagues to the west of Tucson is the populous ranchería of Papagos known as Santa Rosa del Ati, where a foundation would be very appropriate. At almost the same distance to the southwest of it is found a ranchería known as Sonoita, which was a mission of the expelled regulars and which was lost in the uprising of 1751.[81] At present it is inhabited by a considerable number of Indians of this nation. Being in the middle of the Papaguería with a cienega, a permanent arroyo, and good pasturage it offers a favorable chance to reestablish the old mission and continue the conversion of those many gentiles. I have had dealings, Señor, in various places

---

79. Juan Antonio de Mendoza began his military career in 1720 as a cadet in the Spanish infantry. He fought in Africa and Italy, and when he was in Madrid in 1754, he was given a five-year appointment as governor and captain general of the provinces of Sonora and Sinaloa. He received the government in Horcasitas, Sonora, in July 1755. Mendoza waged war on the Seri Indians, attempting to force them to live in reductions (i.e., settled village life under the guidance of priests). In 1756 the Indians sued for peace, and Mendoza spent two fruitless months in the Pimería Alta attempting similarly to reduce the Papago Indians. The governor was killed by a Seri arrow on November 27, 1760 (Almada 1952: 463-464; Bancroft 1884b: 556).

80. Laws 12-16 of Book 6, Title 1 concern the movement of Indians. Law 12, dating from 1536, provides that Indians can of their own free will move from one place to another unless they are in reductions and their moving will damage the encomenderos. Law 13, dating from 1541 and 1568, says that Indians from cold climates shall not be sent to hot climates and vice versa.

Laws 14 and 15 expressly forbid the moving of the "Indians of Santa Cruz" anywhere and the natives of the Philippines from one island to another. Law 16, dating from 1528, 1543, and 1556, says that "Indians shall not be taken to these Kingdoms nor changed from their natural habitats" without permission of the crown or that of the governors and magistrates. Apparently there had been abuses in taking New World natives to Spain.

81. Santa Rosa del Ati has continued to survive as Santa Rosa, the second largest village on the Papago Indian Reservation. One portion of it is known to the Papagos as *aji*, "narrow place." The expelled regulars were the Jesuits, whose Father Enrique Ruhen was martyred at the mission of San Marcello del Sonoydag in late November 1751, during the so-called "Pima Uprising" (see Ives 1955, 1957; Roca 1967: 89-92; 353 n. 19).

during my journey and frequently with the different inhabitants of these rancherías as well as with those of the other seven. I have proposed to them a reducción in their own country at the sites mentioned, and they have joyfully agreed that in their own country they would subject themselves willingly. Foundations at the sites mentioned, Señor, will produce appreciable results, which I do not explain in detail to avoid bothering Your Lordship.

The terrain offers suitable sites for missions in various other places, although one or the other will require more preliminary work than that at Sonoita. The profit realized, however, will be in proportion to the expense. This will be neither great nor excessive. The new missions will cover territory extending to the Gulf of California on the west, to the old missions and the line of presidios on the south and east, and, to the north, to those which may be erected on the Gila. There seems to be no reason to suspect that missions could be a failure. They make possible further increases in religion and the dominions of His Majesty.

The combination of all these facts, Señor, based on knowledge of the country, visual observations, and trustworthy reports as well as on observations made with mathematical instruments, as shown in the map which was made with greatest possible accuracy, offers a multitude of ideas profitable to both religion and the state. Many objectives will be achieved in the Papaguería with the founding of three missions in the pueblos of Vehurichuc, Chuburcabor, and Sutaquison of Gileño Pimas and another two in the ranchería of Sonoita or Ati (this latter mission could be in Aquituni or some other location if it should seem more advantageous). One objective which is not of least importance is a remedy thus provided for that lamentable series of evils which can afflict the Province of Sonora with new Apache attacks.

If this inconstant nation, Señor, badly hurt from the punishment it has received from the troops, should again take up arms, it would meet a great obstacle in these new establishments in the far reaches of the Province on the banks of the Gila. That region is one of their [the Apaches'] points of entry. When it and the other are covered by the line of presidios, they would find it difficult to carry out their acts of violence if they met troops stationed in the interior of the country through which they have to pass to perpetrate their thefts. These conjectures, Señor, become less conjectural when one takes into account the fact that the Apaches were not able to attack that Province so freely when they had to encounter the Sobaipuri nation in the valley of the San Pedro. This river joins its waters with those of the Gila after a short distance. However, as soon as they had achieved the extermination of that nation, whose remaining members are preserved today in the presidio of Santa María, they penetrated to the outer limits of the Province.

The Gileño Pimas themselves, sustained by Spanish weapons, would offer them considerable opposition, since they are used to fighting them. They would close the doors forever to those Apache tribes who might shortly attack the Province. At present they dwell at the confluence of the Gila and Asunción rivers under the name of "Tejuas," or they inhabit the mountains north of the Gileño Pimas under the name of "Tontos." We will be taking only the minimal number of horses and cattle to the new establishments on the Gila though even these few *may excite the cupidity of the barbarians. However, they will not attack pueblos which have been considerably enlarged, for even now they are unable to attack against the resistance of only the Gileño Pimas.*

These new missions, Señor, will soon unite the peoples of the new California with those of the Province of Sonora, and both of them with those of New Mexico — and what great advantages will result from this reciprocal communication! The Apache nation will be encircled by enemies, the Cucapas, Quiquimas, Yumas, Cajuenches, Quemeyas, Jecuiches, and Cuñeil,[82] and will be forced to acknowledge vassalage because they will have nowhere to flee. This may be seen in part on the map [p. 53]. But since I must explain to Your Lordship what must be done to achieve these ends, I must say that these new establishments need the protection of a presidio with a considerable number of soldiers. The best location for it is at the confluence of the Gila and Asunción rivers, where there is plenty of pasture. I am not unaware, Señor, that this cannot be done without cost to the Royal Exchequer. Graciously permit me, Señor, to argue its suitability based on the reasons which I shall present. At least for the time being no new expense will be incurred by the Royal Exchequer to establish a large presidio such as is needed on the Asunción River. I shall, Señor, test the truth of the Asesor's statements in various ways. I beg Your Lordship's understanding that you might accept my feeble efforts to promote religion and the greater glory of our Catholic Monarch. The larger this new presidio, Señor, which is to protect these new acquisitions, the more firmly it will remain and the more copious its fruits. It will continue the reduction of the many neighboring nations. I assert, Señor, that this presidio will not be an additional expense to the Royal Treasury. If Your Lordship will command that it should at first be made up of small detachments detailed from the new presidial companies organized for the Province of Sonora, this will be smoother and more effective for the purpose, since it requires neither the creation of a new presidio nor the removal of any of those already established. A few men from each company will hardly be missed, and when they are joined together they will form a considerable body of troops without any new expense to the Royal Treasury.

What I have just said, Señor, is based on rational suppositions I am permitted to make in view of the present happy state of the Provincias de Sonora. They support my argument that no new expenses are necessary. I even go so far as to prophesy they never will be.

The untamed nation of the Apaches, with their stubborn war, is the chief reason for the existence of those nine companies. The other nations have long since been warned by experience against our weapons, and they do not attack us. That is a ferocious nation, as Your Lordship very well knows. All that Province knows it, and it is now enjoying the state of calm which exists. Consequently, in a short time, some of those companies will be without work, and thus some of them can settle there and protect the new establishments which are now being protected

---

82. See note 23 for information on these tribes.

by all of them. It therefore seems they will never incur new expenses. For all these reasons, Señor, which are in conformity with the Royal Laws, in particular the 2nd and 4th of the 1st Book, Title 1; the 14th of the 2nd Book, Title 2; the 3rd of the 4th Book, Title 4; the 1st from Book 6, Title 3, and others from the Laws of the Indies.[83]

I request and humbly beg Your Lordship in the name of my College of Santa Cruz de Querétaro to make use of his lofty faculties and to order that measures be taken for the foundation of the five missions previously mentioned among the Pimas, Gileños, and Papagos in the places shown on the map. In accordance with all I have said, these locations will be conducive to peace in the Provinces; to the greater growth of our Catholic religion, and the glory of God, Our Lord; to the greater splendor of the Spanish nation; and to the extension of the dominions of our Catholic Monarch.

> *Chihuahua*
> *March 13, 1796*
> *[from] Fray Diego Bringas [to the]*
> *Señor Comandante General*

---

83. In this kind of legal summation for the comandante general, Father Bringas cites laws dating as far back as the early part of the sixteenth century. Book 1, Title 1, Law 2, written first in 1526, is entitled, "When the officers of the king come to any province and discovery of the Indies, they should at once make the Holy Faith known to the Indians."

Law 4, which dates from 1573, reads as follows: "We order our Governors that whenever the natives are unwilling to receive the Christian doctrine in peace the following procedure shall be used in the preaching and teaching of our Holy Faith. They shall try to arrange with a peaceful cacique [Indian leader] nearby to attempt to get them to come to his territory for amusement or something of the sort. The preachers should be there waiting with some Spaniards and Indians who are secretly our friends, and this should be done in some safe way. When the time comes they should disclose themselves to those who have been invited. They should then begin to teach them the Christian doctrine by means of interpreters. In order to encourage more veneration and admiration, the preachers should be vested at least in albs or surplices and stoles and with the Holy Cross in their hands. The Christians present should listen with the greatest attention and veneration so that the pagans will imitate them and be instructed willingly. And if it will attract their admiration and attention any better, they may make use of singers and minstrels. This will motivate the Indians to assemble. Then by other means those who were hostile may be tamed and pacified. Even though they may seem to be friendly and may even ask for preachers to come to their country, this should be complied with very cautiously. The preachers should ask to teach their children and first get them to build churches where they can teach them. By this means, and any others that may seem to be more effective, they should ever continue pacifying and teaching the natives. They should never on any occasion or by any means cause them hurt. All that we desire is their good and their conversion."

Book 2, Title 2, Law 14, dating from 1636, merely requires that the whole Council of the Indies must assemble to decide important government business, including the erection of churches. Book 4, Title 4, Law 3 orders that regular clergy in the Indies who wish to make trips of exploration and to spread the Holy Gospel should be given permission to do so at the expense of the king. And Book 6, Title 3, Law 1, promulgated in 1551, 1560, 1565, 1568, 1573, and 1578 resolves that Indians "should be reduced into pueblos and not live separated by mountains and thus be deprived of spiritual and temporal benefits and without the assistance of ministers." The latter is the legal basis for the entire reduction program (see Spicer 1962: 463-464).

62

We have, Señor, received no other reply to these detailed arguments than the usual one that they have been added to the files. Consequently, since the missionaries have been repeatedly urged by the gentiles to found these new missions, we have finally taken recourse to the Royal piety of Your Majesty.

63

Granted then, Señor, that in 1779 all the nations were at peace with each other and wished to receive the Gospel; that in 1780 two missions were founded for the Yumas, contrary to the normal procedure and in disregard of the arrangements which the Viceroy of Mexico had approved; and granted that for this reason they were lost eight months after being founded, and when an attempt was made to remedy the situation it was obstructed by the new custodia; granted that that calamity is not capable of cooling Your Majesty's burning zeal for the spreading of the faith, just as the continuous failures of the various expeditions sent out for the spiritual conquest of old California, which was still a sterile and poor place inhabited by rational beings who had the misfortune of being gentiles, did not diminish that of the Catholic kings; granted the recent favorable condition of the nations and that they might again return to the status of 1780; granted all the above, we must explain to Your Majesty the means which seem to be most promising for prompt, effective, and permanent reduction of such a large gentile population. We must also explain the causes for the failure of those foundations and of others. These are based on personal experience and knowledge of the situation. These means will make permanent the great benefits which will result for all the Provincias Internas. To make this more clear we insert the following map [see p. 98], which illustrates the countries, nations, and points on which we base our remarks.

64

The causes for the failure of that foundation of the Yuma nation in 1781, reduce substantially to the way in which the foundation was directed by those Señores. Their own zeal and salutory intentions suggested to them that a novelty would be more efficacious than the method accredited by experience and by good results. To prove this truth it is necessary to insert here the instruction which the Caballero de Croix ordered the jefes and missionaries to observe. It is exactly as follows: [84]

---

84. Although Forbes (1965: 185-186) and Croix himself (Thomas 1941: 220) do a good job of summarizing these instructions, this is their first appearance in print in full.

Instructions	*Instruction on the Rules for the Establishment of Two Pueblos of Spaniards and Indians on the Banks of the Colorado River in the Territory of the Yuma Nation.*
Appointment of the Commanding Officer	1. *Having resolved that two new pueblos or missions should be founded on the Colorado River so the Yuma nation might easily attain the knowledge of our true religion and join the Holy Church, in consideration of his so frequently expressed desire of achieving this great benefit and also in consideration of his excellent character, I appoint Don Santiago de Islas, Ensign of the Presidio of Altar, as Comandante Militar and Juez Político of the two pueblos.*[85] *He is to be directly subject to my orders. I hope he will be worthy of this trust and that his zeal and love will be a credit to the Royal service.*
Number of Colonists	2. *Each of the pueblos is to be composed of 25 families not counting that of the Comandante Militar. In the first will live the Comandante and Juez Político, a corporal and nine soldiers, ten residents "de razón," six artisans, and in addition any of the Yuma Indians who wish voluntarily to join either of the pueblos.*
Appointment of Sergeant and Corporals	3. *Sergeant Juan de la Vega, two corporals, and eight soldiers from the Presidio of Tucson, with three more from Altar, have already been appointed for the garrison.*[86] *Six soldiers are lacking. They will be selected from the Presidio of Buenavista. Its garrison is at the disposal of the Comandante Militar. He will choose for this purpose those who are most fit and who have the best qualities.*
The Replacement of the Soldiers from Tucson	4. *The eleven individuals who leave the Presidio of Tucson are to be replaced by three soldiers from Santa Gertrudis del Altar, one from Buenavista and seven from San Miguel de Horcasitas. The replacement and the withdrawal*

---

85. Santiago Islas (or Yslas) became a busy man on receiving this appointment. He gathered supplies and recruited settlers, even as far north as Tucson in September 1780. He and his party reached the site of the intended colonies on December 27, 1780. The shortage of necessary goods among the settlers has moved one historian to comment that "Yslas was a poor choice for commandant" (Forbes 1965: 188-191).

Evidence shows he was harsh with the natives. Early in 1781 he ordered chains that he might detain troublesome Yumas, and he had an Indian lashed for wounding a soldier's horse. Then, late in May or early in June, he imprisoned the son of the Yuma leader. He subsequently released the captive, but the insult had been committed. The Spanish commandant was killed by the Yumas on the morning of July 17 as he was leaving the church of La Purísima Concepción (Forbes 1965: 192, 195, 201).

86. Juan de la Vega came to the presidio of Tucson as a first sergeant in 1778 (Medina 1779).

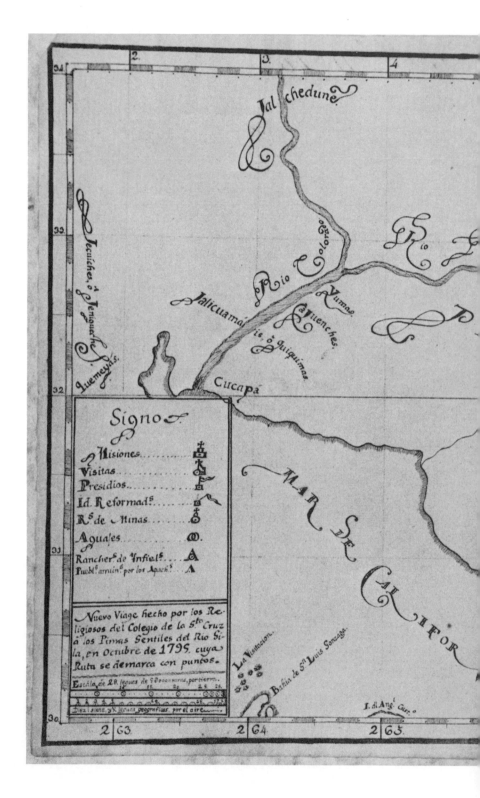

Jalchedune

Río Colorado

Río Colorado

Secuiches, ó Jeniguechi S.

Juemeyás.

Jalicuamais

Yumas.

Avilenches.

is, ó Quiquimas.

Cucapá

MAR DE

CALIFOR

Signos

Misiones ....

Visitas ....

Presidios ....

Id. Reformad.s ....

R.s de Minas ....

Aguales ....

Ranch.ers de Infiel.s ....

Puebl.o arruin.o por los Apach.s

Nuevo Viage hecho por los Religiosos del Colegio de la S.ta Cruz á los Pimas Gentiles del Rio Gila, en Octubre de 1795, cuya Ruta se demarca con puntos.

Escala de 20. leguas de 5000 varas, por tierm.

Diez i siete, y X leguas geograficas, por el aire.

La Visitacion.

Bahia de S.n Luis Sonaga.

I. d.l Ang.l Cust.o

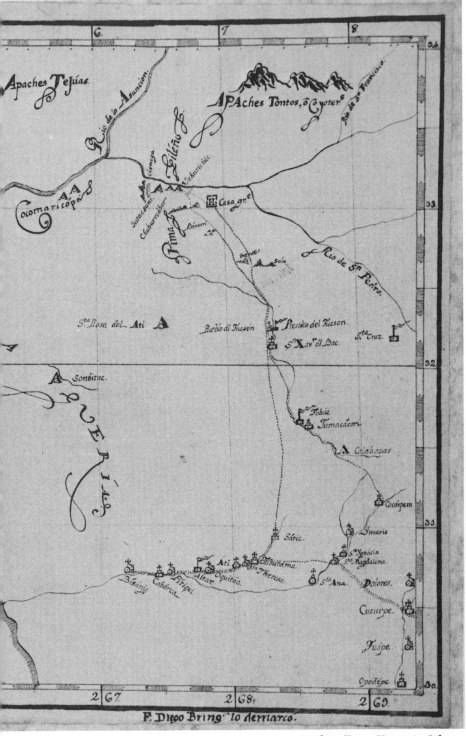

Map 2. Bringas' Map of His Itinerary, October 1795

of the six soldiers from Buenavista whom I ordered to the Colorado River, is to take place on the 1st of next April. Until the end of the current month they must be included in the rolls of their respective companies. Their accounts are to be settled, they're to be given the balance of their pay, and notice is to be sent to the Captain of Tucson of those who are eager to go. Starting with the first of April they are to be mustered in this presidio and be listed separately from those who are not going as replacements until a new order is issued. But it must be understood that although the same provisions are to be made for the six soldiers from Buenavista who are chosen for the Colorado River, the report on what is owed them is to be sent to the Captain of the Presidio of Altar where they should be stationed until the time of departure with this company. The form for the report will be given later and the accounts of these troops will be liquidated. They will march to their respective destinations later, on the 8th of April.

The Attachment of Troops

5. The party of troops destined for the new establishments must be considered as belonging to the Company of Altar. In the future, the vacancies they leave will be filled from it. Consequently, they will be included in the inspection reports with a corresponding separate listing. The Comandante of the detachment will be paid by Altar every month. The monthly inspection reports will be sent when possible to the Captain at Altar.

By Whom the Recruiting Is To Be Done

6. The Ensign, Don Santiago de Islas, shall proceed in this Province to recruit the 20 colonists who are to inhabit the two pueblos. But their choice shall be made with the approval of the Reverend Father Friar Juan Díaz. This religious, as well as the others who may be appointed as ministros of those pueblos, will contribute as much as possible to the success of the recruitment by choosing colonists who are found to be most fit and of best character.

Assistance for the Settlers

7. For the period of a year these settlers are to be assisted with a monthly salary of ten pesos. If necessary this shall be continued for a longer time. This will be attested by the reports of the Comandante made with the help of the reverend father missionaries.

That they might be properly supplied, before they set out two monthly payments shall be advanced to them. In addition, each settler shall be given a yoke of oxen, two cows, one bull, two mares, and one pointed and one blunted hoe on condition that the offspring and the harvests are to be used for reimbursement. All the colonists are to be enrolled by the Comandanté Militar for a period of ten years. The enrollment list shall state the number of children possessed by each.

Recruitment of Workers and Their Pay

8. I charge the Very Reverend Father Friar Juan Díaz and the other religious destined for the establishments to recruit the laborers who will go along also classified as settlers. The monthly wage shall be stipulated in accordance with what is decided to be just and fitting, on the condition that the recruits shall work for two years or more as may be proven necessary by the Comandante and the reverend fathers.

Who Is To Equip Everyone

9. For now the requisitioning of supplies for soldiers, residents and workers shall be in charge of the paymaster at Altar. Distribution shall be up to the comandante of the establishments to which the paymaster will send the needed supplies as per the list or memo which the comandante is to prepare. The paymaster will provide economically for the needs of all. When it should seem more suitable that the management of these affairs should be in charge of a merchant, the paymaster of Altar shall cease to collect and provide supplies. The merchant who is put in charge shall make a contract or assume an obligation to furnish assistance or supplies. He shall prepare a detailed list of the price of each item, including both equipment and food. He must supply goods of high quality and at prices current in the area, adding on the cost of transportation.

Exclusions and Assistance for the Settlers

10. All the officials, soldiers, residents, and laborers shall enjoy the rights, privileges, exemptions, and powers granted by law to new settlers. All must assist either personally or through a representative in the building of a church, the houses of the missionaries and of the comandantes, their own houses, the jail, and other public offices. All shall be of mutual assistance in accordance with the assignments made by the comandantes, not only in these operations but in the indispensible labor of defending the post in case of attack. They shall also form escorts when necessary, although this is chiefly the job of the troops, and a civilian cannot be excused from assisting this anymore than can a soldier be excused when it comes to construction. As to the latter, the Indians who are being reduced may be employed in construction work if they can be induced with love and gentleness to perform it.

Number of Missionaries and Assistance Provided Them

11. In each of the pueblos there will be two missionaries with a salary of 400 pesos each. This will be paid at the Treasury of Arizpe. For the time being 200 pesos each year for each pueblo will be paid for the necessary services of the church and to take care of the most pressing needs of the Indians; to enable the purchase of vestments, sacred vessels, and church utensils; and to pay the missionaries who are to serve the second pueblo. For the expenses of transporting the furnishings mentioned above, 2,000 pesos will be placed at the disposition of the Reverend Father Friar Juan Díaz.

Preparations for the Journey

12. When the recruiting is finished and everything is ready for the journey, and after the *alférez* comandante *has* agreed with the reverend father missionaries as to the time and other circumstances, they shall start the march in whatever order is feasible. If the number of soldiers and residents is too few for the assistance of the families and property being transported, the captains of Altar and Tucson shall offer whatever escort is deemed sufficient to accompany them until they arrive at a safe country.

Formation of the Pueblos

13. After arriving at the Colorado River, the Comandante and reverend father missionaries shall reconnoiter the most suitable locations in accordance with the laws providing for the foundation of settlements. When by common consent sites have been marked off, lots shall be distributed so that they may build their homes. They shall arrange that they be uniform and that the streets be straight in order to avoid disorderly appearance. The same shall be observed in the case of the houses the Indians build when they have been persuaded by the father missionaries to join the pueblos to which they have been attracted by the good example and gentle treatment of the settlers.

Number of Horses

14. Each pueblo must have an exterior wall with a tower at each of the four corners. Within the wall stables shall be built with stalls and sheds so that each soldier can keep a mule and a horse, which are the only mounts they shall have. For this purpose they shall make use of maize stalks, some small amount of maize or barley, and some of the hay or grass which was cut in season and stored in a haystack, and also of the green grass in spring.

Limits of the Pueblos

15. In order that the pueblos may be of mutual assistance they shall be established a short distance from each other. In order to avoid doubts and quarrels, the boundary and jurisdiction of each one shall be drawn at half the distance between them. Some boundary markers shall be erected

in such a way that they may stand out and be recognized. The pasturage, woodlands and other utilities shall be the common property of the two pueblos. In other directions their domains shall remain indefinite for the present, until others have been founded and the areas of each one marked out.

Partition of Lands

16. When the limits of each pueblo have been marked and the lands presently possessed by the Indians set apart for them, together with some more if it is judged necessary, parcels of land shall be set aside in the land that remains. These shall be 400 varas in length and 200 in width. Eight of the best of these shall be set aside as community plots, and their products must be expended for the public good. The remainder of the lands will be distributed among all of the settlers. Officials and soldiers will share in the distribution. It shall be up to the decision of the alférez comandante to grant one, two, or more plots of land to each in consideration of his diligence and industry. When the Indians have a greater understanding, instruction, and knowledge, the same distribution shall be made among them if they voluntarily ask it or desire it.

17. When it is thought proper and the Indians do not oppose it, eight parcels of Indian lands of the same latitude and longitude shall be marked off. All the settlers should share equally in the cultivation of these. A fund will be started with the produce with which future assistance may be given to the church, the ministros may be supported, and the Indians' needs be satisfied. In order that these objectives be more easily attained, 25 cows, two bulls, 100 ewes and four rams shall be immediately placed in each pueblo. They cannot be slaughtered for two years until the increase attained by breeding permits it. Then what the missionaries need for their support shall be provided them at moderate prices. A formal account shall be kept of this so that the amount may be discounted in the Royal Treasury. When these cattle have increased more, some of them may be sold so that the expenses mentioned above may be paid.

Levy of Cattle

18. I charge the Reverend Father President of the missionaries that he should order the missions with cows and sheep to deliver the aforementioned number of them. The cows should be tame so they can be easily driven. Reimbursement shall be made at very moderate prices out of the 2,000 pesos which will be given for the second mission. If there is not enough for this new expenditure, an account should be kept of it for later reimbursement.

**Municipal
Government**

19. *A municipal government shall be formed in each of
the two pueblos. It shall be made up of an* alcalde, *four*
regidores, *and a* síndico *or* tesorero. *They shall be elected at
first by a plurality of votes of the whole pueblo. Those who
are elected shall take over the offices.* Cabos *and soldiers may
also be elected. They shall perform their duties for one year.
The day before the end of the term they shall nominate their
successors. The* comandante oficial *shall notify me so that
I may approve them. The alcalde of each pueblo shall exercise in it and in the territory belonging to it accumulative,
royal, ordinary jurisdiction, and shall keep the comandante
oficial informed. The comandante oficial shall preside at all
council meetings at which he is present and shall have a vote.*

**Management of
Funds**

20. *The management of community plots and their products and of the individuals who handle them shall be under
the direction of one who shall administer the municipal lands
and products as provided for in article 17. For the better
administration of both of these funds, one of the regidores
shall be appointed by the town council. He shall act as* mayordomo *and pay all expenses. He shall also collect the products
and keep complete account of everything. He cannot, however, dispose of anything without an order from the council
through the* procurador síndico. *The latter, as defender of
the common good, shall eliminate any expenditures which are
illegal or which are not being used in accordance with the
purpose designated for the particular fund. The mayordomo
shall keep a formal account and make an annual report to
the council. He shall exhibit the drafts given by the council
as the basis for all expenditures. When these have been
examined and the objections of the procurador síndico have
been heard, the regidores shall make a just decision. This
method and form of government shall be inviolably observed
until eventually another can be set up more suitable for the
progress of the pueblos. I charge and beg the Reverend
Father Missionaries to contribute with zeal and Christian
advice to the better administration and increase of both
funds, making the people see their usefulness to all the
settlers.*

**Spiritual
Government**

21. *Everyone in both pueblos shall recognize the Reverend Father Missionaries as their true and legitimate pastors.
They shall revere them as such. They shall give them whatever assistance they need in the form of escorts and similar
help so that they may attend to the duties of their ministry.
I charge the Reverend Fathers to watch over the preservation
of the Divine Law, frequently exhorting all to lead a Christian*

life. If anyone in the pueblo should be a bad example, despising their admonitions, they shall inform the Comandante Militar. When this report has been made and the crime has been verified, the Comandante Militar should punish the culprit in accordance with the gravity of the offense. The Reverend Fathers should observe the same practice in correcting the Christian Indians, exhorting their respective chiefs strictly to comply with their obligations. When this compliance is lacking they shall inform the juez superior *so that he may impose a just penalty. I also charge the Reverend Fathers to proceed with the reduction of the Indians in conformity with the sovereign laws and many cédulas of their Majesties. They shall teach them with great sweetness and gentleness the certain truths of our religion. Then they shall exhort them to ask for and to receive Holy Baptism of their own accord, after having been instructed in the obligations we have as Christians. By this means they will enter the bosom of Holy Church with greater understanding. The Catholic faith which they profess will take root in them with greater strength.*

22. Finally, I charge the Comandante Militar to provide all the help needed so that the Divine Law will be observed in the new pueblos, so that the settlers may cooperate in the conversion of the gentiles by good example and gentle treatment; and in order that the military discipline of the soldiers shall be excellent. The Comandante Militar shall watch over the stability and progress of the pueblos in the service of both Majesties.

> *Arizpe, March 7, 1780.*
> *El Caballero de Croix.*
> *This is a copy of the original to which I certify:*
> *Arizpe, [March] 12, 1780.*
> *Bonilla.*[87]

65

Your Majesty will know by this set of instructions that there is hardly a clause in it which is not contrary to the rules for conversiones. They are all contrary to

---

87. Antonio Bonilla was the secretaria general under Teodoro de Croix when Croix was comandante general of the Provincias Internas. Bonilla's appointment to this post was made in February 1777. He held this position for six years; was promoted to lieutenant colonel of Dragoons; and in 1787 was made secretaria of the viceroyalty (Almada 1952: 115-116).

the laws and cédulas reales which we have quoted in the preceding sections. These specious dispositions are clearly too full of obstructions if one reflects on each of them and considers them in terms of the goal and of the circumstances of the particular nation, such as distance and terrain, where they should be put into effect.

Everything in them is contrary to the judgment of the missionaries. This is true for some temporal matters and for everything that has to do with the authority for spiritual government. The inconsistency is shocking to us. This can be verified by comparing sections 6, 7, 8, 12, 13, and 20 with 21 and 22 which deal with the spiritual government. In them the hands of the conversores are tied. They are made to depend on the ignorant for the paternal correction of their flock. They are deprived of faculties granted by repeated cédulas reales. Instructions are given for the conversion of the gentiles which are contrary to the experience of three centuries, contrary to the methods of the holy men who have been our examples, and contrary to our personal knowledge of Indians. One must assume the validity of the objections which were made by four chosen and most exemplary ministros, who were objects of veneration in those provinces. If we consider the methods of the holy men mentioned above, it may be concluded that whoever wrote this set of instructions was totally lacking in their kind of experience. And, in the end, it was seen that any apparent disagreements between these holy men and the ministers themselves were merely a matter of words, and that the disaster was caused by laws dictated for founding the two pueblos which they opposed (for in these laws rules appropriate for Spaniards were confused with those for Indian reducciones).

However, Señor, we should not take up Your Majesty's sovereign attention with an extended tale concerning everything that is objectionable in the cited instructions.

It is objectionable that they had decided on two foundations which can be called neither "reducciones" nor "pueblos of Spaniards." They lack many of the requirements for either title, and they abound in nonessentials. They were more than 90 leagues from the older conversiones, and yet a presidio had neither been formally requested nor granted. This was in spite of the fact that they were in the midst of a nation of 3,000 of the most barbarous Indians who were the immediate neighbors of others who were no less numerous and were even more warlike. It is objectionable that an attempt should have been made to establish in that place a government with policies suited only to a foundation in a fertile, peaceful, and civilized land, and not to one in a nation as barbarous as that of the Yuma.

Neither were the missionaries being arbitrary in objecting to this foundation. They had their orders from the jefe to carry it out. Their objections were of no consequence. They expressed their opinions even though they had been intimidated by the experience of having objected on a similar occasion to a foundation which had been planned with the same errors (more or less). They were accused of dereliction of duty before the Viceroy of Mexico. This happened at the founding of the mission of Pitic in the year 1772. Subsequent events proved that the missionaries had been right. They obeyed. The mission was founded without the proper measures. The result was bloody, as it was with the Yumas. After four months the Indians had taken the life of the ministro who was President of the Missions.[88] In spite of this misfortune, which took place only eight years before the Yuma massacre, the rightness of the missionaries was not acknowledged. In the month of July of the following year of 1781, the four ministros sent to the Yumas died — as was to have been expected — and no one can say that any of them was the least bit responsible for the consequences. This is proved in detail by the sworn certification which the commanding officer of the expedition, Don Pedro Fages, gave at the request of the President of the Missions.[89] We have the original in our care. It is as follows:

Certification   *Señor Teniente Coronel Don Pedro Fages.*

Friar Francisco Antonio Barbastro, of the Regular Observance of Our Holy Father Saint Francis, son of the College of Santa Cruz de Querétaro, and President of all the missions of the said college in the Pimería Alta, knowing that you went by order of the Señor Comandante General, Don Teodoro de Croix, as commanding the expedition which His Excellency sent to the devastated missions of the Colorado River, believes that you are aware of everything that happened when they were destroyed. For this reason, he appears before Your Excellency in his own name and that of his Holy College and says:

---

88. He is referring to the martyrdom of Friar Juan Crisóstomo Gil de Bernabé by Seri Indians at the mission of Carrizal in March 1773 (Eckhart 1960: 42-43; Roca 1967: 172-175). See note 124 for a brief biography of Gil.

89. Pedro Fages, a Catalonian volunteer, left Spain for the New World in May 1767. He was in command of a company of the first light infantry battalion, second regiment, destined for temporary duty in Sonora. In January 1769 the young lieutenant was commander of twenty-five troops on board the *San Carlos*, the ship carrying the first contingent of Spaniards to Upper California to annex that area to New Spain (Geiger 1959: I: 207). Fages had had extensive California duty when on September 16, 1781, he set out on an expedition to "lead a punitive force to the Yuma Crossing, rescue or ransom the captives, execute the rebel leaders, and make peace with the other Indians" (Ives 1966: 54). The expedition lasted 106 days and covered about 980 miles. Fages' diary of this journey has been published twice in English (Ives 1966; Priestly 1913).

Although the piety, zeal for souls and virtuous lives of the Reverend Father Preachers Apostolic and sons of my Holy College, Father Juan Díaz, Father Francisco Garcés, Father José Matías Moreno,[90] and Father Juan Barreneche are well known in the Pimería Alta (as can be proven in many ways), a legal deposition is needed. These Fathers were cruelly killed by the gentile neophytes of the Yuma nation, for whose conversion they were working.

First point. Concerning the conduct, zeal, and extraordinary labors with which they were seen to work for the conversion of those gentiles. Also, the attempts they made to get the soldiers and other Spaniards to lead good lives and thus cooperate in converting the Indians and getting them to persevere in their first fervor.

Second point. If they were free of being even the remote cause of disturbances which brought about the ruin of the new missions and if they had labored as much as was possible to prevent this from the time the missions had been in their charge.

Third point. Date and hour of their deaths and instruments with which their lives were taken.

Fourth point. Date their venerable ashes were recovered and the condition in which they were found.

Fifth point. If on the examination of their remains, any circumstances were observed which might be cause for devotion.

Sixth point. If any other circumstances are known which might indicate that their deaths were holy before the Lord.

All this I will receive as a favor and I say, touching my heart, that this, my request, is made for no evil purpose.[91] In order that a proper record may be made, I sign this in the pueblo of Santa Tereza, on February 4, 1782.

FRIAR FRANCISCO ANTONIO BARBASTRO.
President.

---

90. José Matías Moreno was born in Almarza, Spain, either in 1743 or 1744. He began his studies for the priesthood when he was seventeen and became a Franciscan at Logroño in the Holy Province of Burgos. He served briefly out of Querétaro at Tubutama and Caborca in 1779 and 1780 until he was assigned to be compañero of Father Juan Díaz at San Pedro y San Pablo de Bicuñer. He was martyred here — his head cut off on July 17, 1781. Twelve of his thirty-seven years had been in the apostolic ministry (Bringas 1960: 112; Roca 1967: 354 n. 26).

91. These questions were to be asked to help determine whether these men were truly pious religious who were leading exemplary lives of holiness and who gave up their lives for the conversion of Indians. The answers might make possible future canonization of these martyred friars.

In reply to the preceding request for information which Your Reverence addressed to me, dated February 4 of the current year, which contains six points concerning the Reverend Fathers Friar Juan Díaz, Friar Francisco Garcés, Friar José Matías Moreno, and Friar Juan Barreneche, who were inhumanly killed by the gentiles of the Yuma nation. This information is based on declarations which I received under oath and others which I had taken from some male and female prisoners. These investigations were necessary in order to fulfill my obligation as commander of the expedition. I reply to the six points as follows:

To the first I say that the religious cited had acted virtuously and with exemplary modesty and charity. They were dedicated to the holy purpose of attracting the Indians to the knowledge of the faith. They avoided no exertion for this purpose. They went about in the wild country solicitous for all and giving them whatsoever they possessed. Never was there seen in them any other interest than the fervent desire to bring into the flock of the Church those who were without knowledge of it. Simultaneously they persuaded the soldiers and other Spaniards to cooperate to the same end.

As to the second point, I say: In no way did they contribute to the causes of the revolt and the ruin of the aforesaid missions, even remotely. I am convinced that they would not have ceased in cooperating for its prevention with that primitive apostolic fervor.

As to the third, I say: About ten in the morning of July 19, 1781, they beat the Reverend Fathers Friar Francisco Garcés and Friar Juan Barreneche to death. They did the same on the 17th of the same month, about 8:00 in the morning, to the Reverend Fathers Friar Juan Díaz and José Matías Moreno. After his death they cut off the head of the latter with a hatchet. Their venerable ashes were thrown away in the same places where they suffered death.

As to the fourth, I say: The bodies of the Reverend Fathers Friar Juan Díaz and Friar José Matías Moreno were found about 10:00 in the morning on the 17th of last December. The body of the Reverend Father Friar Juan Díaz had the complete and fully articulated skeleton. The head was almost incorrupt. It was recognized by the tonsure, which was complete. The hair was untouched and the fingernails were still on the hands. These signs did not indicate that such a long time had passed since they killed him.

The cadaver of the Reverend Father Friar José Matías Moreno was found with the head missing. Although the skeleton was disjointed, his bones were found together with various small pieces of the holy habit and cord. A crucifix was also found which he doubtless used to wear.

The cadavers of the two, Reverend Friar Francisco Garcés and Friar Juan Barreneche, were found at about 10:00 in the morning of the aforementioned date of last December. They were found buried together in their undergarments[92] in the open country and were almost incorrupt.

As to the fifth point, I say: Captain of Cavalry, Don Pedro Tueros,[93] who was present, reports that both bodies were almost fresh and complete, especially that of the Reverend Father Garcés. At the edge of the place where they were buried a large amount of very fragrant manzanilla had sprung up. Those who were present assured the captain that they had never seen it before anywhere in that neighborhood. Some male and female prisoners disclose that an Indian woman whom they esteemed highly had performed the good work of burying them, leaving as a marker a small cross made of sticks by which the site was recognized.

As to the sixth, I say: The captives declared that when the rebellious attack of the gentiles took place, the Reverend Father Friar Juan Barreneche helped those who were being killed to die well. He called aloud, desiring to confess them and absolve them with no fear that they might kill him as well, who it seemed to them disdained his enemies. They did not succeed in harming him until the end of their enormous crime. They declared that in the pueblo of San Pedro y San Pablo de Bicuñer they had heard sweet songs, and at night it seemed to them that the friars were walking as in procession around the church in whose vicinity the venerable remains of the Reverend Fathers Friar Juan Díaz and Friar José Matías Moreno were discovered. They also declared that this sound aroused fear on approaching the pueblo. It is certain that the four Reverend Fathers mentioned above were

---

92. Franciscans were required by their order to wear a specific type of undergarment consisting of shorts and a tunic. Not to comply was to commit a mortal sin. Had the friars been found without these undergarments, it would have lessened the chances for their possible future canonization.

93. Captain Don Pedro Tueros (or Fueros) was commandant of the royal presidio of Altar and second in command of the Fages expedition to the site of the Yuma massacre in the fall of 1781. Earlier, from 1771 to 1777, Tueros was the military governor of the Real of Cieneguilla in Sonora. He relieved Don Bernardo Urrea as commandant of Altar in 1777. In 1778 he was appointed by Teodoro de Croix to succeed Juan Bautista de Anza as commander of all the military forces in Sonora. In 1782, Tueros was appointed governor of Coahuila in place of Don Juan de Ugalde. He assumed the post in April of 1783 and held the position for more than five years (Ives 1966: 56; Navarro García 1964: 251-254, 324, 470; Thomas 1941: 141).

working constantly for the conversion of the gentiles of that pueblo to attract them to the knowledge of the true law without taking leave to go out in the wild country. They were caring for them in the rancherías and giving them as gifts whatever they had. Also, that the Reverend Father Garcés had gone to perform baptisms as far as the nation of the Jalchedunes,[94] and the Reverend Father Barreneche to the Cocomaricopas without fearing the risk to which they were exposed and with no more reward than that of winning those poor souls for the flock of the Church.

All of this I certify as depositions which I received under solemn oath, as I have already said, and as a proof to whom it may concern, I have signed it in Pitiqui de Caborca on February 16, 1782.

PEDRO FAGES.

The root of this evil is, Señor, in the excessive limitation (contrary to the Royal intentions) placed on the expenditures necessary to make a solid foundation. This limitation has come to produce greater costs and many misfortunes which would have been avoided by handling the affair from the beginning with due seriousness. The Señor Viceroy had ordered that these institutions should be placed on a firm footing; that two presidios were to be planted, one on the Gila and the other among the Yumas.[95] He had ordered that the opinion of the Reverend Father Garcés should be heeded, for he was a very experienced missionary. None of this was done, and the results proved the lack of good judgment.

Another reason for the disaster was the state of those provinces which at that time were under frequent attack by the barbarous Apaches. Troops were few. No decision had been made to found new presidios. As a result, the old presidios were weakened and were unable to furnish the soldiers needed for the new missions.

If, then, we are to express our judgment, we presume, Señor, that first of all it is indispensable that the jefes observe what the laws had prescribed for new

---

94. The Jalchedunes were the Yuman-speaking Halchidhoma, the descendants of whom live in modern times on the Salt River Indian Reservation between Tempe and Mesa, Arizona, and who are known generally to outsiders as "Maricopas" (Dobyns, Ezell, and Ezell 1963: Kelly 1972).

95. The viceroy to whom Bringas refers was either Carlos Francisco de Croix, who was the marqués de Croix; or Antonio María Bucareli y Ursua.

conversiones and take the necessary action. It is certain this cannot be done without expense. But it is equally certain that if the necessary expenditures are made others, which are larger, will be avoided. Thus, not only will the loss of the new missions be prevented, but if these steps are taken, in a short time some of the presidios presently in the middle of the province will be superfluous. When the frontiers where enemies enter are occupied, there is no need for troops in the middle. The complete state of peace in the Provincias de Sonora; communication with the old and new Californias, with New Mexico and New Viscaya; the growth of commerce; the peaceful exploitation of the rich mines in which it abounds; the saving effected for the Royal Treasury; the conversion of 25,000 souls within very few years; the solid establishment of the new Bishopric; the provision of secular ministros for the many pueblos lacking them — these, Señor, are the effects which will certainly be the result of the following measures. Some of them require prompt execution. Others serve only to increase their effectiveness.

To insure the firmness and success of the new foundations, and to build them to our best advantage, they should be initiated as provided by law. No unreduced nation should be left at their back. Accordingly, the first mission should be founded in the Papago nation. This nation bounds on all our missions in the Pimería and extends for 80 leagues from southeast to northwest. This is a very peaceful nation. It has the same language as that of the Pimas. Its land is generally dry. A site quite suitable for a foundation is at a little less than 32°'s lat. and 266°'s longitude from Tenerife.[96] It will be necessary to secure it with troops, but it is not necessary to incur all the expense of a formal presidio solely for it. Such a presidio would be more effective in some other area. For its establishment and support a detachment of forty men will suffice. These can be drawn from the troops in the presidios which we shall later on designate to be necessary. Thus the new mission will be made secure on the east and south by our present missions and by the existing presidios of Altar, Tubac, and San Xavier del Bac [sic][97], and on the west by the coast of the Sea of California. It is only exposed on the north where it borders on other nations. That, however, will be made safe by other measures.

This was formerly the site of a Jesuit mission. The barbarians destroyed it in the general uprising of 1751. To re-establish it will not burden the treasury nor even take from the salary of the ministros. It will only reduce the funds for the detach-

---

96. The site being proposed is that of Sonoita, Sonora, the midway point between the presidio of Altar and the mouth of the Gila River. It was at Sonoita that Father Enrique Ruhen, S.J., was killed by the Papagos in 1751 (see note 81). Sonoita has become an important border crossing for American tourists headed for the Gulf of California.

97. Friar Bringas is mistaken here. San Xavier del Bac was never a presidio. The priest doubtless meant to write San Agustín del Tucson.

ment of troops because of the arrangements we have already suggested. A fund for the foundation has been established already through the pious efforts of some individuals. Only the 1,000 pesos which are customarily contributed by the Royal Hacienda to establish every new foundation will be required — and this only for the first time.

72

The second mission should also be founded in the Papago nation in the ranchería named Santa Rosa del Ati. It is situated a little more than 20 leagues west of the presidio of San Agustín del Tucson. There is a scarcity of water there, and as this is very important for a new foundation, a little more than the usual assistance is needed. When this mission has been established it can be protected by a guard of nine soldiers and an officer from the nearby presidio of Tucson. Its founding will cost the Royal Treasury no more than the usual 1,000 pesos, because the same individuals referred to above have offered to finance the stipends of the four ministros.

73

The third and fourth missions should be founded in the nation of the Gileño Pimas. It is located on the southern margins of the Gila at 33° 10′ latitude. The missions should be placed in the two pueblos of Vehurichuc and Sutaquison. Between them are three other pueblos of the same nation. These five are situated within 2½ leagues of one another. This is a very peaceful nation. For a half-century they have been crying out for the Gospel. Details concerning them and the land they inhabit are given in the report to Chihuahua, which has been inserted here as section 61. However, since this nation is threatened by two numerous groups of Apaches, called the Coyoteros and the Tejuas, as the map [p. 98] shows, this makes the establishment of a strong presidio indispensable for a solid foundation. This presidio should be located near the ancient edifice known as the house of Moctezuma, and located at 33°'s and a few minutes of latitude on the edge of the Gila.[98] We will explain later to Your Majesty the circumstances and the number of soldiers needed to hold this and the other presidio in order to achieve many most important aims.

---

98. This "ancient edifice" is today known as Casa Grande, and it is protected as a United States National Monument. Although its origins remain somewhat in doubt, some archaeologists believe it was built by a Western pueblo people after A.D. 1350 and before A.D. 1650 (DiPeso 1956: 483, 566; Fewkes 1912). The site, not to be confused with the city of Casa Grande, Arizona, lies just north of Coolidge, Arizona, on the highway between it and Chandler.

It is very important that the fifth and sixth missions be founded in the Coco-maricopa nation. It is west of the former and is its ally. Many suitable sites for these missions are to be found at a distance of little more than 20 leagues west of the Gileños and at almost the same latitude. However, since this nation has the Tejua Apaches on the north and on its west and northwest the gentile nations of the Cucupas, Quiquimas, Cajuenches, Yumas, Jalchedunes, Jamajabas,[99] and others, it requires that an equally large presidio be located at the confluence of the Gila and Asunción rivers. The founding and the stipends for these last four missions depend absolutely on Your Royal Majesty's liberality and piety.

These six foundations and two presidios, Señor, are those which are needed most urgently. They will serve to ready a great advance toward the conversion of all the other nearby nations. When these six have been established with a population of 8,000 souls and when in time two other similar presidios are estab-lished, one among the Yumas and the other among the Jaliquamais or Quiquimas (one and the same nation), these conversiones and the Provincias de Sonora will be united with those of both Californias. All these nations will be subdued by having a line of presidios which are not too costly and are, indeed, of considerable importance. They will be located in places where communications are possible without danger of attack. The advances and retreats of the barbarians who attack Sonora will be hindered by these troops and presidios. Thus some of the present presidios will be rendered useless, and their endowment is incomparably more expensive than what we propose to Your Majesty. Consequently, the new expense will be temporary, the provinces will flourish, they will grow considerably, and they will communicate with each other to their own great advantage.

Sonora, in its present state of great decadence, has a little less than 180,000 pesos remaining for the treasury after paying all the expenses which Your Majesty has incurred in it. This money is from the products of the mines previously men-tioned. After the foundation of the six missions and two presidios at a yearly cost of 57,659 pesos, there will still be a surplus for the treasury of more than 120,000 pesos from the products of the mines. After these foundations have been completed, a great deal of land containing rich minerals will be accessible to workers. Trade will flourish and the Royal Treasury will be repaid in a very short time for the expenses it suffers at present.

---

99. See notes 23 and 94 for background on these tribes.

77

The founding of these presidios will be far less expensive than that of any of the others, even though the number of posts is doubled as will be necessary. This, Señor, is a proven truth.

The cause of the greatest expense in the presidial companies presently in that province is that six of them are manned by a total of 437 soldiers, citizens of the country, each of whom draws pay of 240 pesos annually. Added to the 100 other persons — captains, officials, chaplains, et cetera — with their salaries, the cost of these six companies amounts to 153,270 pesos yearly for no more than 537 persons, including officials and soldiers.

78

The plan which we propose offers the opportunity for the foundation of two presidios with a total of 280 men who will cost no more than 53,659 pesos altogether. If at this rate another four should be founded in order to equal the six present companies, there would result a total of 840 men who would require no more than 160,988 pesos. From this it is clear that almost with the same money which 500 men presently cost, Your Majesty will have in his royal service 840 men, and, as we shall make explicit, with improved efficiency.

79

It is a well known fact in the Provincias Internas, Señor, especially in Sonora, that the last peace made with the Apaches and the humbling of this vagabond and barbarous nation is chiefly due to the Opatas and Pimas who make up the presidial companies of Bacoachi, Bavispe, and Tubac. These troops, which are so low class, cost barely half as much as citizens of the country who are paid 240 pesos a year, while an Indian gets only 136 pesos, 7 reales. This is a rate of three reales daily. To this is added the advantage that the Indian companies need no horses. A mule for each soldier suffices. They can thus get to a combat site with no difficulty. This is of value to the new foundations, because horses are the chief object of Apache greed and raids. Thus this motive for their attacks will be lacking.

80

To be sure, it is not at all suitable for the new presidios to be manned by Indians alone. They generally lack the understanding, capacity, and talent necessary for command. They are only good for obeying. This is why they are never promoted in the companies, since the superior officers have learned this by experience. Of course, no rule is without exception. But if the officials and a few others are Spaniards or citizens, as seen in the following chart [the tables of organization which are in the Appendix of this book], it is fitting that the rest should be Indians.

81

It seems to us that the three following charts are sufficient to make all this clear. One represents the present situation, the number of posts and the wages of the royal presidio which Your Majesty is presently supporting in San Agustín del Tucson. It is composed of Spaniards and sons of the country. The second chart shows the same information for the presidial company in the pueblo of San Miguel de Babispe, the frontier of the Province of Sonora, and which Your Majesty is presently supporting. It is composed of Indians of the Opata nation, with officers who are Spaniards and sons of the country. The third shows the same information for the two new presidios, which we propose to Your Majesty in this, our humble plea.

82

By these tables, Señor, it is clearly to be seen that there is a considerable difference in the formation of these new companies in the way in which we propose. With almost twice as many soldiers, they cost much less. The foundations are more secure, and there are many other advantages. We do not, Señor, think we are stepping out of character when we bring to Your Majesty's attention everything we have written from sections 76 to here. All of it is based on reliable, public information, which we know to be dependable from our own experience and knowledge of those provinces. So we consider it our duty to inform Your Majesty of whatever may promote the Glory of the Lord and the Royal Service.

83

The only possible objection is the difficulty of recruiting 200 Indians for each of the presidios. This, however, is overcome when we consider the fact that every year we account for 3,000 Opata Indians, and more than 800 of the nation are capable of bearing arms. There are more than 2,000 Pimas. Thus there would seem to be no difficulty in recruiting 200 men. With this plan it would be unnecessary to pay for chaplains, because the missionaries will minister to the troops with no other recompense than the stipend which Your Majesty's piety grants them.

84

The first and most important step needed to strengthen the well-being of the Pimería missions and to insure them promptly available aid, is the foundation of a second hospice like the one we propose for the Province of Sinaloa. This will encourage the flourishing of morality in the Province of Sonora. It will abundantly succor the needs of the inhabitants; maintain regular discipline among our missionaries; and it will furnish moral and religious relief to those who are weary from illness or age. It will free them from the harsh necessity of having to travel

700 difficult leagues to be able to die at peace in this College. It will also free them from having to remain in a mission when they are incapable of discharging the duties of their ministry and requiring a dispensation from God and Your Majesty.

This hospice ought to be located as near as possible to the gentile frontier. The site which we consider most appropriate for many reasons is the mission of Pitic, located near the Gulf of California at about 30°'s latitude and founded by the missionaries of this College in 1772.

85

We stated in the preceding section, Señor, what can be hoped for from this hospice. It remains for us to explain how it is to be founded with enough support at no expense to the Royal Hacienda. The mission of Pitic is very near the presidio of this name, where Your Majesty pays a chaplain a stipend of 480 pesos annually. In the mission there is a minister from the Province of [Santiago de] Jalisco with a stipend of 350 pesos annually. If Your Majesty should agree to order this mission to be turned over to this College, and that this College should be in charge of the chaplaincy of the presidio to be administered by the religious of the hospice, it is certain that only giving the missionaries the same alms and stipend which Your Majesty orders paid to those presently administering it, the hospice will have 830 pesos for its support. If to these are added the alms for Masses and others begged for in the Province, a number of workers can be maintained which is in proportion to these funds and the present supplies.

86

As a result, the gentile nation which dwells on the Tiburon Island [i.e., the Seri Indians] some 14 leagues to the west of the aforesaid mission will gradually and gently be reduced by our missionaries, and the Province of Sonora will be freed from an enemy who has always fought it and who is so close to its very center. The report we present to Your Majesty made by the most illustrious Bishop of Sonora adds weight to this idea, since he is one who is apprised of all these details and who knows the great harvest which would result from carrying it out.

87

When the two presidios mentioned above have been founded without any new expense, the first mission which we proposed in section 71 will be protected. It is to be located in Sonoita among the Papagos with a detachment of 30 Indian soldiers, nine who are sons of the country, and a commanding officer. This new detachment is necessary, considering the close alliance of the Papagos of Sonoita with the populous Yuma nation and considering the fact that it is at the center of the 80 leagues of the Papaguería. Thus this foundation is well protected from all four directions. It will be a new obstacle to the incursions of the barbarians into the Province. In case of urgent need, it will be easy for them to appeal to the present presidios of Tucson, Tubac, Altar, and the two new ones of La Casa de Moctezuma and the Río de la Asunción.

In section 71 we suggested measures for the founding of the first two missions at no cost to the treasury. As evidence of the wisdom of these provisions, we present the enclosed document to Your Majesty.[100] It was written by the persons who are performing this service for God and Your Majesty. They hope, as do we also, that Your Sovereign piety will not allow this generous sacrifice made in charity for the sake of humanity, religion, and the state to remain useless.

It remains to inform Your Majesty on another point no less important than the foregoing. Although the subject may seem odious, our feeble zeal does not approach it in this spirit, but only in the attempt to remedy the grave evils which the Provincias Internas are suffering because of it. We relate, as we humbly and sincerely assert, only the public facts which are notorious and undeniable. Our spirit will be quieted as we inform Your Majesty, who is the Lord of that vineyard.

The barbarous Apache nation is astonishing for its numbers. It has up to now, during its wanderings, attacked the Provincias Internas of Sonora, Nueva Vizcaya, Coahuilla, and the Nuevo Reyno de León, harassing more than 400 leagues of terrain from east to west and more than 200 from north to south. In addition to this there are many bands of this same nation whom Padre Garcés, a missionary of our College, visited in their own countries. They were so far to the north that they had never approached the aforementioned provinces nor taken up arms against us. This vagabond nation, when persistently pursued by the troops, began to beg for peace eight years ago, but more from fear than from conviction. Some groups came to various presidios and in these nearby locations they were granted peace and were permitted to settle.

The critical and most precious moment for obtaining their complete reduction, when without any doubt fear and humiliation had moved them to make peace

---

100. We have been unable to locate the document to which Bringas refers.

under suitable conditions, was lost, as is common knowledge. From all this sham peace, although it has been much prolonged, no more fruit was gathered than that they dare not return to the mountains from which they came. The simple and truthful explanation of the present state of affairs in which they live in the presidios would suffice to prove this truth and to show the necessity of a remedy for the evils which result from it.

92

The method of bringing peace with the Apaches has, Señor, been this: they were permitted to settle outside the presidios. Every week, at Your Majesty's expense, they were given a ration of maize, meat, tobacco, and sweets. They were also made to obey the ministro, who teaches them the law of God, but they were left the free use of their gentile customs, especially polygamy. The Christian captives whom they made prisoners at a tender age and who were raised in their way and who remain with them as Apaches are not taken away from them. They are permitted the use of weapons and are allowed to take them everywhere. Even the theft of beasts from the residents or travelers is tolerated, and when these protest when they find them in the possession of the Apaches, they are not returned. Many of them are permitted to possess and use firearms.

93

Neither is an attempt made to force them to farm, so that within a few years they might indemnify the Treasury for the considerable sum of pesos with which it supports these disguised enemies. In the Presidio of Bacoachi alone, where there are 40 families of them, Your Majesty has spent 7,000 pesos every year from 1789 on. In the Presidio of Tucson, where there are about 181 souls, the expense is 1,600 pesos. In the Presidio of Janos, where more than 800 reside, the expense is 13,000 pesos in the most moderate year. And it is the same in the other presidios. The government thinks it is feasible to found establishments with police, law, and order among 3,000 Yumas with a force of only 21 soldiers who are 90 leagues away from all help. It is offensive that this very same government does not believe that Apaches who are at peace, who are in the midst of the Provincias Internas right beside the presidios, and who are constantly under threat from the 3,000 men who man the borders of those lands, can also be kept in subjection.

94

If from this disbursement from the Royal Hacienda at least a true peace would be obtained for those provinces, it would be tolerable if only to avoid greater misfortunes. However, there is no way to travel without being attacked. Neither is there any safeguard against their attacks which do not attract attention because they are not as terrible as before. But what will result from this peace,

Señor, is that they do obtain an intimate knowledge of all the provinces simply in order to commit greater crimes when in their instability they return to the wilderness. This already happened in El Paso del Norte, when those who were considered to be at peace rose up last year, killing 57 soldiers and three officials in two days. Thus the expense borne by the Royal Treasury in supporting those ignorant barbarians was wasted.[101]

The report we enclose made by the President of our missions to the Comandante General in response to his request for an opinion on this matter, and which was made with the simplicity proper to a minister of God and loyal vassal of Your Majesty, gives a clear idea of the status of these barbarians.

But we must report to Your Majesty as proof of the great need for a remedy one of the greatest evils which the indolence of the peaceful Apaches has produced. At the close of the year of 1792 there was in the city of Arizpe a little Apache Christian maiden with a good education and signs of true devotion. She was under charge of a settler who had taken her in from the time when they first brought her as a prisoner during the war with the Apaches. One of the gentile Apaches came who had just finished asking for peace, and having heard about her asked the jefe for her. And although the jefe knew that the child was a Christian, in spite of the objection of her *padrinos* and without being moved by the tears of the girl herself, forced them to deliver this victim to a gentile barbarian. This was a scandal to the whole Province and caused injury which can be imagined to a Christian girl who was naturally repelled by union with a pagan. This, Señor, is a deed which needs no amplification.

This College has been and is prepared to undertake the catechizing and the conversion of the Apaches, just as the Procurator told the Comandante General, whenever the necessary measures are taken and these barbarians are placed in a state of subjection and respect such as the laws command. We will do so when there are no serious reasons to fear that ridicule for the ministry and contempt for religion will be the result. The Comandante himself recognized only too late those evil effects which have resulted from not having created a stable peace. He has tried to remedy this, and without success. As proof, Señor, we transcribe

---

101. On July 25, 1795, the Mescalero Apaches of El Paso — for "unknown causes" — rose up and killed twenty-six soldiers from the presidio of San Carlos, a site located in northeastern Chihuahua about eleven miles southeast of modern Lejitas, Texas. Twenty-one Mescaleros were said to have been killed in two battles which took place. "Suddenly the frontier exploded into activity," and prolonged Apache versus Spaniard warfare ensued, one series of episodes lasting into 1796 (Navarro García 1964: 493).

here the following communication which the Comandante General sent to the President of our missions, which is as follows:

I have ordered added to the file concerning this affair the communique of Your P. [Paternity] of the 2nd of last month which was received in the latest mail. In it you insist both by order of and in the name of your Holy College on the establishment of new reducciones among the gentile Pimas who populate the Gila River to the northwest of the Presidio of Tucson. I will advise Your P. when possible of the decision made. In the meantime, although there is a chaplain and ministro doctrinero in the presidio and pueblo of Bacoachi, where there are peaceful Apaches, it seems to me that instruction for these Indians in the catechism could be undertaken by Your P. or one of your religious who merits your confidence. If the Indians come quietly to hear the Divine Word and embrace religion and vassalage it will be easier and less risky than to establish a mission in each place. But this is no more than a hint which I give Your P. I am very pleased by your zeal and prudence. When you have thought the matter over you may tell me what you consider to be the proper course of action.
God keep Your. P. many years.

Chihuahua, March 28, 1795
Pedro de Nava
to the Very Reverend Father
Friar Francisco Antonio Barbastro

 97

In compliance with this order of the Comandante General, the President took pen in hand and made arrangements for the two ministros of Bacoachi and Tucson, where there are peaceful Apaches, to give him a detailed report on the matter. He received from them the two following letters:

Very Reverend Father President Fray Francisco Antonio Barbastro:
I received the letter of Your P. of the 25th of last month. In compliance with its content, I went to the ranchería or rancherías of the Apaches with Marcos, the interpreter. I informed the two captains, Jacinto and Alejandro, who are presently in this Apache settlement, of the King's desire, that of Your P. and of God. They replied for themselves and for all the others of both sexes who were present that the proposal should be put into effect and that they were ready to embrace the Christian religion and to be loyal vassals of the King. These promises cannot become a reality unless the most serious measures are taken to destroy the impediments which could impede a firm and sincere reducción and the necessary means to do this are provided. We must suppose above all that from the beginning to the present day there has been a continuing error in the civil government of these Indians. For this reason they are now full of new vices learned among or from those very same persons who are called "Christians" in addition

to those they had already committed in their pagan state. It seems that of these latter, at least the chief ones such as robbery and murder, have been corrected by the passage of years and the lack of practice. But I consider the correction of the vices which they have recently learned among our people to be very difficult, chiefly because the cause does not cease, which is the bad example of Christians. As proof of this truth the best and most objective witnesses are the gentiles themselves. In the conference I had with them on the afternoon of my visit, when I played a game of chance with them (to which they are highly addicted, and chiefly the "boys" and even women), they told me that this and the other card games they play is the first milk they sucked from the Christians; that in their country they knew nothing of this.[102] They made the same statement about dances, swearing oaths, obscene language and other vices which they have, i.e., that they learned all this from the Christians of Bacoachi. And this cause in Bacoachi has not ceased to exist. There is no lack of games. There are plenty of fandangos in which a thousand improprieties are sung and the most evil movements are made. There is no lack of concubinage, improper speech, oaths, maledictions, insults, envy, and so forth. Then we must confess, although with much pain, that the reduction of the Apaches of Bacoachi can neither be firm nor genuine as long as they remain in contact with the Christians. If one considers this, it is indispensable that the most serious measures be taken against all who are involved in any of the vices mentioned above. They must be punished in the very presence of the gentiles as an example and warning to the rest. If this is not done, the most zealous ministro will wear himself out and will doubtless be exposed to their saying that what he preaches to them is false when they see those who profess that same law practicing the very opposite. Besides this, our experience shows that faith comes to this class of gentiles more through the mouth than through the ears, and their reduction will never be obtained unless special care is taken to give them the rations granted them by the King's piety for their support.

This point, which in my opinion is one of the most important, is observed very carelessly. What I have noticed in this respect is that these unhappy gentiles are left with nothing on the very same day on which they receive their rations. From this evil it follows that since these unhappy beings have nothing to eat they must seek it in the wilderness by hunting, gathering mescal and so forth, without remaining constantly in their rancheria. This could all be corrected if they were forced or if they forced themselves to conserve a ration until they received the next one, or if some other means were found to put an end to their roaming around and to end even the furloughs which are frequently given them for ten, fifteen, or even twenty days. Unless this is done they will pray one day and cease to pray for ten days, and thus the ministro will have to begin all over again and will never

---

102. Precisely when Apaches learned to play cards from the Spaniards is impossible to say, but Father Arriquibar's remarks make an eighteenth-century introduction sound likely. The Apaches created their own versions of card games and of the cards themselves, fashioning the latter out of leather and painting on them in yellow, red, blue and black colors (Hargrave 1966: 179; Wayland 1961). Like virtually all American Indians, Apaches had aboriginal games of chance as well (see Culin 1907).

succeed in completing the task. But even if these gentiles knew how to take care of their rations for a week, they still have to be clothed, and they dress in gamuzas which they hunt in the wilderness. Thus these wanderings cannot be avoided, for it is not proper for them to come to the catechetical instruction naked, especially the women and children. We therefore have this great difficulty to overcome, and only the King can overcome it by making decisions which will result in their being clothed in accordance with the ministro's teachings. If this is not done, the work will be started, but once started, it will not progress. And it's better not to begin at all than to give it up after having started. Your P. will get to the bottom of these matters and call to the attention of our superiors what you may consider most fitting for such a holy work.

Bacoachi, May 20, 1795
FRIAR PEDRO DE ARRIQUIBAR.[103] A copy.

❋   ❋   ❋

Second Letter

Very Reverend Father President Friar Francisco Antonio Barbastro:
I received the letter of Your P. of April 25, and having seen the content, although I was not ignorant of the state of these Apaches, I went to the pueblo of Tucson on the 2nd day of Easter and the teniente *appeared at my request,*

---

103. Pedro Antonio de Arriquibar was born in Vizcaya, Spain, probably in the 1740s. He arrived in Mexico in 1770, bound for the missions of Lower California. From November 1771 until the Dominicans replaced the Franciscans in Lower California in October of 1772, Father Arriquibar served at Santa Rosalía de Mulage. By early 1775, he was at Mission Tumacácori. The last of his entries in the registers of that mission is dated March 27, 1780. His next assignment was the mission of San Ignacio de Cabúrica, where he seems to have remained until 1794 or a little later. It was while he was at San Ignacio that he received a special dispensation from the pope to serve simultaneously as a missionary and as a chaplain in the Spanish army (Stoner and Dobyns 1959: 71-74).

By May of 1795 Arriquibar was at Bacoachi where he was at once doctrinero for the Christianized Indians and civilian non-Indians of the pueblo and chaplain for the troops of the presidio. The Jaliscan friars had tended to the religious needs of Bacoachi as a visita of Arizpe after 1768, but in 1784 a company of Opata Indians placed partly in charge of Spanish officers was organized there. This made Bacoachi a de facto presidio (Bancroft 1884b: 681; Carlisle and Fontana 1969: 183; Roca 1967: 151).

In 1786 Viceroy Bernardo de Gálvez instituted a "peace policy" toward Apache and other hostile Indians, and those who would were urged to live in settlements adjoined to Spanish presidios, where they would enjoy "rations of food, liquor and infectious disease, and indoctrination into the mysteries of gambling" (Dobyns 1959: 442) — as well as poor quality firearms and the opportunity to become addicted to the need for Spanish goods and thereby have to work or trade for them. In this way *establecimientos de paz* ("peace settlements") came into being at the presidios of Bacoachi, Tucson, Janos, Carrizal, San Elizario, Fronteras, and Tubac. The Bacoachi Apaches were said specifically to have been "Chiricaguis" (Gálvez 1951: 36-51; Matson and Schroeder 1957: 351-353; Spicer 1962: 239-240).

By 1797 Father Arriquibar had moved to the presidio of Tucson, where he died as presidial chaplain in 1820 (Stoner and Dobyns 1959: 75).

because the capitán *was away on the New Mexico Commission.*[104] *We spoke about the subject. He told me the Apaches are very obedient and ready for whatever they're ordered to do, and are desirous of being Christian. His opinion is that there will be no difficulty at all in their reduction. We could not talk with them personally, as they were out hunting.*

Many have still not returned, but others were here today. They understood me and said they were quite satisfied and wanted it to be done right away. However, this does not mean much because these are new things. They do not understand their purpose nor the fact that they must give up their vicious customs and superstitions. Nor do they understand the war which the Enemy will wage against them on this account. I know that the yoke of the law will indeed be heavy for them, as it would not have been when they first came down here, because now in addition to living licentiously, they have learned from the bad examples they have seen in the Spaniards. However, we may have hopes of converting all the youth and little by little of reducing some of the adults by industry and patience on the part of the ministro. In my opinion, though, the following things must be done:

First. The Father Minister must govern them in both temporal and spiritual affairs. The Comandante must not interfere except with the approval of the Father, or unless he requests help to force them to respect and obey him.

Second. They must be informed of the law immediately and made to know the penalty or punishment which is to be given those who break it. All possibility of evasion must be denied them.

Third. They must be settled in the pueblo of Tucson with a detachment of ten soldiers and a captive interpreter who will be under obedience to the Father in Indian affairs, because if the Apaches are away from the presidio and far from the eyes of the Father and the church we risk all and gain nothing.

Fourth. Schooling is to be given them at once. All the youths, who are many, have indicated that they want to know how to read.

Fifth. They are to be given the land of a settler and of the alférez Sosa which immediately adjoin the pueblo, as well as the contiguous lands of the island which are owned by the pueblo.[105] *Thus they may manage them by themselves by means of the canal in the middle which belongs to the pueblo, with a fourth part of the water. The settler mentioned above, together with another who is on the island*

---

104. The *capitán* of the Tucson presidio at the time was Don José de Zuñiga, who had transferred to this post from the presidio of San Diego in Upper California in 1792. On March 31, 1795, he was commissioned by Manuel de Echeagaray, military commander of arms of Sonora, to open a direct trade route between Sonora and Santa Fe, New Mexico, which would be shorter than the road via El Paso. Zuñiga took 150 men with him, including eight Apache scouts from Bacoachi. He left Tucson on April 9, 1795; reached Zuñi, New Mexico, on May 1; he was back in Tucson by May 29 (Dobyns 1964: 41; Hammond 1931; Navarro García 1964: 507).

105. It seems likely that *alférez* (ensign) Sosa was José María Sosa, who in 1778 was a second corporal in the cavalry which made up the Tucson presidial garrison. By 1782 he had been promoted to sergeant, a key position which often qualified its holder for advancement to the officer status of ensign (Dobyns 1964: 10, 28-30).

and also the *alférez*, can have the lands which the Apaches now possess and which are much below the presidio, thus avoiding vexation and trouble.

Sixth. At first each head of a family should be given a hatchet, a hoe, a sickle, and a plowshare. For one year they are to receive their support from the hands of the Father so that they may devote themselves to the land and lose the desire to go to the mountains to hunt at various times. The equipment mentioned is to be given them by the Father, who will be careful to get it back so they don't lose it. Finally, if these Apaches are properly regulated at the very start all will be achieved in a short time. They are not like those of Bacoachi, but are all very alert. They greet one with the *Ave María Santísima*, and there is no instance of their having hurt anyone. Whenever any of them have had to be manacled or put in the stocks they have borne it well, and for this reason they have been considered to be very obedient and docile.

The difficulty which will arise on the part of the Pimas in admitting them to the pueblo and giving them access to their land I have already overcome, although this took a lot of work. In spite of all I have said I will not venture to assure their loyalty, for we have examples to the contrary. So Your P. should report whatever you deem fitting. No doubt if it is God's work it will succeed.

Bac. June 2, 1795.

FRIAR JUAN BAUTISTA LLORENS.[106] A copy.

98

The sincerity with which these letters were written, the experience acquired over 23 years, and the certainty of being correct encouraged the President to present to the Comandante General all that was important for the service of God and Your Majesty in the report which follows:

I send Your Grace a faithful copy of the opinions which have been sent me by the reverend fathers Friar Juan Bautista Llorens, Minister of San Xavier del Bac, and Friar Pedro de Arriquibar, interim minister of Bacoachi, thus to reply to Your Lordship as I was ordered to do in a communique of March 28 of this present year. I characterize these reports, Señor, as truthful narratives and as being very prudent in the measures they indicate as necessary firmly to establish the planned conversiones. Without hesitation I can add my opinion to theirs, keeping in mind that it is in the interests of both religion and state that these gentiles be made secure by means of the establishments proposed. I wish to speak my opinion or, better, to corroborate that of the Fathers. So I say this:

The Apaches have given their consent to receive baptism and vassalage. The ministros are ready. It only remains for us to bear in mind all the circumstances

---

106. See note 40 concerning Father Llorens.

surrounding these gentiles and to consider seriously the measures which should be taken to attain and perpetuate this new Christian community and to put these measures into effect. The Fathers predict great difficulties, and I foresee many others. But this does not frighten me because Your Lordship has been especially charged to found these establishments and has been given the authority and power to overcome difficulties. My opinion, Señor, is that for the Apaches to be properly instructed they ought to be completely separated from all the Christians in Bacoachi and Tucson. Pueblos should be founded for them with their own church and missionaries who would have no other occupation. This should be in their own country or at least a league away from both presidios so that they do not learn everything contrary to what is preached to them. If this were done the company of Opatas should be divided between the two pueblos as a safeguard for the church and the ministros. It is certain that the Apaches fear the Opatas and that these latter will be more docile under the direction of the ministros. They and their women will present a more devout appearance in church than any other troops when in the presence of gentiles. Finally, Señor, they are themselves Indians who share certain common Indian characteristics. This is very useful, and it is the reason why Tlaxcaltecan Indians were brought for the foundations made for the implacable Chichimecas in New Spain.[107] But even if the pueblos are established adjoining the presidios, communications with the gente de razón *are always to be avoided. It is widely known in the province that great injury has resulted to the gentiles from this, as regards both their customs and their temporal affairs. They are frequently without rations and naked as a result of the games they have learned. Even though the ministro of San Xavier is of the opinion that the Apaches of Tucson might live with the Pimas, in spite of the difficulty I confess I see in that, I still consider even this method very risky and I judge a total separation to be more appropriate. To reduce and teach Apaches very special regulations are necessary. They must be made to understand the obligations they undertake. Because they have seen and heard so many things which are contrary to the law they are to profess they must be taught repeatedly that these Christians whom they have seen living with so much license will be severely punished by God. The penalties owing to the public vices of any person must be imposed immediately in order to bring about the correction of the Apaches who have contracted them.*

All this, Señor, is so necessary that if it is not put into practice there is no hope for the conversion of the gentiles. The only result in that case will be to waste the Royal Hacienda fruitlessly, and the ministros will wear themselves out in pain.

---

107. In general, "Chichimec" was a term used by Spaniards in the sixteenth century to refer to hostile tribes along New Spain's northern borders. The word, however, also applies to a group of Indians who lived in the vicinity of Querétaro and who spoke dialects of a common language. In 1591 these particular Chichimecs capitulated to the viceroy of New Spain with the understanding they would receive annuities from the Spaniards and would allow the Spaniards to settle them in special colonies made up of Christianized Indians. It was thus that four hundred families of Tlaxcaltecan Indians were brought to live in four new colonies with Chichimecs under the direction of Franciscan friars and Spanish military authority. "Here the Tlascaltecs and Chichimecs continued to live in peaceful community, though they never would intermarry nor dwell together in the same house" (Bancroft 1883a: 763-764).

Concerning the support of these gentiles: as for the ration which the King will continue to give them in their status as catechumens — they should be forbidden to sell it or gamble it away and, least of all, to do so with those who are not Apaches. If this should ever happen, the settler who bought it or won it should be obliged to return it, even though he has paid for it, because this is a purchase or a trade with a minor which was made contrary to the law. Forbidding this is only putting into effect what has already been commanded for the Indian.

It is indispensable that a piece of land be given to each one and a large section to the community. This should be done in proportion to the farming tools available. The ministro of San Xavier explains that idleness predominates in the Apaches and that it must be rooted out. Otherwise, their vices increase, and they think nothing but their personal affairs and amusements. We know that these people do not farm and that this work will be unpleasant to them. However, it is necessary for them to begin in this way, and they must be taught it. This is particularly difficult. There should therefore be temporarily assigned to them a community field where they may work together under the direction of some intelligent Opata soldier whose authority they will acknowledge. This working together will serve as a school of agriculture. It does not really merit the name of "work," but rather of "play." In addition to instruction, it has the great advantage of preventing idleness. It is necessary to place a yoke of oxen, cart, and harness in each village in care of the mayordomo. If the Opata soldiers will make an effort and a piece of land is given them for an orchard, the Apaches will learn from them to cultivate the earth, and their women will learn to spin and sew. In this way some day the King, Our Lord, will not have to pay for their rations. If they are kept busy they can be refused passes which permit them to roam about and steal under the pretext of going hunting. These passes are the main stumbling block to a foundation among the Apaches. In order to avoid it, a decision was made to give them a ration. However, this accomplished nothing, because they have never learned to conserve, use, and be satisfied with it.

We have treated of the food, and it remains to discuss clothing.

The Apache nation neither plants nor knows how to make use of cotton. Consequently, for clothing they have to hunt gamuza. They make footgear from the hide. However, this nation differs from all others in going clothed and shod from childhood. This is the most pressing motive for letting them go hunting. However, when one sees how this roaming about makes their education impossible, it is necessary to consider some means to supply this lack.

They must immediately be made to sow cotton and to learn to use it. They can learn this from the Opata soldiers. As all must assemble for catechism, and as they should not be permitted to be present while indecently naked, it is essential they be provided with blankets or cloaks or coverings because in the catechumenal status, in which I consider them to be, they must be provided with clothing as well as food.

Up to this point, I have been discussing the Apaches in general. Some problems have arisen concerning placing them in a mission which are so grave that only the authority and power of Your Lordship can surmount them. Now I must distinguish between Apache adults and Apache children, i.e., those of twelve years and younger. Once this distinction has been made, one is encouraged. This is because for the instruction of these children there are no such great mountains of difficulty as we have seen in the case of the adults. With this in mind we can enter upon the founding of missions with enthusiasm, for the youths of both sexes are exempted from the vices of the adults. Naturally, an agreement must be made with the parents that they too will come to the doctrina for the sake of their children. No one must be permitted to absent himself under any pretext. In Bacoachi the ministros worked very hard at this. The Governor gave the Indians this order, but it is clear that nothing was accomplished. At first, some came. Then, only a few. And finally, no one. They say their parents don't want to come. It is necessary that this not be overlooked. If they do not assemble frequently, the youth cannot be taught, and it is not permissible to baptize the small children. Besides the difficulty of teaching the adults, there are many other difficulties which do not arise in the case of children. However, if the problems which occur in the case of children are not overcome, the mission will have only a nominal existence. Señor, if we are merely to hope that the Apaches will ask for ministros and that they will come voluntarily and send their children to the doctrina, it will never happen. They will give verbal consent, but we must not hope they will continue to comply if left to their wishes. To handle and characterize a single unusual case by the general rules is impossible because all rules have exceptions and no rule covers all situations. Thus, if such a measure as the one requested seems to be contrary to the general law of liberty, it is not really so when brought down to the specific case of these gentiles. The Apache says he wishes to be a Christian and that his children should be Christians. Consequently, he must also desire those means which are necessary in order to be a Christian. Once he has been baptized he must be forced to do what he promised. It is for this purpose that authority exists.[108] Their transgressions of the Divine and ecclesiastical laws cannot be overlooked. The same treatment should be given to the captives who are among them and to Apaches who have been baptized when in danger of death. When the Moorish kingdoms in Spain had no rulers left, many begged for baptism. It was given them. After some time had passed it was noticed that they assembled at night to celebrate Ramazan and other Mohammedan rites. Bishops and Curas began to declaim, and a great controversy arose. Those who had an interest in the continuance of these rites defended them. The true Catholics, however, were of the opinion that the converted Moors should be obliged to keep their promises. The first promise was to renounce Satan and all his works. As the controversy heated, a conference of the greatest jurists, canonists, and theologians in the kingdom was held in Madrid. They heard the allegations of the Moors and their lawyers, saying that the Moors had been baptized without the proper intention solely out of fear and human respect; that if they were obliged by force completely to give up their rites, they

---

108. By the law of the church, only baptized individuals are subject to the jurisdiction of the church. Therefore, an unbaptized Apache could not be forced to perform any Christian act. Once baptized, however, he could be forced to comply. However, lack of baptism did not free one from the threat of secular (military) coercion, and military force could be used to bring Indians into proximity to religious, thereby making them candidates for baptism.

would go to hear Mass and would assist at prosecutions. All these allegations and more were considered by the Assembly. Nonetheless they decided unanimously that Ramazan and all Mohammedan gatherings or rites contrary to Christianity should be prohibited. The decision was that all that the Moors had alleged was invalid.[109]

Now let Your Lordship consider if our present situation is not the same as this. Even though we overlook something in the case of adults, no exceptions can be made in the case of children. To start to provide schooling for young people of both sexes is most important, because the success or failure of a republic depends on the good or bad training of its youth.

Let us now discuss the ministro and his activity. Concerning this, I repeat what I have already told Your Lordship, namely that my College desires only to have its religious occupied in the propagation of the faith. It is ready to send as many as are requested of it. The mind of the Sovereign is made clear in the law which orders that two ministros are to be placed in the new missions with the alms necessary for their support. This is a matter of charity and justice, for he who sacrifices himself for the soul of his neighbor must not neglect his own soul. If the ministro is provided with a companion he has someone with whom to consult. He has someone to help him. If he should become ill or die the work among these new conversiones and the converts will not stop. Thus, the jurisdiction of the missionaries is extended in a generous way and infinite good is wrought for souls. For this reason I say that in conformity with the spirit of the law the government of the reducciones ought to be put in the hands of the ministro in temporal affairs as well as spiritual. The separate administration of these two areas is very damaging to the Indian conversiones. Even the Sovereign himself has told the ministros that when they receive their orders they should take the special conditions of the territory into account and if they find the orders would cause harm they should not carry them out.

The salvaguardia, Señor, is necessary in view of the nature of these gentiles. The name itself indicates its purpose, i.e., that it is not given so that the Comandante can give the orders in the conversión but so that the person of the ministro is secure, and to give authority and effectiveness to his orders as is expressly provided in the cédulas reales of November 13, 1744 and December 4, 1747.[110] If I should have erred in my judgments, it will not be of any great matter.

Aconchi, June 29, 1795
Friar Francisco Antonio Barbastro
[To] Comandante General, Don Pedro de Nava

---

109. Ramazan (or Ramadan) is the ninth month of the Moslem year, one spent in fasting from sunrise to sunset. The entire matter of attempts in Spain to convert Moslems to Christians (*Moriscos*) is summarized in Chapman (1918: 276-280). Matters came to a head in the early years of the seventeenth century when most Moriscos were expelled by decree and forced to go to Africa.

110. See note 19 for discussion of these two cédulas reales.

The result of this report, whose content we have largely abridged, has been silence. The Apaches continue to suffer from the bad example of the other Indians. It is much to be feared that after having increased the expenses of the Royal Treasury they will again withdraw to the wilderness with all the more detriment and harm to the provinces, especially since during these many years they have acquired a practical and personal knowledge of all our affairs. They have learned the use of firearms and the vices of the bad Christians, and none of their virtues. All that we have said to Your Majesty up to this point is based solely on the truth. Its only motivation is true zeal and the desire to remedy the grave injury which the provinces are suffering contrary to Your Majesty's pious wishes.

Our interest in this matter, Señor, is not temporal. All that moves us is the discharge of our ministry, the glory of God, the well-being of the provinces, the reformation of manners, the conversion of the gentiles, and the happiness owed to Your Majesty. If, Señor, our interest were in perishable things, we would have made use of the affection and liberality of persons who give their wealth, inclining them to make this sacrifice for the benefit of Our College and not for these new foundations. In these we seek only labor, danger, and weariness, and then we give them up as soon as they are in such a state that the secular clergy can easily administer them while we go on as faithful ministros of the Lord and humble vassals of Your Majesty in search of new bitter experiences which will increase the flock of Jesus Christ and add brilliance to the crown of Your Majesty, whose burning and generous zeal animates us.

Therefore, we beg Your Majesty, full of confidence in the Lord's providence and in the Royal clemency and Catholicism of Your Majesty, to deign to grant us your Royal permission for the founding of the two hospices; the turning over of the mission at Pitic and the assistance of its presidio; the faculties needed for the restoration, stabilization, and enlargement of the eight missions of the Pimería Alta in accordance with the rules established for the conversiones; and the doubling up of ministros in each reducción. We also request Your Majesty to accept the generous offer of those persons who give their riches for the two new missions, and to grant permission for their foundation as well as for that of the four others which we desire in the three nations of the Papagos, Pimas Gileños, and Cocomaricopas. We also request the erection of the two presidios which will strengthen these new establishments and further the conversion of so many thousands of gentiles. We further request an increase of twenty more religious in addition to the forty we have already asked of Your Majesty in order to carry out all these details.

But if our humble supplications are neither acceptable nor agreeable to Your Majesty, we still submit to your Royal will as loyal vassals. Finally, we add the request that Your Majesty should deign to command that the government of the Provincias Internas should not impede the entrance of missionaries into the neighboring gentile areas.

As we have explained to Your Majesty, the piety of the faithful has provided what is necessary to support four ministros among the gentiles. The cries of these poor souls are continuous. They often visit the most remote missions. They beg the ministros to settle among them. We are sure of their love for us. Their loyalty has been tested over many years. We find nothing unsuitable and find instead much satisfaction and glory to God in allowing some of the many religious who desire it eagerly to go and establish themselves among the Gileño Pimas, the Papagos, and Cocomaricopas. Thus these poor nations may finally receive that incomparable benefit they so much desire of the knowledge of God and the exercise of our Holy religion. We humbly request Your Majesty's approval, and hope that in the royal clemency you will order put into effect what we have asked. Thus, provisionally, the ministros will continue to manage the reducciones without needing a salvaguardia and at no cost to the Royal Treasury.

If this, our humble petition, should have the happy fortune of pleasing Your Majesty, then due to our own practical knowledge of how conversiones should be managed and as a result of the grave troubles which this College has experienced during the long period of a hundred years, we beg Your Majesty to condescend to command strictly that in these missions which are to be founded no Spaniard shall be permitted to establish himself under any pretext. The consequences which would otherwise follow would be extremely harmful to the Indians, and for this reason they are to be prohibited.

We have shown that experience has taught us that the Comandancia of Provincias Internas pays no attention (perhaps because it cannot) to the affairs and petitions of the missionaries of this College. Our missionaries got along more happily when they were in charge of the Viceroys of New Spain. Consequently, we also beg Your Majesty to command that the missions of the Pimería Alta and all the missions which are to be newly founded should be under the sole government of the Viceroy, like those of the Californias. They are identical, and this fact makes necessary one and the same administration for both establishments. This measure doubtless will be one of the most efficacious and effective causes for the progress and happiness of the missions.

For all these reasons, which are conducive to the glory of God, the exaltation and growth of the Holy Faith, the service of Your Majesty and the extension of your dominions, we beg Your Majesty with complete submission and humility, to deign to use that sovereign power which the Lord has placed in your Royal Hands to order and provide as we have requested.

APOSTOLIC COLLEGE OF SANTA CRUZ DE QUERÉTARO.

FRIAR BRINGAS' APPENDIX TO HIS REPORT

TABLES OF ORGANIZATION

Table of Organization [1. San Agustín del Tucson]

Which shows the present state and number of spaces and salaries for the Royal Presidio for which His Majesty pays at present in San Agustín, Mission of Tucson, on the frontier of the Province of Sonora, composed of Spaniards and sons of the country distributed as follows:

Officers and Soldiers	Positions	Salaries
Captain	1	3000
Chaplain	1	0480
Lieutenant	1	0700
Ensigns	2	0500
		0500
Sergeants	3	0324
		0324
		0324
Drummer	1	0144
Corporals	6	0276
		0276
		0276
		0276
		0276
		0276
Carabineers	6	0270
		0270
		0270
		0270
		0270
		0270
Armourer	1	0272
Soldiers each with salary of 240 pesos	84	20160
Totals	106	30004 pesos

[135]

Table of Organization [2. San Miguel de Babispe]

Which shows the present status of forces and salaries of the Presidial Company which Your Majesty is now paying in the Pueblo of San Miguel de Babispe, on the frontier of the Province of Sonora, composed of Indians of the Opata Nation, with Officers who are Spanish and sons of the country, distributed as follows:

Officers and Soldiers	Positions	Salaries
Captain, a Lieutenant commanding	1	700
Chaplain	1	480
Lieutenant	0	000
Ensign	1	450
Sergeants	2	324
		324
Drummer	0	000
Corporal	0	000
Native Captain	1	400
Carabineers	0	000
Armourers	0	000
Soldiers each one with the salary of 3 reales daily which amounts in a year to 136 pesos 7 reales	80	11771:2
Totals	92	14449:2

Table of Organization [3. Model Presidio]

Which shows the forces and salaries of each one of our Presidios which we consider
necessary for the foundation of new Misiones on the Gila River, composed of Indians of
the Opata and Pima nations with Officers who are Spanish and sons of the country, located
at 33 and 34 degrees of North Latitude: contains the model of a single Presidio.

Officers and Soldiers	Positions	Salaries
Captain	1	3000
Chaplain	1	000
Lieutenant	1	700
Ensigns		
Sergeants	2	324
		324
Drummer	1	144
Corporals	3	276
		276
		276
Carabineers	3	270
		270
		270
Armourers	1	272
Soldiers of the Country with 240 pesos salary	26	6240
Indian Soldiers with 3 reales daily which makes 136 pesos 7 reales a year	100	13687:4

[Table of Baptisms 1. Caborca, 1768 – 80]

Ministers	Souls	Nations	Age Years	Months	Days	Place	Year	Month	Day
V. F. Juan Díaz	19	Papagos	Infants	0	0	Caborca	1768	June	8
"	1	"	28	0	0	"	"	Nov.	28
"	1	"	50	0	0	"	1769	Feb.	11
"	1	"	2	0	0	"	1770	May	27
"	1	"	4	0	0	"	"	"	"
"	1	sold in war [111]	12	0	0	"	1771	May	27
"	1	"	13	0	0	"	"	"	"
"	1	"	9	0	0	"	"	July	21
"	1	"	10	0	0	"	"	"	"
"	1	"	9	0	0	"	1772	Feb.	28
"	1	Nijora	Adult woman	0	0	"	"	Dec.	26
Fr. Ambrocio Calzada	1	Papago	12	0	0	"	1773	Sept.	17
"	1	"	7	0	0	"	1774	March	6
"	1	"	9	0	0	"	"	"	7
"	1	"	10	0	0	"	"	"	8
"	1	"	7	0	0	"	"	"	13
"	1	"	9	0	0	"	"	"	26
"	1	"	7	0	0	"	"	"	"
"	1	"	12	0	0	"	"	May	16
"	1	"	10	0	0	"	"	Sept.	23
"	1	"	9	0	0	"	"	"	"
"	1	"	20	0	0	"	"	Nov.	20
"	1	"	4	0	0	"	1775	March	9

111. This term, "Vendidos" in Spanish, probably refers to Indian children who were captured in warfare and subsequently bought by Spaniards or others, but who were not regarded as slaves. In contrast, "Nixoras" or "Nijoras," who were not a tribe, were likely to have been from groups hostile to Spaniards and were regarded as slaves (see note 41).

[Table of Baptisms 1. Caborca, 1768–80] (cont.)

Ministers	Souls	Nations	Age Years	Months	Days	Place	Year	Month	Day
V. F. José Moreno	1	Papago	5	0	0	Caborca	1775	May	2
P. Calzada	1	"	4	0	0	"	"	"	9
V. Moreno	1	Nijora	20	0	0	"	"	July	19
"	1	"	6	0	0	"	"	Nov.	23
"	1	"	7	0	0	"	"	"	"
"	1	Papago	0	Infant	0	"	1776	Jan.	4
P. Calzada	1	Nijora	7	0	0	"	"	March	24
"	1	"	3	0	0	"	"	Nov.	4
"	1	Papago	0	Infant	0	"	1777	Feb.	9
"	1	Nijora	5	0	0	"	"	"	24
V. Moreno	1	Seri	4	0	0	"	"	Sept.	27
Fr. Francisco Yturralde[112]	1	Nijora	10	0	0	"	1778	March	9
P. Calzada	1	Papago	0	0	0	"	1773	June thus the priest testifies	18
"	1	"	15	0	0	"	1779	Nov.	7
V. Moreno	1	"	4	0	0	"	1780	March	15
"	1	"	65	0	0	"	"	June	2
"	1	Nijora	14	0	0	"	"	Oct.	24
Total	58								

112. Friar Francisco Yturralde, from the holy province of Cantabria in Spain, went to the College of Querétaro in 1770. He spent most of his missionary career in Sonora, and much of that at Tubutama. He was at Tubutama in 1776, at Caborca in 1778, at Caborca and Tubutama in 1784, and at Tubutama in 1790 and from 1792 to 1799. He completed the church begun there by Father Barbastro. He became president of the missions in 1795, and in 1797, he made an official tour of the Pimería Alta. He died at the College of Querétaro on April 5, 1817, and was buried there "in the common burial of the religious" (Querétaro 1776–1856: Entry No. 266; Yturralde 1797; Dobyns and Ezell 1959: 54; Kessell 1976; Moyano 1803; Roca 1967: 379 n. 102).

[Table of Baptisms 2. Caborca, 1780–84]

Ministers	Souls	Nations	Age Years	Months	Days	Place	Year	Month	Day
V. Moreno	2	Nijoras both	17	0	0	Caborca	1780	Oct.	24
P. Calzada	1	Seri	7	0	0	"	"	Nov.	19
F. Juan Gorgoll[113]	1	Nijora	5	0	0	"	1781	March	16
F. Antonio Ramos	1	Seri	9	0	0	"	"	Sept.	25
"	1	Seri	6	0	0	"	"	Oct.	13
"	1	Nijora	11	0	0	"	"	Dec.	21
"	2	Seris	9	0	0	"	"	"	"
"	1	Papago	0	6	0	"	1782	Jan.	6
"	1	Nijora	12	0	0	"	"	"	"
"	1	Papago	2	0	0	"	"	Feb.	8
"	1	"	4	0	0	"	"	"	25
"	1	"	8	0	0	"	"	March	26
"	1	"	6	0	0	"	"	"	"
"	1	"	5	0	0	"	"	"	"
"	1	"	4	0	0	"	"	April	2
"	1	"	3	0	0	"	"	"	3

---

113. Friar Juan P. Gorgoll signed the church registers at Ati from 1773 until 1787, and at Caborca from 1772 until 1786. He took care of San Xavier del Bac in 1774 during the absence there of Father Francisco Garcés during the first Anza expedition to California (Roca 1967: 380 n. 129).

[Table of Baptisms 2. Caborca, 1780–84] (cont.)

Ministers	Souls	Nations	Age Years	Months	Days	Place	Year	Month	Day
P. Calzada	1	Nijora	10	0	0	Caborca	1782	May	8
P. Ramos	1	Papago	12	0	0	"	"	July	27
"	1	"	16	0	0	"	"	"	"
"	1	"	8	0	0	"	"	Sept.	18
"	1	"	5	0	0	"	"	"	"
"	1	Nijora	7	0	0	"	"	Nov.	24
"	1	"	7	0	0	"	1783	Feb.	13
"	1	"	7	0	0	"	"	Nov.	15
"	1	"	7	0	0	"	"	"	"
"	1	"	8	0	0	"	"	Dec.	5
"	1	"	6	0	0	"	"	"	"
"	1	Seri	18	0	0	"	"	"	19
"	1	Nijora	5	0	0	"	1784	Jan.	10
"	1	"	9	0	0	"	"	May	23
"	1	"	4	0	0	"	"	Aug.	7
"	1	"	5	0	0	"	"	"	"
"	1	"	5	0	0	"	"	"	"
"	1	"	8	0	0	"	"	"	"
"	1	"	7	0	0	"	"	Oct.	8
"	1	"	7	0	0	"	"	"	18
"	1	"	6	0	0	"	"	"	"
"	1	"	8	0	0	"	"	Nov.	19
"	1	Papago	0	5	0	"	"	Dec.	12
"	1	Nijora	5	0	0	"	"	"	15

142

Ministers	Souls	Nations	Age Years	Months	Days	Place	Year	Month	Day
P. Ramos[114]	1	Nijora	6	0	0	Caborca	1784	Dec.	20
"	1	Papago	0	5	0	"	"	"	26
"	1	Nijora	8	0	0	"	"	"	30
"	1	"	6	0	0	"	1785	Jan.	5
"	1	"	7	0	0	"	"	"	6
"	1	Papago	0	Infant	0	"	"	Feb.	9
"	1	Nijora	6	0	0	"	"	Sept.	11
"	1	"	5	0	0	"	"	"	"
P. Francisco Moyano[115]	1	Papago	2	0	0	"	"	Dec.	12
"	1	Nijora	13	0	0	"	1786	Feb.	21
"	1	Papago	20	0	0	"	"	June	2
"	1	Nijora	12	0	0	"	"	July	3
"	1	Jalchedunes	9	0	0	"	"	"	–

114. Antonio Ramos was at Tubutama and Ati in 1774; at Ati in 1775; and at Saric as president of the missions of Pimería Alta in November of 1776, when the place was attacked by Apaches, Seris, and "Cimarrones." Father Ramos served Caborca and its visita of Pitiqui (Pitiquito) from 1781 until his death at the visita of Santa Teresa on January 12, 1793 (Font 1776; Querétaro 1776–1856: Entry No. 208; Roca 1967: 109, 374 n. 48). The only entry Father Bringas lists for him in 1785 in these tables is that for September 12, recorded at Pitiqui, suggesting that he may have spent most of the year 1785 elsewhere.

115. Francisco Moyano was one of the nineteen Franciscans recruited by Bishop Reyes in Spain in 1782 to serve in the Custodia de San Carlos de Sonora which was formally organized in 1783. Coming from the province of Granada in Spain, Father Moyano was at Caborca and its visitas of Pitiqui and Bísanig from 1785 to 1789. In 1790 he moved to Ati, serving here and at Oquitoa until his death in the "Missions of Sonora," word of which reached Querétaro on January 18, 1818. Father Moyano became president of the missions of Pimería Alta in 1801 (Dobyns and Ezell 1959: 54; Querétaro 1776–1856: Entry No. 269; Moyano 1801; Roca 1967: 379 n. 103).

Ministers	Souls	Nations	Age Years	Months	Days	Place	Year	Month	Day
P. Moyano	1	"	5	0	0	Caborca	1786	July	–
"	1	Nijora	9	0	0	"	"	"	–
"	1	"	5	0	0	"	"	"	–
"	1	"	4	0	0	"	"	"	–
"	1	"	7	0	0	"	"	"	–
"	1	"	10	0	0	"	"	"	–
"	1	"	7	0	0	"	"	"	–
"	1	"	10	0	0	"	"	Sept.	17
"	1	"	7	0	0	"	"	Oct.	2
P. Ramos	1	"	7	0	0	"	1787	Dec.	18
"	1	"	7	0	0	"	1788	April	27
"	1	Papago	56	0	0	"	"	June	5
"	1	Nijora	7	0	0	"	"	Dec.	4
"	1	Papago	8	0	0	"	1789	Feb.	2
"	1	Nijora	8	0	0	"	"	May	13
P. Moyano	1	"	10	0	0	"	"	"	31
P. Ramos	1	Papago	18	0	0	"	"	Aug.	18
"	1	Nijora	23	0	0	"	"	Dec.	30
"	1	"	9	0	0	"	1790	Jan.	30
"	1	Papago	60	0	0	"	"	March	18
"	1	"	0	10	0	"	"	April	23
"	1	"	0	1	0	"	"	"	24
"	1	Nijora	8	0	0	"	"	May	25
"	1	Papago	13	0	0	"	"	"	15
P. Moyano	1	"	50	0	0	Santa María Bísanig	1789	Jan.	18
P. Ramos	1	Nijora	8	0	0	Caborca	1790	May	28
"	1	"	17	0	0	"	"	Sept.	10

144

Ministers	Souls	Nations	Age Years	Months	Days	Place	Year	Month	Day
P. Ramos	1	Papago	33	0	0	Caborca	1790	Sept.	13
"	2	(1) "	14	0	0	Pitiqui	"	Nov.	13
		(2) Nijora	13	0	0				
"	1	Nijora	8	0	0	Caborca	1791	May	3
"	1	Papago	90	0	0	"	"	Sept.	21
"	1	Nijora	9	0	0	"	1792	Jan.	23
"	1	Gileño	0	0	8	"	"	March	28
"	1	Nijora	8	0	0	"	"	May	1
"	1	Yuma	24	0	0	"	"	"	3
"	2	Papagos	24	0	0	"	"	"	4
			18						
Fr. Angel Collazo[116]	1	"	70	0	0	"	1793	April	23
"	1	"	80	0	0	"	"	June	4
"	1	"	3		0	"	1794	Jan.	15
"	1	"	24	0	0	"	"	"	30
Fr. Mariano Bordoi[117]	1	"	0	Infant	0	"	1795	Dec.	7
V. Díaz	2	(1) Pima	17	0	0	Pitiqui	1772	March	18
		(2) Yuma	12			visita			
"	2	Pimas	18	0	0	"	"	April	6
			19						
"	1	"	12	0	0	" .	"	July	13
Fr. José Soler[118]	1	Nijora	17	0	0	"	1773	July	26
P. Calzada[119]	1	"	9	0	0	"	1774	Feb.	22

116. Father Angel Collazo remains something of a mysterious friar. His name does not appear in the death registers for Querétaro, and like Paul Roca (1967: 383 n. 186), we have been able to find no reference to him other than in connection with this brief service at Caborca.

117. Mariano Bordoy (Bordoi), who was born on Mallorca and who became a Franciscan there, arrived at the College of Querétaro in 1789. He served a stint as missionary at Tumacácori in the Pimería Alta in 1796–1799 (Jackson 1951: 39; Whiting 1953), but because of ill health, his activities, although geographically widespread, were somewhat limited. He played the organ and heard confessions in Querétaro, Guatemala, Zacatecas, Mexico City, and Nicaragua. He died at the College of Querétaro on October 6, 1819 (Querétaro 1776–1856: Entry No. 271).

118. According to Roca (1967: 380 n. 128), "José Soler, O.F.M., was one of the original band of fourteen Franciscans who came to Pimería Alta, taking charge of Atil [Ati] in the summer of 1768. He stayed until 1774, but his name shows on the books at Caborca in 1773."

119. Father Ambrosio Calzada was born in the province of Burgos in Spain. He came to Sonora in 1770, and served at Caborca from 1773 until his death there from a stroke on the Feast Day of Saint Francis Xavier, December 3, 1782 (Querétaro 1776–1856: Entry No. 164; Roca 1967: 383 n. 184).

[Table of Baptisms 4. Caborca and Pitiqui, 1769–82] (cont.)

Ministers	Souls	Nations	Age Years	Months	Days	Place	Year	Month	Day
P. Calzada	2	Nijora	12 12	0	0	Pitiqui visita	1774	Feb.	25
"	1	"	9	0	0	"	"	May	1
V. Moreno	1	"	12	0	0	"	1776	March	25
"	1	"	5	0	0	"	1777	Feb.	15
"	1	Papago	very old	0	0	"	"	May	23
"	1	Nijora	5	0	0	"	"	Aug.	26
"	1	Seri	4	0	0	"	1778	Jan.	28
V. F. Francisco Garcés	1	Nijoras	16	0	0	Caborca	1779	April	3
"	4	"	16,12, 16,15	0	0	"	"	"	"
V. Moreno	1	Seri	14	0	0	"	"	"	"
F. Pedro Font	1	Yuma	18	0	0	Pitiqui	1780	Jan.	21
"	1	Papago	20	0	0	"	"	Feb.	2
"	1	Apache	7	0	0	"	"	"	25
"	1	Papago	20	0	0	"	"	March	3
"	3	Seris	3,1,6	0	0	"	"	Oct.	8
"	1	Papago	10	0	0	"	1781	July	21
"	1	Seri	20	0	0	"	"	Aug.	9
"	1	Nijora	18	0	0	"	"	Oct.	8
P. Ramos	5	1 Nijora 2 Seris 2 Nijoras	8 6,5, 7,4			"	"	Dec.	14
"	2	Nijoras	9,9	0	0	"	1782	Jan.	31
"	1	Papago	35	0	0	"	"	Feb.	2
"	1	Nijora	9	0	0	"	"	May	21
"	1	Cajuenche	18	0	0	"	"	Aug.	9
"	1	Seri	5	0	0	"	"	Oct.	25
"	1	Nijora	8	0	0	"	1783	Feb.	10
"	1	Papago	14	0	0	"	"	March	21
"	1	Nijora	10	0	0	"	"	Dec.	15
"	1	Seri	40	0	0	"	1784	Jan.	8
"	1	Nijora	12	0	0	"	1785	Sept.	12
P. Moyano	1	"	7	0	0	"	1786	July	10
P. Ramos	1	"	8	0	0	"	1788	April	30
"	1	"	7	0	0	"	"	Nov.	10
"	1	"	23	0	0	"	1790	Feb.	11

There follow the entries in the book of the Pueblo of Santa María del Pópulo del Bísanig, visita of the mission of Caborca. All the preceding have been taken from the books of Caborca, and of San Diego del Pitiqui which is the second visita of the aforesaid mission of Caborca. It must be noted that from here on the missionaries are not specified, because they are alternatively (i.e., in turn, or as they come up) the same ones which are shown in the four preceding tables. They are all sons of this Apostolic College of Santa Cruz de Querétaro.

✿   ✿   ✿

[Table of Baptisms 5. Bísanig, Caborca, and Pitiqui, 1769–82]

Souls	Nations	Age in Years	Place	Year	Month	Day
2	Nijoras	12,13	Pitiqui	1769	Sept.	23
1	Pima	12	Caborca	"	"	"
6	Pimas Vendidos [who were sold]	10,10,12, 13,14,17	"	1771	March	3
5	"	9,12,11, 12,10	"	"	Nov.	24
5	"	8,8,8, 16,15	"	"	"	"
2	1 "	14				
	2 Papago	13	"	"	March	2
2	Pimas	12,12	"	"	June	2
1	Nijora	3	"	1774	Jan.	23
1	Papago	25	Bísanig	"	April	2
1	Nijora	36	Caborca	1775	Jan.	22
1	"	60	"	"	Feb.	14
2	"	5,5	"	1776	Oct.	27
1	Papago	6	"	1778	Sept.	27
1	"	24	"	1779	March	28
1	Apache	6	Bísanig	1781	Oct.	30
1	Papago	5 mo.	in the wilds	1782	Jan.	1
1	"	4	Bísanig	"	"	"

[Table of Baptisms 6. Bísanig and Caborca, 1782–92]

Souls	Nations	Age	Place	Year	Month	Day	147
1	Papago	8	Bísanig	1782	Jan.	15	
1	"	50	"	"	"	27	
1	"	30	"	"	"	28	
1	"	36	"	"	Feb.	18	
1	"	14	"	"	May	8	
1	"	13	"	"	"	"	
1	"	40	"	"	June	2	
1	"	20	"	"	"	"	
1	"	10	"	1783	Oct.	13	
1	"	18	"	"	Feb.	23	
1	"	6	"	1784	Jan.	28	
1	Nijora	9	"	"	April	26	
1	"	10	"	"	May	30	
1	"	8	"	"	Dec.	27	
1	"	7	"	"	"	"	
1	Papago	90	"	1785	Jan.	6	
1	"	1	"	"	Feb.	15	
1	Nijora	8	"	"	April	8	
1	"	7	"	"	"	"	
1	"	6	Caborca	"	Nov.	24	
1	"	8	Bísanig	1786	Jan.	28	
1	"	5	"	"	"	"	
1	"	5	"	"	July	9	
1	"	12	"	"	Sept.	9	
1	"	9	"	"	"	"	
1	"	6	Caborca	1787	Nov.	29	
1	"	6	Bísanig	1788	Aug.	10	
1	"	7	"	1789	Feb.	12	
1	"	7	"	"	June	24	
1	"	24	Caborca	"	Nov.	30	
1	"	7	Bísanig	"	Oct.	17	
1	Papago	13	"	1791	Feb.	2	
1	"	13	"	"	"	16	
1	"	24	"	1792	Jan.	6	
1	Nijora	13	"	"	June	17	
1	"	12	"	"	"	18	
1	Papago	16	"	"	"	"	
1	Nijora	9	"	"	Aug.	26	

Ministers	Souls	Nations	Place of Baptism	Year	Missions
The V.P.F. Francisco Garcés, and the Padres Fr. Juan Belderrain and Fr. Juan Llorens	99	Nijoras and Papagos	Mission of San Xavier and its visita Tucson	From May 2, 1768 to Jan. 1796	Mission of San Xavier del Bac
V.P. Garcés	58	Pimas Gileños	On the Gila river in *articulo mortis* [death throes]	During his trips from 1768 to 1780	
"	5	Nijoras	In gentile country and in the same circumstances	The same period	
"	32	Yumas	On the Colorado river in the country of the Yumas	The same period	
Fr. Juan Bautista Llorens	30	Papagos	Tucson	1795	
"	27	"	"	1795	
"	53	"	San Xavier and San Agustín del Tucson	from 1790 to 1795	
Fr. Esteban Salazar[120] and others up to F. Francisco Yturralde Presidente and present ministro	44	Papagos	Tubutama and its visita Santa Teresa	1768 to 1796	Mission of San Pedro and San Pablo de Tubutama
"	21	Yumas	"	"	

120. Esteban Salazar arrived at the College of Querétaro from the province of Burgos, Spain, in 1749. One of the fourteen original Queretarans to serve in Pimería after the expulsion of the Jesuits, he was first at Ures in 1768, but the following year found him at Tubutama. He was still at Tubutama in 1772. Later that same year he became guardian of the College of Querétaro, a post he held until 1784. He subsequently "became ill and lost his memory to such an extent that he finally remembered nothing at all. He neither spoke nor recognized anyone and did not even know how to eat. He was like the fourth of four suckling children, and even worse off. He lived on this way for five or six years" before dying at Querétaro on August 6, 1797 (Querétaro 1776–1856: Entry No. 217; Roca 1967: 378 n. 96).

[Table of Baptisms 7. San Xavier, San Agustín del Tucson, and Others, 1768–96] (cont.)

Ministers	Souls	Nations	Place of Baptism	Year	Missions
F. Juan de Agorreta[121] and others up to the present F. Florencio Ybáñez[122]	7	Papagos	In Saric	"	Mission of N.S. de los Dolores del Saric
"	4	Yumas	"	"	
"	5	Nijoras	"	"	
"	3	Apaches	"	"	
F. Diego Martín García[123] up to Fr. Pedro Arriquibar	11	7 Nijoras 3 Apaches 1 Papago	In San Ignacio and its visita Santa Magdalena	"	Mission of San Ignacio
V.P.F. Juan Crisóstomo Gil de Bernabé[124]	19	Papagos	San José Tumacácori	May 2, 1768	Mission of San José de Tumacácori

121. Father Juan José Agorreta, who went to Saric in 1768 as the first Franciscan to be stationed there in the wake of the Jesuit expulsion, was still at this station in September 1773. He died at the College of Querétaro on November 22, 1789 (Querétaro 1776–1856: Entry No. 199; Roca 1967: 373 n. 28).

122. Father Florencio Ybáñez (or Ibáñez), who was in charge at Saric from 1783 to 1798 and who constructed the church of fired brick and lime mortar there, was born in Tarragona, Spain, in 1740. In 1770 he arrived at the Franciscan College of San Fernando in Mexico, where he remained until his health failed four years later. From 1774 to 1781 he recuperated at a convent in Michoacán, and from 1781 until 1798 he served in Sonora out of the College of Querétaro. Ybáñez saw some service at Ati before 1790 and at Caborca in 1796. In 1800 he returned to the jurisdiction of the San Fernandoans, and subsequently spent the remainder of his life at Mission San Antonio and Mission Soledad in California. He died at Soledad on November 26, 1818, where he was buried in the church (Moyano 1803; Roca 1967: 374 n. 49).

123. Father Diego Martín García was among the fourteen Franciscans to enter the Pimería in 1768 to replace the expelled Jesuits. He was assigned to San Ignacio, where he remained at least until 1772. He died at the College of Querétaro on February 9, 1789. Roca makes a mistake in confusing Diego Martín García with the San Fernandoan, Diego García who served at Mission Soledad in California beginning in 1791 (Engelhardt 1930: II: 472). He also errs in saying that the present report implies that Diego Martín García was at San Ignacio in 1796. It clearly states in the chart: "F. Diego Martín García up to Fr. Pedro Arriquibar" (Querétaro 1776–1856: Entry No. 196; Roca 1967: 364 n. 67).

124. The first Franciscan to serve at Mission Guevavi after the Jesuit expulsion, Friar Juan Crisóstomo Gil de Barnabé was born in Alfambra, Spain, about 1729. He remained at Guevavi from 1768 to 1772, being forced to leave because of illness. He succeeded Friar Mariano Antonio de Buena y Alcalde as president of the missions and founded a mission among the Seri Indians at Carrizal in November 1772. He was stoned to death there by an Indian on March 7, 1773, and six months later was reburied in the church at Ures. Friar Juan's ministerial zeal was such that Father Barbastro was later to call him a saint (Kessell 1970: 190; McGee 1898: 80–81; Roca 1967: 352 n. 22).

[Table of Baptisms 7. San Xavier, San Agustín del Tucson, and Others, 1768–96]
(cont.)

Ministers	Souls	Nations	Place of Baptism	Year	Missions
F. Gaspar Clemente[125]	8	5 Nijoras 3 Apaches	San José Tumacácori	1771	
"	5	Apaches	"	1773	
"	8	4 Nijoras 3 Apaches 1 Papago	"	1774	
F. Pedro Arriquibar	7	Papagos	"	From 1776 to 1780	
F. Baltazar Carrillo[126]	30	Papagos	"	From 1780 to 1789	The mission of Tumacácori
Fr. Baltazar Carrillo	12	1 Apache, 5 Yumas, 6 Papagos	Tumacácori	From 1790 to 1794	Continues
Fr. Narciso Gutiérrez[127]	4	2 Yumas 2 Papagos	"	1795	
V.P. Friar Juan Díaz and others	278	They are listed in the six preceding tables	In Caborca and its visitas, Pitiqui and Bísanig	From 1768 to 1796	Mission of La Purísima Concepción de Caborca

125. Friar Gaspar de Clemente was minister of Mission Tumacácori in June 1774, during the inspection of Friar Antonio Ramos (Baldonado 1959: 21–23).

126. Friar Baltasar Carillo was born in Titero, Navarra, in 1723. He was in charge at Cucurpe in 1771, and by 1780 he was at Tumacácori, his station until his death and burial there on October 10, 1795. In 1822 his remains were exhumed and reburied on the Gospel side of the altar in the sanctuary of the new church at Tumacácori. Still not to be left at peace, his bones were again dug up and transplanted in February of 1935 to be reburied beneath the floor of the mortuary chapel at Mission San Xavier del Bac (Fontana 1963: 22; Querétaro 1776–1856: Entry No. 212; Roca 1967: 387 n. 57).

127. Narciso Gutiérrez was born in Calahorra, Rioja, Spain, about 1765. "He took the habit in the Convent of San Julian de Agueda, the Recollect House of the Holy Province of Burgos. He departed from Santo Domingo de la Calzada for this College [Querétaro] in the month of July in the year 1789 and arrived on the 23rd of March in the following year. He stayed in the College doing missionary work among the faithful and the infidels. He died at the age of 55 years and was buried in the same mission [Tumacácori]" (Querétaro 1776–1856: Entry No. 275). Gutiérrez's service at Tumacácori began in 1794 and lasted there until his death in mid-December 1820. He also had a brief stint of service at Tubutama from 1796 through 1797. Like Father Carrillo's remains, this priest's body was removed to San Xavier del Bac more than a century later (Fontana 1963: 22; Roca 1967: 379 n. 105).

Lexicon of
Spanish Words

alcalde. Governor of a town or justice of the peace, often with civil, police, and judicial authority. *Alcaldes* were judges for minor crimes as well as councillors on municipal councils. Indian *alcaldes* usually had only civil jurisdiction, their criminal jurisdiction being limited.

alcalde mayor. Municipal judge with ordinary jurisdiction. Also the presiding officer of an *audiencia* (defined below).

alférez. Ensign. Also a chief or second in command.

alférez comandante. The ensign in command; an ensign is a standard-bearer.

armero. Armorer; gunsmith; keeper of arms or armor.

á salvo. Safe, secure.

asesor. Legal counsel, judge, consultant to a judge.

audiencia. Advisory or judicial body assisting the viceroy. *Audiencias* existed at various levels of government, from the viceroyalty on down.

cabo. Corporal.

capellán. Chaplain or priest.

capitán. Military captain; commander of a company.

capitán de la nación. Indian official equivalent to the rank of captain; a native captain.

carabinero or *caravinero.* Soldier armed with a carbine.

cédula real. A law or measure passed through the Council of the Indies, and with the authority of the king.

chamiza or *chamizo.* Fourwing saltbush, *Atriplex polycarpa.*

comandancia. The office, province or district of a commander; also the office of a comandante general (defined below).

comandante and *comandante militar.* Military commander.

comandancia general. Office of the comandante general.

comandante general. Official in charge of the office of the comandancia general.

comandante oficial. Official or military officer in charge.

comisario. Commissary; person commissioned to carry out an order; inspector.

compañero. Companion.

conversión. An Indian mission in a primitive state. See also *misión, reducción, doctrina.*

conversor. Priest in charge of a *conversión.*

corporales. Cabos or corporals (military).

cura. Priest in charge of a *curato;* pastor.

curato. Type of parish presided over by a *cura.* A *curato* is a full-fledged parish made up of Catholics, i.e., neither pagans nor new Christians.

custodia. A Franciscan ecclesiastical subdivision in mission territory. An incipient province or *provincia;* a "custody."

custodio. Ecclesiastical official in charge of a *custodia.*

discretos. Persons elected as assistants in the councils of some religious houses.

doctrina. A pueblo of Indians not yet advanced to the status of a parish. The missionary charged with the spiritual care of the Indians in a reduction was called a *doctrinero,* since his principal duty, besides the administration of the sacraments, consisted in teaching the Christian doctrine; the reductions were thus also called *doctrinas.*

doctrinero. Pastor of a *doctrina,* defined above.

encomendero. See below.

encomienda. A system of tributary labor established in Spanish America. It was developed as a means of securing an adequate and cheap labor supply. It required Indians to pay tribute from their lands which were "granted" (from the Spanish verb *encomendar*) them. This often included personal services as well. In return the *encomendero* (holder of the grant) was obliged to protect his wards (*encomendados*), teach them the Catholic Faith, and defend their right to use the land for their own subsistence.

entrada. Entrance; journey of exploration.

establecimientos de paz. This term refers to settlements near presidios in which Spaniards hoped the Apaches could be persuaded to live and keep the peace due to the food and other benefits they would receive.

expediente. A file.

fanega. A measure of grain and seed of about a hundredweight, or an English bushel: sometimes called faneague in English.

gamuza. Antelope.

gente de razón. All classes of society in which there was an admixture of white blood.

guardián. The superior of a Franciscan convent.

hacienda de campo. Country estate; *finca rural.*

hacienda real. Department of public finance. *Real Hacienda* meant more than treasury or exchequer; it included all the royal possessions.

hediondilla. Probably the creosote bush *Larrea tridentata.* It was called "Hediondilla" in the Piman area. Farther south it was called "Gobernadora."

hijo del país. A person born in the New World.

indios reducidos. Converted Indians; Indians forming a *reducción, doctrina,* or *conversión.*

jefe. Chief, superior, or boss.

juez político. Civil judge.

juez superior. A higher judge in charge of a particular affair.

justicias. Magistrates or tribunals of various ranks.

legua. League. A term of variable meaning at the time of Bringas. Approximately 4,180 meters, or 2.6 miles.

leyes de partida. Also referred to as the *Siete Partidas,* the laws of Castile. The first codification of Spanish law, which occurred under King Alphonso the Tenth (A.D. 1252–84), it was subject to revision at various times.

lugar. Place; a village or very small town.

manzanilla. A shrub common to the area. The term is applied to several different plants.

mayordomo. Major-domo, superintendent, steward.

mineral. A mine containing metals, minerals, or precious stones. Also a *real de minas,* or mining settlement.

ministro. Ministro de Dios, or priest.

misión. See also *conversión, doctrina, reducción.* Most literally "a sending." The term had two meanings in Bringas' time: (a) travel undertaken by priests and other religious persons to propagate religion and (b) the area in which activities for the conversion of natives were undertaken. The individual who performed the *misión* was a missionary, or *misionero.* Modern usage in the American Southwest applies the term to the actual church building in such an area.

misionero. The priest or religious in charge of a mission.

morizcos or *moriscos*. Moors who remained as Catholics in Spain at the time of the Restoration. In Mexico this term also refers to the descendants of mulatto and European parents.

Nixoras, or *Nijoras*. Indian captives sold to Spaniards by friendly Indians. This term is elucidated further in note 111.

órdenes reales. See *reales órdenes*.

padrinos. Godparents or protectors.

partida, leyes de. See *leyes de partida*.

patronato. Literally, patronage; in the context of this work it refers to prerogatives over the churches of America conferred on the Catholic kings of Spain by the pope. These prerogatives chiefly had to do with the conferring of a benefice and the appointment of bishops and other prelates.

patronato personale. A Latin term designating a right belonging to a person who is in possession for the time being of an office or status position with which a patronage is connected, for example, the office of the king of Spain.

patronato real. A Latin term designating a right belonging to a person as such, i.e. the right ceases only with the death of the person.

personale. A Latin term meaning "personal" as distinguished legally from *reale* or "real," for example, the distinction between "personal" and "real" property. See also *patronato personale* above.

peso. A silver coin generally weighing twenty-five grams. The term *peso de oro* is used in the Americas and has the approximate value of two silver pesos.

presidente. The *presidente* of the missions was the priest-missionary having supervision of all the missions in a given area.

procurador síndico. Literally, syndic procurator; attorney in charge of town management. In the Franciscan Order, an individual designated to hold property and transact business for the friars.

provincias internas. Interior Provinces. The *provincias internas* were reorganized into a new *comandancia general* (defined earlier) under José de Gálvez, visitor-general of New Spain from 1765 to 1771.

pueblo. Town, village, nation, people.

pueblo de visita. A chapel or locality attached to a main mission or church and attended to by the mission clergy, who come to "visit" it.

ranchería. A settlement, usually of Indians. Originally applied by the Spaniards in New Spain to the place where food was distributed to laborers or soldiers.

real. A monetary unit. Eight *reales* = one *peso* (defined earlier). Also a mining camp.

real de los álamos. The Alamos mining camp, which became the modern-day Alamos in Sonora.

real de minas. In New Spain, a mining camp having silver mines in the vicinity.

reales órdenes. Royal orders. Measures adopted by the king without the intervention of the Council of the Indies.

recopiladas. Codified laws. Also used for the *Recopilación de Indias* or the codified laws of the Indies (defined below).

Recopilación de Indias. The Laws of the Indies. In 1542 a Royal Junta of ecclesiastical and juridical experts drafted regulations for the better government of the provinces of the Indies. These received the royal approval and, after being somewhat enlarged upon, were published in Madrid in 1543 under the name of "The New Laws." These "New Laws," together with other legislation for the Indies, were codified in the year 1680 under the title of *Recopilación de Indias* by the Council of the Indies.

reducción. An area into which Indians were collected for intensive missionary effort. See also *conversión, doctrina, misión*.

regidores. Members of a town council.

salvaguardia. Safeguard, security, protection, bodyguard. Used in the expression "to place men *á salvo,*" i.e., to place them in safety.

sargento. In modern times, as in the American army, a non-commissioned officer ranking above a corporal. Formerly, one of the chief judges in a province; also in the old military organization a high-ranking officer close to the field marshal.

sargento mayor. The highest governing military official in a province, for example, a captain general may also be a *sargento mayor.*

síndico. City attorney. Also a layman who received the alms and disbursed them for the needs of the Franciscan friars.

soldados del país. Literally, soldiers of the country, i.e., soldiers of Spanish descent.

tambor. Drum, drummer.

teniente. Military rank directly below that of captain.

teniente comandante. Second in command.

teniente coronel. Lieutenant colonel, i.e., the military rank immediately below that of colonel.

tesorero. Treasurer.

vara. A linear measure of approximately eighty-four centimeters (ca. 2.75 feet).

vendidos. Those who were sold; in this case probably Indians of various tribes redeemed by the missionary from the Apaches. This term is further elucidated in note 118.

villa. A village; a place smaller than a *pueblo* (town) and larger than an *aldea* (hamlet).

villa de Sinaloa. The town of Sinaloa; i.e. Culiacán.

visita. A sub-station of a mission or church. Also the inspection of a *visitador* (defined below) sent to America to examine the enforcement of particular rules, regulations, or laws.

visitador. Visitor or inspector. Also an official of the Franciscan Order with equivalent inspection and correction duties.

REFERENCES

Ahlborn, Richard E.
  1974 *The sculpted saints of a borderland mission: los bultos de San Xavier del Bac, with notes on the statues of Tumacacori.* Tucson, Southwestern Mission Research Center, Inc.

Almada, Francisco R.
  1952 *Diccionario de historia, geografía y biografía sonorenses.* Chihuahua.

Arricivita, Juan D.
  1792 *Crónica seráfica y apostolica del colegio de propaganda fide de Santa Cruz de Querétaro en la Nueva España.* Mexico City, Don Felipe de Zúñiga y Ontiveros.

Austin, Mary
  1924 *The land of journey's ending.* New York and London, The Century Company.

Bahr, Donald M.
  1973 "The Pima-Papago: social organization." Unpublished manuscript, copy on file with its author at the Department of Anthropology, Arizona State University, Tempe, Arizona.

Bahr, Donald M.; Juan Gregorio; David I. Lopez; and Albert Alvarez
  1974 *Piman shamanism and staying sickness (ká:cim múmkidag).* Tucson, The University of Arizona Press.

Bailey, Lynn R.
  1966 *Indian slave trade in the Southwest.* Los Angeles, Westernlore Press.

Baldonado, Luis
  1959 Missions San Jose de Tumacacori and San Xavier del Bac in 1774. *The Kiva,* Vol. 24, no. 4 (April), pp. 21-24. Tucson, Arizona Archaeological and Historical Society.

Bancroft, Hubert H.
  1883a History of Mexico. Vol. 2. 1521–1600. *The Works of Hubert Howe Bancroft,* Vol. 10. San Francisco, A.L. Bancroft & Company.

  1883b History of Mexico. Vol. 3. 1600–1803. *The Works of Hubert Howe Bancroft,* Vol. 11. San Francisco, A.L. Bancroft & Company.

  1884a History of California. Vol. 1. 1542–1800. *The Works of Hubert Howe Bancroft,* Vol. 18. San Francisco, A.L. Bancroft & Company.

  1884b History of the North Mexican States and Texas. Vol. 1. 1531–1800. *The Works of Hubert Howe Bancroft,* Vol. 15. San Francisco, A.L. Bancroft & Company.

Beaver, R. Pierce
  1966 *Church, state, and the American Indians.* St. Louis, Concordia Publishing House.

Berlandier, Jean L.
  1969 *The Indians of Texas in 1830.* Edited by John C. Ewers; translated by Patricia R. Leclercq. Washington, Smithsonian Institution Press.

Bernstein, Marvin D.
  1963 Latin America. *Encyclopaedia Britannica,* Vol. 13, pp. 743-744J. Chicago (etc.), Encyclopaedia Britannica, Inc.

Bihl, Michael
n.d.   "Historical compendium of the Order of Friars Minor." Mimeographed; 16 pps.
         Copy in the Oblasser Memorial Library, Mission San Xavier del Bac, Tucson,
         Arizona.
Bolton, Herbert E., *translator and editor*
1914   *Athanase de Mézières and the Louisiana-Texas frontier, 1768–1780.* Two vol-
         umes. Cleveland, The Arthur H. Clark Company.
1930   Correspondence. *Anza's California Expeditions,* Vol. 5. Berkeley, University of
         California Press.
Bolton, Herbert E.
1960a   *The mission as a frontier institution in the Spanish-American colonies.* El Paso,
         Academic Reprints, Inc.
1960b   *Rim of Christendom.* New York, Russell & Russell.
Bonfíl Batalla, Guillermo
1972   The Indian and the colonial situation: the context of indigenist policy in Latin
         America. In *The situation of the Indian in South America,* edited by W. Dostal,
         pp. 21-28. Geneva, World Council of Churches.
Boudinhon, A.
1912   Secular clergy. *The Catholic Encyclopedia,* Vol. 13, pp. 675-76. New York, The
         Gilmary Society.
Brinckerhoff, Sidney B., and Odie B. Faulk
1965   *Lancers for the king.* Phoenix, Arizona Historical Foundation.
Bringas, Diego Miguel de
1960   *Crónica apostólica y seráfica del Colegio de Propaganda Fide de la Sta. Cruz de
         Querétaro.* Tercera parte. Querétaro, Ediciones Cimatario.
Carlisle, Charles R., and Bernard L. Fontana, *translators and editors*
1969   Sonora in 1773. Reports by five Jaliscan friars. *Arizona and the West,* Vol. 11,
         no. 1 (Spring), pp. 39-58; no. 2 (Summer), pp. 179-190. Tucson, The Univer-
         sity of Arizona Press.
Castañeda, Carlos E.
1942   The mission era: the end of the Spanish regime, 1780–1810. *Our Catholic Heri-
         tage in Texas, 1519–1936,* Vol. 5. Austin, Von Boeckmann-Jones Company.
Chapman, Charles E.
1918   *A history of Spain.* New York, The Macmillan Company.
Culin, Stewart
1907   Games of the North American Indians. *Annual Report of the Bureau of Ameri-
         can Ethnology,* Vol. 24, pp. 1-826. Washington, Government Printing Office.
Díaz, Juan
1930a   Diary kept by Father Fray Díaz . . . during the journey which he is making in
         company with the Reverend Father Fray Francisco Garcés . . . In *Anza's Cali-
         fornia Expeditions,* translated and edited by Herbert E. Bolton, Vol. 2, pp. 245-
         290. Berkeley, University of California Press.
1930b   Diary kept by Father Fray Juan Días . . . during the journey which he made
         from the mission of San Gabriel, in northern California, to the presidio of San
         Ygnacio de Tubac . . . In *Anza's California Expeditions,* translated and edited
         by Herbert E. Bolton, Vol. 2, pp. 291-306. Berkeley, University of California
         Press.
DiPeso, Charles C.
1956   The Upper Pima of San Cayetano del Tumacacori. *The Amerind Foundation,
         Inc.,* no. 7. Dragoon, Arizona.
Dobyns, Henry F.
1959   "Tubac through four centuries. An historical resume and analysis." Three
         volumes. Ms., copy on file in the Arizona State Museum Library, The University
         of Arizona, Tucson.
1964   *Lance, ho! Containment of the Western Apaches by the royal Spanish garrison
         at Tucson.* Lima [Peru], Editorial Estudios Andinos.
1972   Military transculturation of northern Piman Indians. *Ethnohistory,* Vol. 19, no. 4
         (Fall), pp. 323-343. Tucson, American Society for Ethnohistory.

Dobyns, Henry F., and Paul H. Ezell
    1959   Sonoran missionaries in 1790. *New Mexico Historical Review,* Vol. 34, no. 1 (January), pp. 52-54. Albuquerque, Historical Society of New Mexico and the University of New Mexico.

Dobyns, Henry F.; Paul H. Ezell; and Greta S. Ezell
    1963   Death of a society. *Ethnohistory,* Vol. 10, no. 2 (Spring), pp. 105-161. Bloomington, American Indian Ethnohistoric Conference.

Dobyns, Henry F.; Paul H. Ezell; Alden W. Jones; and Greta S. Ezell
    1960   What were Nixoras? *Southwestern Journal of Anthropology,* Vol. 16, no. 2 (Summer), pp. 230-258. Albuquerque, University of New Mexico.

Domínguez, Francisco A.
    1956   *The missions of New Mexico, 1776.* Translated and annotated by Eleanor B. Adams and Angélico Chávez. Albuquerque, The University of New Mexico Press.

Eckhart, George B.
    1960   The Seri Indian missions. *The Kiva,* Vol. 25, no. 3 (February), pp. 37-43. Tucson, Arizona Archaeological and Historical Society.

Engelhardt, Zephyrin
    1930   *The missions and missionaries of California.* Second edition, revised. Two volumes. Santa Barbara, California, Mission Santa Barbara.

Espinosa, Isidro Félix de
    1964   Crónica de los colegios de propaganda fide de la Nueva España. New edition, with notes and introduction by Lino Gómez Canedo. *Publications of the Academy of American Franciscan History, Franciscan Historical Classics,* Vol. 2. Washington, D.C.

Ewing, Russell C.
    1966   Major historical themes. In *Six Faces of Mexico,* edited by Russell C. Ewing, pp. 1-63. Tucson, The University of Arizona Press.

Ezell, Paul H.
    1956   Fray Diego Bringas, a forgotten cartographer of Sonora. *Imago Mundi,* Vol. 13, pp. 150-158. The Hague, Mouton & Co.

    1958   An early geographer of the Southwest: Father Diego Bringas. *El Museo,* new series, Vol. 2, no. 2 (May), pp. 18-30. San Diego, California, Museum of Man.

    1961   The hispanic acculturation of the Gila River Pimas. *Memoirs of the American Anthropological Association,* no. 90. Menasha, Wisconsin, American Anthropological Association.

    1963   The Maricopas. An identification from documentary sources. *Anthropological Papers of the University of Arizona,* no. 6. Tucson, The University of Arizona Press.

Farriss, N. M.
    1968   Crown and clergy in colonial Mexico, 1759–1821. *University of London Historical Studies,* Vol. 21. London, The Athlone Press.

Fewkes, Jesse W.
    1912   Casa Grande, Arizona. *Annual Report of the Bureau of American Ethnology,* Vol. 28, pp. 25-180. Washington, Government Printing Office.

Fisher, Lillian E.
    1926   Viceregal administration in the Spanish-American colonies. *University of California Publications in History,* Vol. 15. Berkeley, University of California Press.

    1929   *The intendant system in Spanish America.* Berkeley, University of California Press.

Font, Pedro
    1776   [Letter to Father Diego Ximenez, Father Guardian of the College of Santa Cruz, written from Imuris on November 30.] Ms., Civezza Collection 201/79; Film 305, The University of Arizona Library, Tucson.

    1930   Diary of an expedition to Monterey by way of the Colorado river, 1775–1776. *Anza's California Expeditions,* Vol. 4, translated and edited by Herbert E. Bolton. Berkeley, University of California Press.

Fontana, Bernard L.

1963 Biography of a desert church: the story of Mission San Xavier del Bac. Revised edition. *The Smoke Signal,* no. 3. Tucson, The Westerners.

1974 Man in arid lands: the Piman Indians of the Sonoran desert. In *Desert Biology,* Vol. 2, edited by George W. Brown, Jr., pp. 489-528. New York, Academic Press.

Forbes, Jack D.

1960 *Apache, Navaho, and Spaniard.* Norman, University of Oklahoma Press.

1965 *Warriors of the Colorado; the Yumans of the Quechan nation and their neighbors.* Norman, University of Oklahoma Press.

Forde, Cyril D.

1931 Ethnography of the Yuma Indians. *University of California Publications in American Archaeology and Ethnology,* Vol. 28, no. 4, pp. 83-278. Berkeley, University of California Press; London, Cambridge University Press.

Franco, José L., *compiler*

1961 *Documentos para la historia de Mexico existenes en el archivo nacional de Cuba.* La Habana, Impreso en los Talleres del Archivo Nacional de Cuba.

French, Rachel

1962 Alamos — Sonora's city of silver. *The Smoke Signal,* no. 5 (Spring). Tucson, The Westerners.

Gálvez, Bernardo de

1951 Instructions for governing the Interior Provinces of New Spain, 1786. Translated and edited by Donald E. Worcester. *Quivira Society Publications,* Vol. 12. Berkeley.

Garcés, Francisco

1776 [Letter to Father Diego Ximenez, Father Guardian of the College of Santa Cruz, written from San Ignacio, December 25.] Ms., Civezza Collection 201/18; Film 305, The University of Arizona Library, Tucson.

1777 [Letter to Father Diego Ximenez, Father Guardian of the College of Santa Cruz, written from San Ignacio (?), mid-1777.] Ms., Civezza Collection 201/19; Film 305, The University of Arizona Library, Tucson.

1778 [Letter to Father Diego Ximenez, Father Guardian of the College of Santa Cruz, written from Tucson, February 19.] Ms., Civezza Collection 201/20; Film 305, The University of Arizona Library, Tucson.

1900 *On the trail of a Spanish pioneer; the diary and itinerary of Francisco Garcés (missionary priest).* Two volumes. Translated and edited by Elliott Coues. New York, Francis P. Harper.

1930a Diary of the expedition which is being made by order of his excellency the viceroy, don Antonio Maria Bucareli y Ursua . . . to open a road by way of the Gila and Colorado rivers to the new establishments of San Diego and Monte Rey, under command of Captain don Juan Baptista de Ansa. In *Anza's California Expeditions,* translated and edited by Herbert E. Bolton, Vol. 2, pp. 307-360. Berkeley, University of California Press.

1930b Garces's brief account. In *Anza's California Expeditions,* translated and edited by Herbert E. Bolton, Vol. 2, pp. 361-372. Berkeley, University of California Press.

1930c Garces's diary of his detour to the Jalchedunes. In *Anza's California Expeditions,* translated and edited by Herbert E. Bolton, Vol. 2, pp. 373-392. Berkeley, University of California Press.

1965 *A record of travels in Arizona and California, 1775–1776.* Translated and edited by John Galvin. San Francisco, John Howell-Books.

Geary, Gerald J.

1934 The secularization of the California missions (1810–1846). *The Catholic University of America Studies in American Church History,* Vol. 17. Washington, D.C.

Geiger, Maynard J.
1959   The life and times of Junípero Serra. Two volumes. *Publications of the Academy of American Franciscan History, Monograph Series,* Vol. 5. Washington.

Gifford, Edward W.
1932   The southeastern Yavapai. *University of California Publications in American Archaeology and Ethnology,* Vol. 29, no. 3, pp. 177-252. Berkeley, University of California Press; London, Cambridge University Press.

1933   The Cocopa. *University of California Publications in American Archaeology and Ethnology,* Vol. 31, no. 5, pp. 257-334. Berkeley, University of California Press; London, Cambridge University Press.

1936   Northeastern and western Yavapai. *University of California Publications in American Archaeology and Ethnology,* Vol. 34, no. 4, pp. 247-354. Berkeley, University of California Press; London, Cambridge University Press.

Gómez Canedo, Lino, *editor*
1971   Sonora hacia fines del siglo XVIII. Un informe del misionero franciscano Fray Francisco Antonio Barbastro, con otros documentos complementarios. *Documentación Historica Mexicana,* no. 3. Guadalajara, Librería Font, S.A.

Gómez Hoyos, Rafael
1961   *La iglesia de América en las Leyes de Indias.* Madrid, Instituto Gonzalo Fernández de Oviedo y Instituto Colombiano de Cultura Hispánica de Bogotá.

Goodwin, Grenville
1969   *The social organization of the Western Apache.* Tucson, The University of Arizona Press.

Hammond, George P.
1931   Zúñiga journal, Tucson to Santa Fe. The opening of a Spanish trade route, 1788–1795. *New Mexico Historical Review,* Vol. 6, no. 1 (January), pp. 40-65. Albuquerque, The Historical Society of New Mexico and the University of New Mexico.

Hammond, George P., and Agapito Rey, *translators and editors*
1953   Don Juan de Oñate, colonizer of New Mexico, 1595–1628. *Coronado Cuarto Centennial Publications,* 1540–1940. Vol. 5. Albuquerque, University of New Mexico Press.

Hargrave, Catherine P.
1966   *A history of playing cards.* New York, Dover Publications, Inc.

Huonder, A.
1911   Reductions of Paraguay. *The Catholic Encyclopedia,* Vol. 12, pp. 688-700. New York, The Gilmary Society.

Ives, Ronald L.
1955   Mission San Marcello del Sonoydag. *The Records of the American Catholic Historical Society,* Vol. 66, no. 4, pp. 201-226. Philadelphia.

1957   Enrique Ruhen, S.J. — Borderland martyr. *The Kiva,* Vol. 23, no. 1 (October), pp. 1-10. Tucson, Arizona Archaeological and Historical Society.

1966   Retracing the route of the Fages expedition of 1781. *Arizona and the West,* Vol. 8, no. 1 (Spring), pp. 49-70; no. 2 (Summer), pp. 157-170. Tucson, The University of Arizona Press.

Jackson, Earl
1951   Tumacacori's yesterdays. *Southwestern Monuments Association Popular Series,* no. 6. Santa Fe.

Kelly, Marsha C.
1972   The society that did not die. *Ethnohistory,* Vol. 19, no. 3 (Summer), pp. 261-265. Tucson, American Society for Ethnohistory.

Kessell, John L.
1965   Father Eixarch and the visitation at Tumacácori, May 12, 1775. *The Kiva,* Vol. 30, no. 3 (February), pp. 77-81. Tucson, Arizona Archaeological and Historical Society.

1969   Father Ramon and the big debt, Tumacácori, 1821–1823. *New Mexico His-iorical Review,* Vol. 44, no. 1 (January), pp. 53-72. Albuquerque, University of New Mexico Press.

1970   *Mission of sorrows; Jesuit Guevavi and the Pimas, 1691–1767.* Tucson, The University of Arizona Press.

1976   *Friars, soldiers, and reformers: Hispanic Arizona and the Sonora mission frontier, 1767–1856.* Tucson, The University of Arizona Press.

Loomis, Noel M.
1969   Commandants-general of the Interior Provinces, a preliminary list. *Arizona and the West,* Vol. 11, no. 3 (Autumn), pp. 261-268. Tucson, The University of Arizona Press.

Lynch, John
1958   Spanish colonial administration, 1782–1810: the intendant system in the vice-royalty of the Río de la Plata. *University of London Historical Studies,* Vol. 5. London, The Athlone Press.

Mathiot, Madeleine
1973   A dictionary of Papago usage. Vol. 1. B - K. *Language Science Monographs,* Vol. 8, no. 1. Bloomington, Indiana University.

McCarty, Kieran
1962   Apostolic colleges of the propagation of the faith — old and new world back-ground. *The Americas,* Vol. 19, no. 1 (July), pp. 50-58. Washington, D.C., Academy of American Franciscan History.

1973   "Franciscan beginnings on the Arizona-Sonora desert, 1767–1770." Unpublished Ph.D. dissertation, The Catholic University of America, Washington, D.C.

1975   The Colorado massacre of 1781: María Montielo's report. *The Journal of Arizona History,* Vol. 16, no. 3 (Autumn), pp. 221-225. Tucson, Arizona Historical Society.

McCarty, Kieran, *translator*
n.d.   "Reyes report of 1772. A report on the existing conditions in the missions of Sonora administered by the fathers of the Propagation of the Faith College of the Holy Cross in Querétaro, Mexico, by Antonio María de los Reyes, O.F.M." xx + 48 pp., unpublished manuscript, copy on file in the Oblasser Memorial Library, Mission San Xavier del Bac, Tucson, Arizona.

McCloskey, Michael B.
1955   *The formative years of the missionary college of Santa Cruz of Querétaro, 1683–1733.* Washington, D.C., Academy of American Franciscan History.

McGee, William J.
1898   The Seri Indians. *Annual Report of the Bureau of American Ethnology,* Vol. 17, pp. 1-344. Washington, Government Printing Office.

Matson, Daniel S., and Albert H. Schroeder, *editors*
1957   Cordero's description of the Apache. *New Mexico Historical Review,* Vol. 32, no. 4 (October), pp. 335-356. Albuquerque, Historical Society of New Mexico and the University of New Mexico.

Medina, Roque de
1779   "Revista del real presidio de Tucson, May 3, 1779." Unpublished manuscript in the Archivo General de Indias, Sevilla, Spain, Audiencia Guadalajara 271.

Moorhead, Max L.
1968   *The Apache frontier: Jacobo Ugarte and Spanish-Indian relations in northern New Spain, 1769–1791.* Norman, University of Oklahoma Press.

Morfi, Juan A.
1935   History of Texas, 1673–1779. Translated, with biographical introduction and annotations, by Carlos E. Castañeda. *Quivira Society Publications,* Vol. 6, part 1. Albuquerque.

1967   Diario y derrotero, 1777–1781. *Publicaciones del Instituto Tecnológico y de Estudios Superiores de Monterrey,* no. 5. Monterrey.

Moyano, Francisco
1801 [Letter to the Bishop, written from Oquitoa on April 5.] Ms., Archivo del Gobierno de la Mitra de Sonora, Hermosillo, Legajo de 1801–1802. Film no. 422, roll 24, L1, University of Arizona Library, Tucson.

1803 "Report of the missions which the Religious of the College of Santa Cruz of Querétaro administer in said province, their growth to the year of 1802, the number of missionaries serving them, the income which they enjoy, and the total number of souls by castes and sexes." Unpublished translation by William W. Wasley, copy on file in the Arizona State Museum Library, the University of Arizona, Tucson. The original document in Spanish is in the Archivo General de Indias, Sevilla, Spain, Audiencia de México, Legajo 2736.

Navarro García, Luis
1959 *Intendencias en Indias.* Sevilla.

1964 Don José de Gálvez y la comandancia general de las Provincias Internas del Norte de Nueva España. *Publicaciones de la Escuela de Estudios Hispano-Americanos de Sevilla,* 2nd series, whole no. 148. Sevilla.

Ocaranza, Fernando
1933 *Los franciscanos en las Provincias Internas de Sonora y Ostimuri.* México.

Opler, Morris E.
1946 Childhood and youth in Jicarilla Apache society. *Publications of the Frederick Webb Hodge Anniversary Publication Fund,* Vol. 5. Los Angeles, Southwest Museum.

1965 *An Apache life-way.* New York, Cooper Square Publishers, Inc.

Parry, John H.
1963 Indies, laws of the. *Encyclopaedia Britannica,* Vol. 12, pp. 255-56. Chicago [etc.], Encyclopaedia Britannica, Inc.

Polzer, Charles W.
1972 "The evolution of the Jesuit mission system in northwestern New Spain, 1600–1767." Unpublished Ph.D. dissertation, Department of History, The University of Arizona, Tucson.

Porras Muñoz, Guillermo
1966 *Iglesia y estado en Nueva Vizcaya (1562–1821).* Pamplona, Universidad de Navarra.

Pradeau, Alberto F.
1959 La expulsión de los Jesuitas de las provincias de Sonora, Ostimuri, y Sinaloa en 1767. *Biblioteca Histórica Mexicana de Obras Inéditas,* no. 24. Mexico City, Antigua Librería Robredo de José Porrúa e Hijos.

Priestly, Herbert I., *translator*
1913 The Colorado River campaign, 1781–1782: diary of Pedro Fages. *Publications of the Academy of Pacific Coast History,* Vol. 3 (May), pp. 135-233. Berkeley.

Priestly, Herbert I.
1916 José de Gálvez, visitor-general of New Spain (1765–1771). *University of California Publications in History,* Vol. 5. Berkeley, University of California Press.

Querétaro, Colegio de Santa Cruz de
1776– "Libro de partidas de los hijos difuntos de este colegio de la Santa Cruz desde
1852 el dia 25 de julio de 1776 [hasta el dia 8 de junio 1852]." ACQ [Acta Colegii Queretarensis], Libro de Muertos, II. [Microfilm copy on file in the Oblasser Memorial Library, Mission San Xavier del Bac, Tucson, Arizona.]

Rivera, Juan Francisco
1795 Lista de los religiosos sacerdotes que existen en el colegio; Rivera, CSCQ, Sept. 22. Archivo General de Indias, Guad 2737. Seville.

Roca, Paul M.
1967 *Paths of the padres through Sonora.* Tucson, Arizona Pioneers' Historical Society.

Russell, Frank
1908 The Pima Indians. *Annual Report of the Bureau of American Ethnology,* Vol. 26, pp. 3-389. Washington, United States Government Printing Office.

Sägmüller, Johannes B.
    1939   Patron and patronage. *The Catholic Encyclopedia,* Vol. 11, pp. 560-62. New York, The Gilmary Society.

Scholes, France V.
    1937   Church and state in New Mexico, 1610–1650. *Historical Society of New Mexico Publications in History,* Vol. 7 (June). Albuquerque, University of New Mexico Press.

Segesser, Philipp
    1945   The relation of Philipp Segesser. Translated and edited by Theodore Treutlein. *Mid-America,* Vol. 27, no. 3 (July), pp. 139-187; no. 4 (October), pp. 257-260. Chicago, Loyola University.

Simmons, Marc
    1968   *Spanish government in New Mexico.* Albuquerque, The University of New Mexico Press.

Simpson, Leslie B.
    1950   *The encomienda in New Spain.* Berkeley and Los Angeles, University of California Press.

Sonnichsen, Charles L.
    1958   *The Mescalero Apaches.* Norman, University of Oklahoma Press.

Spicer, Edward H.
    1962   *Cycles of conquest.* Tucson, The University of Arizona Press.

Spier, Leslie
    1933   *Yuman tribes of the Gila river.* Chicago, The University of Chicago Press.

Stagg, Albert L.
    1974   The making of a bishop. *The Journal of Arizona History,* Vol. 15, no. 1 (Spring), pp. 61-72. Tucson, Arizona Historical Society.

Stoner, Victor R., and Henry F. Dobyns
    1959   Fray Pedro Antonio de Arriquibar, chaplain of the royal fort at Tucson. *Arizona and the West,* Vol. 1, no. 1 (Spring), pp. 71-79. Tucson, The University of Arizona Press.

Tejas Galleries
    1974   *Rare maps catalogue 13.* Austin, Texas, Tejas Galleries.

Thomas, Alfred B.
    1941   *Teodoro de Croix and the northern frontier of New Spain, 1776–1783.* Norman, University of Oklahoma Press.

Tibesar, Antonine S.
    1957   The Franciscan *doctrinero* versus the Franciscan *misionero* in seventeenth-century Peru. *The Americas,* Vol. 14, no. 2 (October), pp. 115-124. Washington, D.C., Academy of American Franciscan History.

Toro y Gisbert, Miguel de
    1948   *Pequeño Larousse ilustrado; nuevo diccionario enciclopédico.* Paris, Librería Larousse.

Torres Lanzas, Pedro
    1900   *Relación descriptivo de los mapas, planos, etc., de México y Floridas existentes en el archivo general de Indias.* Two volumes. Sevilla, El Mercantil.

Twitchell, Ralph E.
    1914   *The Spanish archives of New Mexico.* Two volumes. Cedar Rapids, The Torch Press.

Underhill, Ruth M.
    n.d.   "Papago economics." Unpublished manuscript, copy on file in the Arizona State Museum Library, The University of Arizona, Tucson.

    1939   Social organization of the Papago Indians. *Columbia University Contributions to Anthropology,* Vol. 30. New York, Columbia University.

    1946   Papago Indian religion. *Columbia University Contributions to Anthropology,* Vol. 33. New York.

    1968   *Singing for power.* Berkeley and Los Angeles, University of California Press.

Warman, Arturo
1972   *La danza de moros y cristianos.* México, Secretaría de Educación Pública.

Wayland, Virginia
1961   Apache playing cards. *Southwest Museum Leaflets,* no. 28. Los Angeles, Southwest Museum.

Whiting, Alfred F.
1953   The Tumacacori census of 1796. *The Kiva,* Vol. 19, no. 1 (Fall), pp. 1-12. Tucson, Arizona Archaeological and Historical Society.

Wilhelm, J.
1908   Councils, general. *Catholic Encyclopedia,* Vol. 4, pp. 423-435. New York, The Gilmary Society.

Wilson, H. Clyde
1964   Jicarilla Apache political and economic structures. *University of California Publications in American Archaeology and Ethnology,* Vol. 48, no. 4, pp. 297-360. Berkeley, University of California Press.

Yturralde, Francisco
1795   [Letter to Fray Diego Bringas, written from Tubutama, December 12.] Ms., Civezza Collection 203/2; Film 305, The University of Arizona Library, Tucson.

1798   "Visita de las misiones de la Pimería por el P. Yturralde, Presid.te. Tubutama." Franciscan archives, Rome. Unpublished, a copy of the original is on file with Bernard Fontana, Arizona State Museum, The University of Arizona, Tucson.

INDEX

Acapulco, Mexico: 84 n. 70
Aconchi, Sonora: 4, 18, 70, 70 n. 46, 129
Aculco, Hidalgo, Mexico: 2
Agorreta, Fr. Juan José: 18; baptized Indians
  at Saric, 149; biographical sketch, 149 n. 121
Agueda, Convent of San Julian de, Spain:
  150 n. 127
Ak Chin: *see* Aquituni, Sonora (Papago
  ranchería)
Alamos, Sonora: 2, 42, 43, 45, 45 n. 15
Alcantara, Saint Peter of: 60 n. 30
Alcantarines: 60 n. 30
Alejandro (Apache captain): 121
Alfambra, Spain: 149 n. 124
Almarza, Spain: 108 n. 90
Alta California: 4, 8, 9, 20, 21, 25, 49 n. 19,
  52 n. 21, 94, 112, 114, 124 n. 104, 132;
  Anza expedition to, in 1774, 84 n. 69, 85 n.
  72, 140 n. 113; Custodia de San Gabriel,
  38 n. 2; Fages in, 107 n. 89
Altar presidio, Sonora: 9, 65, 68, 91, 110 n. 93,
  112, 112 n. 96, 118; to send supplies to
  settlements among the Yumas, 101;
  to supply escort for missionaries, 102;
  to supply troops for settlements among the
  Yumas, 97, 100; to supply troops for
  Tucson presidio, 97
Altar River: 23, 66 n. 40
Amorós, Fr. Pedro: 41 n. 10
Antonianum College, Rome: vii
Anza, Juan Bautista de: expedition to Alta
  California in 1774, 84 n. 69, 85 n. 72, 140 n.
  113; replaced by Pedro Tueros, 110 n. 93
Apache Indians: 4, 9, 10, 25, 45, 52, 57, 74, 80,
  88, 90, 91, 94, 111, 113, 115; attack San
  Xavier del Bac, 84 n. 69; attack Saric, 142 n.
  114; attack Sonora, 93; captives, 67, 67 n. 41,
  73-74, 75, 82, 89; card playing, 122, 122 n.
  102; "Chiricaguis" at Bacoachi, 123 n. 103;
  Chiricahua, 52 n. 23; classification of tribes,

52 n. 23; clothing, 127; Coyotero, 52, 52 n.
  23, 113; *estáblecimiento de paz* at Bacoachi,
  121-123; *establecimiento de paz* at Tucson,
  123-125; *establecimientos de paz*, 119-130;
  in table of baptisms for Bísanig, Caborca,
  and Pitiquito, 146; in table of baptisms for
  Caborca and Pitiquito, 145; in table of
  baptisms for San Xavier del Bac, San
  Agustín del Tucson, and others, 149-150;
  Jicarilla, 52 n. 23; lack of agriculture, 127;
  learn vices from Christians, 121-122; Lipan,
  52 n. 23; Mescalero, 52 n. 23; Mescaleros of
  El Paso, 120, 120 n. 101; of Bacoachi, 125;
  prisoner returned to, 120; raids in the
  Provincias Internas, 118-119; scouts from
  Bacoachi, 124 n. 104; "tame," 10, 30, 119-
  130; Western, 52 n. 23; White Mountain
  group, 52 n. 23. *Also see* Tejua (Yavapai)
  Indians; Tonto Indians.
apostolic brief: *see* pontifical brief
apostolic college: 42, 72; described, 11-12
Aquituni, Sonora (Papago ranchería): 66, 72,
  72 n. 54, 75; mission proposed for, 93
Aquistuni, Sonora: *see* Aquituni, Sonora
  (Papago ranchería)
Aragón, Spain: 70 n. 46, 84 n. 69
Archbishopric of Seville, Spain: 85 n. 72
Archivo General de Indias: 43 n. 12
Arivechi, Sonora: 18
Arizona: 37 n. 1, 85 n. 72
Arizpe, Sonora: 7, 18, 67, 86, 86 n. 73, 105;
  Apache prisoner at, 120; *cabecera*, 123 n.
  103; treasury of, 102
Arricivita, Fr. Juan D.: 27
Arriquibar, Fr. Pedro Antonio de: 30, 63 n. 36,
  122 n. 102, 125, 149 n. 123; baptized Indians
  at San Ignacio, Magdalena, and Tumacácori,
  149-150; biographical sketch, 123 n. 103;
  report on "tame" Apaches of Bacoachi,
  121-123

[165]

Buen Retiro, Madrid, Spain: 48, 49 n. 19, 65
Buena y Alcalde, Fr. Mariano Antonio de: 18, 149 n. 124
Buenavista presidio, Sonora: 9-10; to supply troops for settlements among Yumas (Quechans), 97; to supply troops for Tucson presidio, 97, 100
Burgos, Spain, Franciscan province: 108 n. 90, 144 n. 119, 148 n. 120, 150 n. 127

Caballero de Croix: *see* Croix, Teodoro de
Caborca, La Purísima Concepción de, Sonora: 18, 52, 91; *cabecera* in Pimería Alta, 39 n. 7; church, 59 n. 26; in table of baptisms for San Xavier del Bac, San Agustín del Tucson, and others, 150; served by Fr. Calzada, 144 n. 119; served by Fr. Collazo, 144 n. 116; served by Fr. Díaz as first Franciscan, 18, 85 n. 72; served by Fr. Gorgoll, 140 n. 113; served by Fr. Moreno, 108 n. 90; served by Fr. Moyano, 142 n. 115; served by Fr. Ramos, 142 n. 114; served by Fr. Soler, 144 n. 118; served by Fr. Ybañez, 149 n. 122; served by Fr. Yturralde, 139 n. 112; table of baptisms for 1768–1780, 138-139; table of baptisms for 1780–1784, 140-141; table of baptisms for 1784–1790, 142-143; table of baptisms for, including Bísanig, 147; table of baptisms for, including Bísanig and Pitiquito, 146
Cabúrica, San Ignacio de, Sonora: 18, 52; *cabecera* in Pimería Alta, 39 n. 7; church, 59 n. 26; construction by Fr. Francisco Sánchez Zúñiga, 59 n. 26; in table of baptisms for San Xavier del Bac, San Agustín del Tucson, and others, 149; Piman troops stationed at, 9; served by Fr. Diego Martín García as first Franciscan, 18, 149 n. 123; served by Fr. Francisco Sánchez Zúñiga, 59 n. 26
Cahuilla (Jecuiche) Indians: 52 n. 23, 94
Cajuenche Indians: *see* Kohuana (Cajuenche) Indians
Calahorra, Rioja, Spain: 150 n. 127
California: *see* Alta California; Baja California
Calleja, Felix María (general): 2
Calzada, Fr. Ambrosio: baptized Indians at Caborca, 138-141; baptized Nixoras at Pitiquito, 144-145; biographical sketch, 144 n. 119
Canals, Fr. Antonio: 18
Cañas, Río de las: 42, 43, 43 n. 12
Cantabria, Spain, Franciscan province: 139 n. 112
Caraygorta, Fr. Andrés: 41 n. 10
Carlos I, king of Spain: *see* Charles I
Carlos II, king of Spain: *see* Charles II
Carlos III, king of Spain: *see* Charles III

Carmelites: as mendicants, viii
Carrillo, Fr. Baltasar: 63 n. 36, 150 n. 127; baptized Indians at Tumacácori, 150; biographical sketch, 150 n. 126
Carrizal, Sonora: mission, 46 n. 16, 83 n. 68, 107 n. 88, 149 n. 124
Carrizal presidio, Nueva Vizcaya: Apache "peace settlement," 123 n. 103
Casa Grande, Arizona: city, 113 n. 98; prehistoric ruin, 113 n. 98; presidio proposed for area near prehistoric ruin, 113, 118
Catalonian volunteers: 107 n. 89
Cavorca, La Purísima Concepción de, Sonora: *see* Caborca
Caxa, Fr. José Antonio: 18
Cebrián y Agustín, count of Fuenclara: 48, 49 n. 19, 65
cédula real: 13, 41, 45, 47, 60, 61, 76, 77, 78, 79, 106; defined, 6; in chronological order: *1591,* 60 n. 28; *Jan. 30, 1607,* 15, 48, 48 n. 17; *Dec. 5, 1608,* 15, 48, 48 n. 18; *1621,* 60 n. 28; *Sep. 24, 1668,* 59-60, 60 n. 27; *Nov. 13, 1744,* 48, 49 n. 19, 65, 68, 76, 76 n. 62, 129, 129 n. 110; *Dec. 4, 1747,* 48, 49 n. 19, 65, 68, 76, 76 n. 62, 129, 129 n. 110; *Oct., 1749,* 16; *June 1, 1754,* 44, 44 n. 13; *Feb. 27, 1767,* 17; *Sept. 10, 1772,* 74 n. 58; *Aug. 22, 1776,* 84 n. 69; *Feb. 14, 1777,* 85; *Oct. 16, 1778,* 70, 70 n. 48; *Oct. 24, 1781,* 73, 73 n. 57, *Feb. 8, 1782,* 70, 71 n. 49; *May 20, 1782,* 21, 38, 38 n. 2, 69, 69 n. 43, 87; *Jan. 20, 1785,* 71, 71 n. 50, 78-79, 79 n. 63; *July 16, 1790,* 38, 38 n. 2, 70, 70 n. 47; *March 24, 1791,* 60, 61 n. 31; *Aug. 17, 1791,* 22, 38 38 n. 4, 70, 70 n. 47; 87; *Nov. 23-24, 1792,* 75 n. 60; *Aug. 20, 1793,* 71, 71 n. 51; *June 23, 1796,* 71, 71 n. 53
Chandler, Arizona: 113 n. 98
chaplain: salary, 65, 68. *Also see* Franciscans.
Chapman, Charles E.: cited, 129 n. 109
Charles I, king of Spain: 85 n. 71
Charles II, king of Spain: 60 n. 27
Charles III, king of Spain: 7, 15, 70 n. 48, 79, 84, 85 n. 71, 87; biographical note, 38 n. 2; creates Franciscan custodies, 38; expels Jesuits, 17
Chemeguaba Indians: *see* Chemehuevi (Chemeguaba) Indians
Chemehuevi (Chemeguaba) Indians: 52 n. 23
Chichimeca Indians: 126, 126 n. 107
Chihuahua, Villa de, Mexico: 9, 41, 54, 61, 67, 75, 75 n. 60, 83, 95, 113, 121
Chiricahua Apache: *see* Apache Indians
Chuburcabor, Sonora (Pima ranchería): 88; mission proposed for, 93
Chuburrcabon, Sonora: *see* Chuburcabor
church and state: separation, 5-6
Cieneguilla, San Ildefonso de la, Sonora: 40, 110 n. 93
Cimarrone Indians: attack Saric, 142 n. 114

173

The Documentary Relations of the Southwest

This volume is one in a series entitled The Documentary Relations of the Southwest, *which includes three major categories:*
> *The Jesuit Relations of the Southwest,*
> *The Franciscan Relations of the Southwest,*
> *The Civil-Military Relations of the Southwest.*
These three divisions reflect the primary sources of documents for Southwestern history and ethnohistory. By their very nature they provide geographical, chronological, and topical control for the rich and complex resources in Southwestern studies.

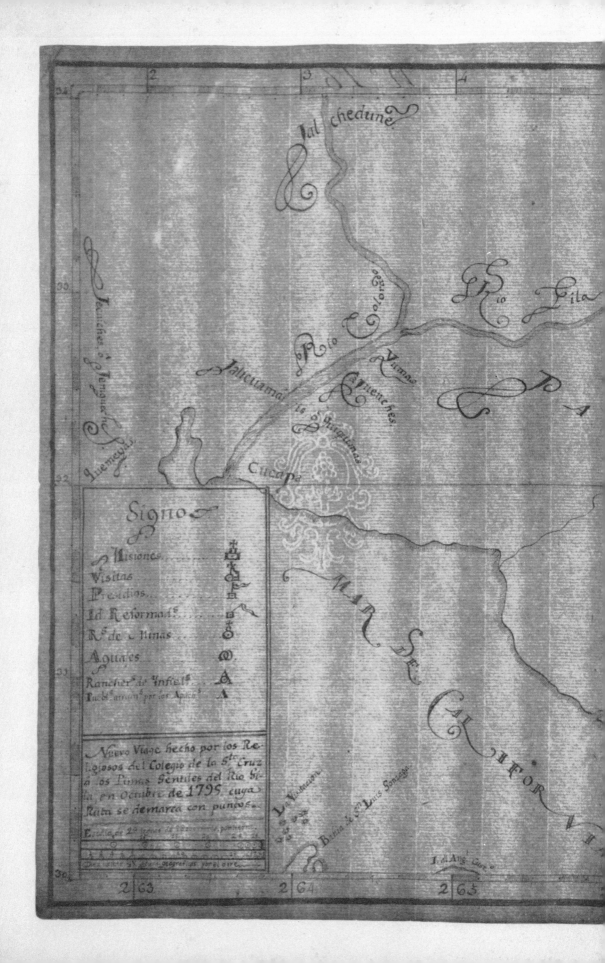